## Advance Praise

"A page-turning, superbly written, and warmhearted book of narrative practices for how to help clients re-story their lives, gain agency, and find purpose and meaning in life. A great read that fully addresses life's struggles—the good, the bad, and the ugly—as well as possibilities of change with hope, courage, and an open heart.

—**Marlene F. Watson, PhD, LMFT,** author of *Facing the Black Shadow* and coauthor of *Facing the White Shadow: How to Tame Your Racism and Become a True Ally to People of Color*

"Readers will appreciate Dr. Kamya's engaging blend of storytelling, scientific exploration, and therapeutic acumen used to illustrate the power of narrative theory and practice. Each chapter reflects his vast clinical experience working with diverse individuals, couples, and families. They are also deeply personal, drawn from his immigration and spiritual journeys. Altogether, Dr. Kamya's book lends powerful insight into the mechanisms and application of narrative practice that will benefit learners as well as inspire seasoned practitioners."

—**Shelley Cohen Konrad, PhD,** author of *Child and Family Practice: A Relational Perspective* and *Social and the Arts: Expanding Horizons*

"*Narrative Practices for Resilience and Hope* by Dr. Hugo Kamya offers a rigorous and timely contribution to narrative therapy, trauma studies, and clinical practice. Drawing on his Ugandan upbringing and clinical expertise, Kamya bridges the art of storytelling with contemporary narrative practice. Addressing trauma, oppression, and multigenerational harm, the book advances practices of witnessing, externalization, and reauthoring stories, using the metaphor of a 'crack in the window,' where light, reconnection, and hope illuminate pathways to agency and resilience."

—**Johnnie Hamilton-Mason, PhD, MSW,** professor and associate dean of faculty development, Simmons University SSW; Fulbright Scholar; private practitioner and coauthor of *Systemic Racism in the United States: Scaffolding as Social Construction*

"It is difficult to overstate the magnificent analysis and deconstruction articulated in these chapters. This is in part captured by Kamya's ingenious reference to the transformative power of curiosity. *Narrative Practices for Resilience and Hope* guides therapists in witnessing and walking with clients from trauma to resilience and beyond. Let the stories be told and retold."

—**Jay T. King, PhD, MEd,** former supervisor for the AAMFT, former faculty at Brown University, the University of Rhode Island, and Boston College; former assistant dean and founding member of the Boston Institute for Culturally Affirming Practices

# Narrative Practices for Resilience and Hope

## REWRITING STORIES OF TRAUMA IN CLINICAL WORK

Hugo Kamya

**Norton Professional Books**

*An Imprint of W. W. Norton & Company*
*Independent Publishers Since 1923*

Note to Readers: This book is intended as a general information resource for professionals practicing in the field of psychotherapy and mental health. It is not a substitute for appropriate training or clinical supervision. Standards of clinical practice and protocol vary in different practice settings and change over time. No technique or recommendation is guaranteed to be safe or effective in all circumstances, and neither the publisher nor the author(s) can guarantee the complete accuracy, efficacy, or appropriateness of any particular recommendation in every respect or in all settings or circumstances.

All case studies in this book are composites. Any URLs displayed in this book link or refer to websites that existed as of press time. The publisher is not responsible for, and should not be deemed to endorse or recommend, any website other than its own or any content that it did not create. The author, also, is not responsible for any third-party material.

Weingarten's Four Witnessing Positions used with permission of John Wiley & Sons - Books, from "Witnessing, Wonder, and Hope," Kaethe Weingarten, in *Family Process, 39*(4), 2000; permission conveyed through Copyright Clearance Center, Inc.


Printed in the United States of America
First Edition



For information about special discounts for bulk purchases, please contact W. W. Norton Special Sales at specialsales@wwnorton.com or 800-233-4830

Manufacturing by Versa Press
Book design by Beth Steidle
Production manager: Gwen Cullen

ISBN: 978-1-324-02007-3

W. W. Norton & Company, Inc., 500 Fifth Avenue, New York, NY 10110
www.wwnorton.com
W. W. Norton & Company Ltd., 15 Carlisle Street, London W1D 3BS

Authorized EU representative: EAS, Mustamäe tee 50, 10621 Tallinn, Estonia

1 2 3 4 5 6 7 8 9 0

**Dedicated with love and gratitude**

*to my mother, Immaculate Namakula,*
*and my father, John Chrysestom Kazibwe,*
*whose love for stories and storytelling*
*taught me the enduring value of listening.*

**To Ponsiano,**

*whose love for life was boundless.*

**In memory of**

*Everett, Liz, Hannah, Joseph,*
*Henry, Robert, and Anne.*

# Contents

# Acknowledgments

I could never have imagined how profoundly my life would change when I first met Henri Nouwen. At the time, I didn't know how I would afford my education, but the invisible hand of grace was already at work, opening unexpected doors.

I was sitting on the steps of Andover Hall at Harvard—both excited at the possibility of being there and weighed down by the fear and sadness that it might never happen. As I sat there, I reflected on my journey, my hopes, and my experience as an immigrant in the United States. Then, a man in his early sixties appeared.

He asked me about my interests and the books I was reading. I shared how deeply I admired Henri Nouwen—the spiritual author whose reflections on hospitality, ministry, and woundedness had inspired me to work with people living with physical and mental challenges. At that moment, I didn't know that the very man I was speaking about was Henri Nouwen himself.

Our conversation stayed with me. His interest in my story and his encouragement to pursue my education planted seeds of hope. Then, in an act of profound generosity, he offered to sponsor my education. Through him, new doors opened, and I began to see how the invisible hand of God was writing—and rewriting—my life story.

That meeting marked the beginning of a decade-long friendship, lasting until Henri's death in 1996. During those years, our lives took different paths—Henri remained at Harvard, while I was at

L'Arche. Eventually, I left L'Arche, entered Harvard, and began my academic journey. Though we lived in different places, our friendship deepened. Henri became both a mentor and a spiritual companion. He would write to ask about my coursework and my continued commitment to people living with mental illness. I, in turn, devoured more of his books and reflected more deeply on questions of meaning and purpose.

Often, I wondered why grace had touched my life in such an extraordinary way—especially when so many of my friends back home had been killed. When Henri walked into my life, I knew something sacred had occurred. His presence was an invitation to extend the same hand of compassion to others who also wait—sometimes in silence—for love and hope.

At the heart of this book is a commitment to cultivating hope, especially in times and places where hope seems absent. Over the years, I've learned that hope is not only felt but also practiced. Hope has been a guiding force in my life. I have clung to a stubborn optimism even in moments of despair. Hope carried me and my family when our father was taken from us. Hope became the light shining through a crack in the window. It is the same hope I hold for my clients as we work together to re-story their lives.

As I reflect on the journey that shaped this book, I'm filled with gratitude for my mother's strength and courage throughout our childhood. I want to thank the many teachers, mentors, and village members who stepped in to support us when my father was in detention. They became the community that raised us. Indeed, it takes a village!

I am especially thankful to Sr. Martina, who gave my mother a job so she could provide for us, and to Fr. Shorter, who inspired my love for books and learning. I'm grateful to Fr. Edward, who introduced me to mindfulness and prayer, to Fr. Cousins, who believed in me, and to L'Arche, where I volunteered with men and women living with mental disabilities. There, I learned how little separates us—and how much binds us—in our shared humanity and need for belonging.

I extend my deep thanks to Iola, who welcomed me into her home, supported me, and helped me thrive. I am also grateful for the incredible colleagues I've had the privilege of working with throughout my career. Stephanie, with whom I've worked for many years, has taught me that refugees never truly say goodbye. The BICAP group in Boston has been central to my growth—our challenges have been a source of personal renewal. I especially thank Jay, a friend whose unwavering support spans over 40 years.

At Simmons School of Social Work, I am thankful for my colleagues, particularly Johnnie, my writing partner, and at Smith School for Social Work, Dean Yoshioka, who has supported this project wholeheartedly. My friend Robert, who walked into Harvard with me, has remained a steadfast companion in both academia and life. I am deeply grateful to Carol Bonner, a mentor and friend, who introduced me to Shelley. Shelley's close reading and thoughtful feedback on this manuscript were invaluable. She embodies hope for me. I am deeply grateful to Leslie who challenged and steadfastly assisted me in writing. I am grateful to Judy Florio who worked with me in the early stages of this manuscript. I am deeply thankful to Ken Hardy who believed in me and introduced me to Deborah Malmud. A very special thank you to Deborah, Jamie, McKenna, and the staff at Norton for your patience and generosity throughout the process of this project.

My students have been a lightning rod in my life—their questions continue to push me toward deeper inquiry and learning. I have learned so much from my clients, whose courage and resilience have taught me to hope in the face of hopelessness, to be patient with life's unfolding, to ask questions, and to question the answers.

To my beloved family, Norah, Sarah, and Elizabeth—thank you for being my greatest cheerleaders. Your love and support have carried me through every chapter of this journey. Thank you for the gifts of your presence in my life. I am also grateful to my extended family in Uganda, especially Hilda, who has followed the progress of this book with care and encouragement.

Finally, I dedicate this book to my mother and father. Even after raising their own children, they took on the responsibility of raising their grandchildren and other children in my village. My mother, especially, dedicated her final years to caring for children—regardless of where they came from. Her spirit of unconditional love and compassion is a lasting gift she has passed on to us all. She embodies the *it takes a village* spirit toward resilience and hope.

# Introduction

Throughout my childhood in Uganda stories were an intrinsic part of my family's culture. My parents used stories to teach us lessons, learn about our African culture, and help us make sense of natural and relational worlds. They were also a means to communicate important messages and, when times were tough, they were used as a survival mechanism to keep us safe. Stories were also a source of entertainment, rich with folklore and tales based in African traditions. For my family, it was a way not only of preserving our history, culture, and identity—it was a way to bring them alive in our day-to-day lives.

Oral literature is a collection of stories, both myth and history, that ensures people's cultural and historical traditions are not forgotten, used as sources of insight, reflection, and guidance. Folktales, legends, proverbs, and epics serve multiple purposes, from educating children to imparting societal values. As a communal activity, storytelling becomes a collective experience, one that connects us as human beings to one another and helps us form a spiritual relationship to the divine balance of nature.

In African tradition, animal characters possessing extraordinary wisdom, wit, and perseverance often populate stories, each symbolizing different qualities and lessons. These characters represent lives in nature and are used to impart essential relationships between human beings, the natural world, and the universe's origins. For example, the tales of *Anansi*, the spider, is known for cleverness and ability to overcome challenges; *Kamuje*, the hare, is celebrated for agility, strength, and wit; and *Nfudu*, the slow-paced turtle, is recognized as a symbol of grace and wisdom. These animal figures serve to teach various lessons through their actions.

Along with characterizations, metaphor, proverbs, and aphorisms are used to teach moral lessons and create a collective language that binds people together in community. Some share simple messages, such as "The person who hunts two rats catches none," which emphasizes the importance of focus and attention. Others are more complex, like "The person who asks questions cannot avoid the answers." When my grandmother used proverbs, they provided us with a moment to pause and reflect, as they often revealed profound and enduring life lessons.

My grandmother often told us stories before bedtime. Some took place by the warmth of the outdoor fireplace; others were told in fields under the moonlight. One such evening, as we sat outside in the dark, I recall her saying, "When the moon is not full, the stars shine more brightly." I looked up and noticed how brightly the stars shone that night. Another of my grandmother's stories that has stayed with me reminded us about the importance of remaining steadfast in any endeavor. She always ended it with a saying: "A strawberry blossom will not sweeten dry bread." She explained that it's important to earn what one reaps.

Stories are told in multiple ways. They are performed through music, the spoken word, and dance. For example, among the Baganda of Uganda, elaborate dances were performed at harvest time. The dances are carefully choreographed to celebrate the yield from the harvest of crop. Exuberant dance celebrates a good yield while subdued movements signal a poor yield of harvest. Visual art is another potent storytelling medium. Paintings, sculptures, beadwork, masks, and icons tell stories through images that transcend language and cultural barriers. More recently, film, plays, and digital platforms have been added as mediums of storytelling.

Stories are inescapable: They give meaning, provide direction, and reveal what truly matters in life. I firmly believe, and I've learned from people, that the meaning of any event is shaped by the story we tell about it. I love telling and listening to stories, and over the years my fascination with them has only deepened. As a therapist, I have been invited to bear witness to clients' stories and to explore with them the complexity and diversity of their lives. This narrative journey has opened my eyes to the importance of active listening, suspending assumptions, and willing to be open to multiple and sometimes conflicting perspectives.

The chapters of this book are in themselves stories. They seek to engage readers in learning from a range of narratives offered from different perspectives, including those we tell about ourselves and those that are told about us, ones that contribute to who we are and who we are becoming. They are stories of how we make meaning of relationship with others and of the world that are both ordinary and extraordinary, tales of individuals and community. Last, they are stories that come with privilege—to be allowed into others' stories and to be a respectful observer in the process of meaning making and healing.

It is important to acknowledge that while I bring my personal stories and understanding to this work, I am mindful that the narratives within this book are incomplete. All case studies presented, whether titled "vignettes" or "stories," are composites, created by combining information from different clients' stories. With that in mind, I hope that they illuminate the power and beauty of stories and advance your understanding and use of narrative practices.

In Chapter 1 I tell my story, and by doing so, I invite the reader to do the same. I believe that clinicians have an obligation to stay connected to the telling and retelling of their stories as they influence how we listen to and make sense of the stories clients share. We need to remain cognizant of how formative experiences shape our lives and inform our beliefs, how they significantly impact what we deem important and worthy. When I reflect on my story, certain key elements stand out: my family of origin, my parents' humble beginnings, the politics of turmoil, searching for our spiritual roots, stories told, and stories not told. This chapter welcomes readers to examine their own stories, to find meaning and inspiration in them, and raise awareness of how they may collide with clients' stories in nontherapeutic ways. Being aware and open with oneself about the influence of inner narratives increases the likelihood that one can authentically connect with the people who become our clients (Koenig et al., 2020).

Chapter 2 lays the foundation for understanding narrative practice. Using composite client case material, I discuss key concepts of narrative practice within the framework of culture. Culture is a dynamic and intersectional process that takes many forms, including but not exclusive to one's ethnic, regional, community, or intersectional identities. Narrative approaches appreciate the relevance of contextualizing therapy within a cultural framework, and from the position that clients are experts in their cultural knowledge and experience. In this chapter, we explore and apply these foundational principles through narratives and their analysis.

Chapter 3 explores the transformative power of questions to foster a "not-knowing" and curious stance within narrative practice. According to feminist theorists, "not knowing" is a conscious process of remaining open to understanding another. It requires a willingness to challenge one's assumptions and explore diverse perspectives achieving a deeper and authentic understanding of those we encounter (Belenky et al., 1986). Questions matter and therapy is about seeking answers to life questions. It is also about learning to live with uncertainty knowing that the answers to some questions might never be revealed. Collaborating with clients through narratives is a process of re-storying that leads to new learning and the discovery of new knowledge. Narrative practitioners focus on the generative effects of questions, emphasizing their role in shaping and facilitating meaning making. This chapter presents a range of prompts and questions that help clinicians facilitate collaborative story exploration and foster deeper understanding of client narratives.

Questions are inherently embedded in language. Chapter 4 explores the various forms and functions of language, examining how language influences thought, shapes reality, and is, in turn, shaped by reality. The chapter delves into the dynamic relationship between language and power, highlighting its capacity to both empower and disempower, privilege, and marginalize. Language also plays a formidable role in fostering human connection and relational accountability, which underscores its significance in narrative practices and meaningful interactions.

Stories of trauma are complex and challenging for practitioners, calling them to be present to pain and suffering and engage in witnessing practices. Chapter 5 explores these practices through narratives of clients who have experienced various forms of trauma. Clinicians are positioned to be key witnesses and play a vital role in holding hope and accompanying clients as they restore meaning in the aftermath of trauma. The chapter draws on Kaethe Weingarten's (2000) seminal work on witnessing, and Marie-Nathalie Beaudoin's (2005) exploration of choice and agency, providing insights into how relational practices can help clients reclaim their sense of self and agency.

Chapter 6 poignantly illustrates the potency of narrative therapy from Rwandan survivors of the 1994 genocide as they continue to reconstruct their lives through narratives and storytelling. It acknowledges the role of colonialism in Africa as a significant factor in the events leading to the Rwandan genocide. The suffering endured is conveyed through the stories by individuals like Rudeka as well as from the descendants of genocide survivors. The chapter highlights various storytelling tools and techniques, such as the use of metaphor and expanding the audience. Additionally, it emphasizes the importance of double listening: attending to both stories of suffering and stories of resilience (White, 2004).

Chapter 7 explores narrative practices in therapy with couples that bring intricate, highly complex, and multifaceted stories to the therapeutic spaces. Couples present both individual and shared narratives as they work toward a centering story for their relationship. Intercultural couples navigate complex dynamics as they seek connection and understanding.

Addressing these layered realities requires a sensitive, informed, and holistic approach in therapy. The chapter draws on the influential work of John Gottman (2011), Mona Fishbane (2019), Peter Fraenkel (2023), Jill Freedman and Gene Combs (1996), Thomas Carlson and Amanda Haire (2014), and Michele Scheinkman (2017), whose contributions provide valuable insights into supporting couples in their relational journeys.

Chapter 8 explores illness narratives that often resist categorization and are frequently overlooked. Collaboration with clients is essential to access their insider knowledge of illness, recognizing that these narratives are deeply personal and complicated especially when their stories have been dismissed by others, including health providers and family. In the face of uncertainty, therapy involves holding reasonable hope for clients

(Weingarten, 2022). While modern medicine often prioritizes curing, the need for compassionate care for those with chronic and life-limiting illness has never been more necessary. Clinicians play a pivotal role in witnessing, believing, and embodying such care.

Chapter 9 examines spirituality as a search for purpose, connection, and meaning. Making sense of senselessness, suffering, and often unimaginable circumstances is an invitation to embrace social justice. "Spirituality and justice-seeking are inextricably linked" (Perry & Rolland, 2009, p. 384), and in tandem with commitment to social justice and an ethic of care, they foster meaningful relationships and help people cope during the toughest of times. This chapter brings to light the role of spirituality, beliefs and practices toward healing and recovery.

Chapter 10 focuses on the significance of personal stories as shaped by social identities especially those that exist at the intersection of marginalization and privilege. Client narratives celebrate social identities as they challenge systemic forces of oppression. To be effective, clinicians need to understand how social identities relate to a client's sense of self, their relationship to community narratives, and to the broader cultural discourses, which may restrict the rich and unspoken stories in people's lives.

In the concluding chapter, the epilogue, I return to the image of the crack in the window, a defining moment in our family. The crack speaks to how we connect to stories in our life and those of our clients. It also highlights the role of metaphors in storytelling.

No single volume can reflect all perspectives, nor do justice to honor the contributions and legacies of narrative theorists and practitioners, including Michael White, David Epston, Marie-Nathalie Beaudoin, Gerald Monk, Jill Freedman, Gene Combs, Kaethe Weingarten, Sallyann Roth, Bill Madsen, David Denborough, Cheryl White, and many more who have written eloquently in this field. That said, I fully recognize that the following chapters are personally constructed from many sources; what I have learned from those before me, from my own stories, and from the spaces and social identities I inhabit as a Black, African man, immigrant, academic, narrative therapist, social worker, son, father raising children of color, and spiritual and religious person. Like everyone, my life story is a slice of a tapestry—woven from the narratives that I have chosen to share. It is my hope that elevating stories and the important roles they play in therapeutic conversations will inspire you to value your own stories as well as those that are shared with you in your personal and professional encounters.

# Narrative Practices for Resilience and Hope

CHAPTER I

# Narrative Practice and Storytelling

## Stories and Storytelling

As storytellers and story listeners, we engage in universal and vital human activities in our everyday lives. Through stories, we build spaces for connection and healing as well as explore issues of power and powerlessness. Stories inform the way people view themselves, perceive others, and make meaning of the interactions between them. Some stories originate from folklore or tales, while others communicate facts or express criticism. Storytelling in all forms contributes to how people construct a sense of self, one that is coherent and connected to the different elements of our internal and external identities (Schutz & Luckmann, 1974). Stories also build relational connection between individuals and promote collectivity across communities. Through writing and telling stories, people find and cement bonds with each other.

In effect, we are born into a world of stories (Schutz & Luckmann, 1974) that forges cultural pathways between the past, present, and future. Some stories frame social and moral expectations while others are meant to inspire individual growth, promote community unity, and keep traditions alive through the generations (Hodge et al., 2002). Others aim to challenge privileged and dominant narratives that are promoted through public discourse, such as the news and social media.

They seek to uplift the voices of those who are too often unheard due to marginalization and systemic oppression. Such stories must be told by those with intimate knowledge and lived wisdom. As I explore in this book, they must be listened to with openness and a willingness to unpack and counter issues of power and powerlessness.

Stories anchor the work that therapists do with clients. They permit us to enter into clients' inner lives—their truths and regrets, pain, and resilience. It is to be expected that they affect us in ways that touch upon our own vulnerabilities as people. David Browning (2003) reflects upon the reciprocal encounter with vulnerability when we invite clients to share their stories: "We encourage [clients'] narratives to unfold not knowing what it is we will hear and not understanding how these stories will affect us," he writes. "In many respects we meet clients at times of heightened vulnerability, and we greet them from a place within ourselves that is perhaps equally vulnerable" (p. 335).

Being consciously aware of the manifest and latent content of our stories makes practitioners better equipped to receive other peoples' stories. Such reflection reminds us that we are never neutral in relationship to others. The therapeutic process is inherently intersubjective, and thus, we need to be cognizant of how the practitioner's story (as in our own stories) interweaves with those of the people we work with. For me, this takes the form of continuous self-reflection and scrutinizing of my social identities—including my experience as an immigrant—and how, altogether, they shape my understanding of clients and their unique circumstances.

This chapter centers my own story, and I use it as a bridge to understand clients' stories. I have used my own story to understand myself and to bring resilience and hope to my practice. It is about how we create space to listen to people's stories and provide a sense of hope and empowerment. I also use stories about culture and naming to anchor key points in the therapeutic process.

In many respects, the therapeutic process is a series of stories that has many points of entry, and narrative practice is an approach that allows us to enter these healing portals. Narrative theory values the reciprocity of telling *and* listening, of recognizing the shared humanity that emerges through the therapeutic process. I often reflect upon the many ways that my own story can be told and how it can best be heard. The narrative that follows is my personal story of immigration, of the assault on my family, our escape to a new and unfamiliar country, and to establishing a new life in the United States. No single moment can describe the dramatic and traumatic events endured nor the touchpoints that led to my journey. My immigrant story is where I begin.

## Leaving Home

I was born in Uganda during a time when the country was under British colonial rule (1894–1962). Precolonial Uganda was characterized by distinct ethnic groups and kingdoms with varying levels of political organization. Bantu-speaking kingdoms lay in the south and Nilotic and Sudanic groups were in the north. The kingdom of Buganda, located in the south, was particularly significant as it was the largest ethnic group and had an established political organization. My family was born and lived there.

In October 1962, Uganda became an independent African nation, but freedom from the British led to intense political rivalries and tyrannical regimes. One such regime was led by Idi Amin, the Ugandan dictator who belonged to the Kakwa tribe, a small ethnic group in Uganda from the West Nile region. It was during the dictatorship of Idi Amin, the third president of Uganda (1971–1979), and considered one of the most brutal leaders in history, that my family made our escape. We had been targeted by the government because my father belonged to an ethnic group that had opposed Amin's policies. We had no recourse but to leave our home. I was a 19-year-old student living apart from my family at the time. My family went into hiding without me in Uganda, and I didn't learn their location until several months later. I fled to Kenya, Uganda's neighboring country, with the clothes on my back along with a few childhood friends. We decided to go to Kenya because it was a neighbor to Uganda, but more important, because I knew certain people there who were sympathetic to the cause in Uganda and who might help me start a new life.

Along the way, I met fellow travelers. We traveled at night to avoid detection, carrying very few belongings and leaving most things behind. Some of the time we walked, at other times we took the chance of hitching rides from strangers, never knowing whether we would survive the ride. On one occasion, we got picked up by a minibus that was already carrying 13 or 14 travelers. We rode in motionless silence, staring into space, none of us daring to say a word or make eye contact. No one spoke about why we were traveling or where our destination would be. Everyone was suspect. No one could be trusted, so I was guided by caution and fear. Although I yearned to make contact, I maintained distance to not invite anyone's interest or allow them to sense my unease. We were tightly packed together, but the emotional space between us was vast; we needed to feel protected. As we crossed the border into Kenya, each of us in turn carefully paid the driver with our precious unwrapped notes of paper currency. The silence was deafening, our journey uncertain.

It was during this flight that I became aware of how language can both bring richness to stories and act as an impenetrable, frightening cultural barrier. At various roadblock identity checks, Amin's soldiers would pull us out of vehicles yelling at us in Swahili; this was a language none of us spoke and most had come to associate with intimidation and brutality. The name on your identification card could determine your fate. If you belonged to a tribe the government opposed, you were considered an enemy.

Fate also depended on the whims of soldiers stationed at each checkpoint. Some passengers were hauled out, interrogated, and roughed up before being allowed back into the vehicle. Others were not so lucky. Guns were pointed at them, and some were struck with the butts of rifles or had barrels aimed at their heads. Some people were killed. No laws protected us. This situation reflects how quickly the structures of law and justice can erode under authoritarian rule, replaced by randomness and terror. It also speaks to how systemic violence can dehumanize not just individuals but entire communities through the manipulation of language, identity, and power.

When I reflect on the time when my family was together prior to fleeing for safety, there was no reassurance or safety. Not surprisingly, a pervasive distrust seeped into all our relationships, even with those we once called neighbors. We lived in constant fear, desperate to escape the intimidation, brutality, and uncertainty. At times, we knew who our enemy was; at other times, we were left in the dark, unsure of where the next threat would come from. My life became consumed by anger as I struggled to identify the oppressor, seeking clarity in an oppressive and shadowy reality.

Once I arrived in Kenya, I began the arduous task of rebuilding my life. I was now faced with re-creating myself in an unfamiliar and daunting culture all while trying to make sense of Swahili, a language I did not speak. Learning a new language triggered thoughts and emotions reminiscent of the turmoil I had just escaped. It also came with recurring reminders of what I had lost. The marauding soldiers and unpredictable violence I had just survived was now replaced by suspicion. My identity was questioned. Some people wondered if I had been a collaborator with Uganda's regime.

Having fled with only the bare minimum, I couldn't provide documentation that would qualify me for employment—I had none, so I couldn't find work. Employers were acutely aware of my country's political and social upheaval and understandably felt compelled to protect themselves from anyone associated with it. I was forced to balance a range of emotions, but in the end, survival had to be my primary focus. I needed to endure. I had to be strong and maintain hope that my host country, though initially unwelcoming, would eventually accept me.

When in survival mode, finding and carrying personal documents isn't a priority, so many of us failed to bring along the proper forms as proof of identity. With more Ugandans fleeing persecution to relocate, the Kenyan government increased its scrutiny of immigrants. One such program, *Kipandilisho*, meaning "documented" in Swahili, required all foreigners to carry a verified 4 × 6 identity card that had to be regularly stamped to confirm one's status. Verification was a constant and stressful challenge, and at times it took much effort to convince the authorities that I was the person I claimed to be.

Gradually I found my footing in Kenya, taking on menial jobs, and fruitlessly holding hope that there would be change in my country making it possible for me and my family to return home. Meanwhile,

I obtained my academic records, which allowed me to restart my educational pursuits and begin building a future. But Kenya was not to be my final home. Four years later, at the age of 23, I took the next step of my journey by moving to another unfamiliar landscape: the United States. New York City was the first place I landed, where I stayed for a few days until I left for Syracuse to become a volunteer in a home for people struggling with mental illness. This was my introduction to the therapeutic world.

Leaving Kenya and traveling to the United States brought mixed emotions. I felt excited to take residence in a country renowned for its embrace of diversity and freedom. Yet the United States was another unfamiliar culture that required me to make many emotional and existential adjustments. Things I once took for granted no longer held significance. For example, back home, people stopped to say hello to each other, whether they were strangers or not. In the United States, this was not the case.

I did encounter other immigrants who also suffered from the devastating effects of war. Their stories were different from mine, but our legacies were similar and our struggles the same. I did my best to speak English, or so I thought. But my pronunciation often raised eyebrows, and people frequently commented on my accent by asking me where I was from. At times, feelings of alienation and of being an outsider resurfaced, and I found myself reliving traumas I had thought were left behind. To counteract this, I pressured myself to be assertive, to constantly achieve and prove my worth. I had to define who I was.

Growing awareness of race, of being a Black man in America, was perhaps the most startling aspect of redefining myself. In Uganda, despite its long history of White colonization, Blackness had never been central to my self-identity. This is because most of the population is Black; it is the norm, not the exception. In other words, Blackness in Uganda is a default state—unmarked and unchallenged—rather than a marker of difference or marginalization. However, soon after arriving in the United States I became acutely aware of negative racial stereotypes. I was a Black man, and that simple aspect of my identity based solely on how I looked and sounded, caused me to be labeled and categorized—even hated—by some. I wanted to be seen and treated as a respectable human being, but as a Black person, I soon felt a form of Othering from White people.

Equally jarring were assumptions other people of color made about me. I recall while walking down the streets of New York one day, a Black man yelled out. He called me "brother!" But I didn't feel like his brother. I was an African Black man in a country not my own trying to figure who I was and where I belonged.

When I was growing up in Uganda, Whiteness was idolized—a discriminatory preference that is shared by people in many countries in the global south. Confronting Whiteness and racial attitudes in America felt like reliving colonization. My early experiences in the United States highlighted how race is so often reduced to a binary of Black and White. Over time, I learned and experienced some of what many Black people go through—being followed in stores under suspicion of theft, having one's intelligence or competence questioned in academic or professional settings, or being spoken over or ignored in conversations until a White voice echoed the same thought. I witnessed the ways Black people are policed differently, how things like a simple traffic stop could escalate into a life-threatening encounter, and how grief and outrage often go unheard unless they are legitimized by non-Black allies.

I began to feel the psychological burden of code switching, of having to modulate how I speak, dress, and behave to avoid being stereotyped. These experiences revealed the pervasive, and often invisible, labor that comes with navigating a society that views Blackness through a lens of suspicion, limitation, or exoticism. They also served to distinguish and illuminate how my experience of Blackness in Uganda was starkly different from those of Black Americans. My racial identity was woven by my culture and its stories. How would these build upon the tapestry of my new identity as a Black African man in America?

## Stories and Culture

Culture matters, and within every culture, there are countless stories that interact and build upon one another. As I discussed above, one of the most surprising and continuous narratives I encountered early in my journey is the story of being Black. I quickly learned that, to a great degree, my identity in America was viewed through my skin color. Before coming to the United States, I had never used the term "Black" to describe myself. The American cultural narrative had imposed this on me, and it was not without struggle that I came to accept it.

I realize now that this internal conflict was a natural outgrowth of transformation and increased self-awareness. I loved my country and was forced to flee it. Holding true to identity kept me close to the many things I'd lost. Allowing new circumstances to reshape me felt disloyal and wrong. I could not allow external forces to influence my essential self. I wrestled with profound questions: Who am I? Will this new culture accept me? Do I matter, and how do I truly belong? And yet, despite these reservations and fears, my story was evolving.

I have come to embrace new parts of myself, mindful of how stories by necessity change us. I relish the self-understanding, and ultimately, the sense of belonging I now feel. Acceptance has also brought me closer to African Americans whose stories of struggle have found a place within my skin color and my Black identity. I'm aware that many clients come to me because I am Black, while others seek me out because of my African heritage, accent, and name. These aspects of identity create connection and are elements of psychological safety for some who haven't felt able to open up with practitioners of different backgrounds and races. Sometimes, people make erroneous assumptions based only on my external identities. For example, based on the spelling of my name one young man assumed I was from India, while in another instance, a woman seeking therapy thought I was Japanese. When I met these clients, their previously constructed stories about me dissolved and new and richer stories emerged.

Stories unfold in particular ways influenced by culture and context and also by distinctive biological, psychological, sociocultural, and spiritual constructions. I often reflect upon how clients' identities are impacted by their cultural stories, self-stories, and by dominant societal norms that affect their well-being. One never knows how stories will unfold and what influences will be most meaningful. What visible and invisible identities will clients bring to the therapeutic encounter and how they will interface with my own?

## The Centrality of Whiteness

The centrality of Whiteness is ever present in psychotherapy spaces. In my office, I watch as clients scan my diplomas and certificates scrutinizing my credentials. Even now, this act weighs heavily on me and causes self-doubt. I have to remind myself that I have much to offer in our interactions. Still, sometimes I question my own skills and wonder whether I deserve the fees for my services.

Because of the dissonance and uncertainty engendered by Whiteness I sometimes feel, it has been important for me to show a strong sense of confidence. Even now, as I am writing these words, I am acutely aware that I cannot escape the centrality of Whiteness (Hardy, 2022). My training as a therapist has been within White institutions, and most of my teachers have been White, influenced by Eurocentric theories.

As a Black man, I have to navigate Whiteness with White clients as well as with non-White clients. With White clients, I am acutely aware of what Mangram (2022) calls "performances of survival" (p. 39). I have struggled with the pressure to play the "affable Black man" who poses no threat to White clients, even as they seek my services. My self-confidence becomes tempered with self-effacement and not wanting to seem too self-assured. It is a balancing act of clashing stories and underlying racism. With clients of color, the challenges that bring them to therapy can reawaken my fears as a Black man in predominantly White spaces. Their stories often mirror my own silent negotiations: of how to exist, succeed, and stay safe in environments where their presence is constantly questioned and scrutinized.

I carefully observe how people's stories are performed within the context of Whiteness and remain diligently aware of their bidirectional influences. I actively listen to what they choose to speak about and what remains unsaid. I am keenly aware that despite our commonalities, we are in fact different, and that in this relationship I must deal with issues of power between us. With clients of color, managing the power dynamic is critical to maintaining trust. I am constantly making decisions about how to navigate tensions without reproducing the oppressive structures clients experience in their lives.

Mangram's (2022) metaphor of the elephant in the room encapsulates the experience of being a Black person inhabiting the White domain of therapy. "The elephant (whiteness) is not *in* the room. Whiteness, in the context of the United States, IS THE ROOM" (p. 47). I am acutely aware that Whiteness is part of the air we breathe, even in therapy spaces. In listening to people's stories, it is key to name Whiteness and to navigate conversations about race. I listen with a "third ear" to what may not be said in the stories and utterances clients bring to therapy. Narrative practice offers a space to bring to light both told and untold stories and to celebrate them.

## Reframing Stories

People are not defined by the stories told about them or that they tell themselves. Narrative practice opens up opportunities to reframe and positively "re-story" deficit-saturated narratives, to create a new positive, empowering narrative. The story of a male client, Woo [not his real name], illustrates how telling can pave the way to transform a narrative following experiences of war.

Woo had escaped the killing fields of the war in Sudan. He consulted with me shortly after arriving in the United States. His life had been consumed by the atrocities of war. When he first immigrated, he had hoped for a life free of those fears—that is, until he was confronted by anti-Blackness in his new community. Racism compounded his ability to move forward in multiple ways. He described how no one would hire him because "he had no skills" to put on his job application. Internalized racism and low self-worth conspired to lead him to believe these stereotypes about him. He dismissed his own skills, put himself down, and felt altogether worthless.

I knew that helping Woo meant re-storying his war and immigration experiences. I listened as he retold the perils he had endured, reframing his experiences at critical junctures. His was a story of escape: he had escaped being killed by wild animals as well as being slain by warlords. From a narrative perspective, escape from the killing fields was also a powerful story of valor, crisis management, and ingenuity that he used to flee from his persecutors and stay alive. Reframing his story through these positive lenses gave Woo a renewed sense of agency. He became aware of the many skills he possessed and was able to celebrate them. These were skills he could now articulate and use to seek employment.

Woo's story was not just about a lack of employment opportunities. It reflects a deeper struggle with self-identity that is shaped by racism and internalized racism. Therapy sought to help him see that the issue was not *him* but the racism and social messaging that contributed to a distorted view of himself. Through this, he could begin to recognize the skills and strengths he had undervalued or dismissed. Over time, therapy supported the rebuilding of his self-esteem through strengths-based approaches, such as highlighting lived experiences, resilience, and resourcefulness as valid—and highly valuable—forms of competence.

## The Stories Clients Tell

Stories invite us to listen intently and attentively, as they come in many different forms and have different starting points. White and Epston's (1990) work on "thin and thick self-descriptions" highlights the importance of being open to diverse and evolving storylines. Simply put, clients often begin their stories from a singular, problem-saturated perspective: one that has negatively pervaded their lives. White and Epston refer to these as "thin" and "thick" stories. Narrative work seeks to help clients retell their stories, adding nuance and detail that counteracts the negativity and integrates positive elements and outcomes of experience. These so-called thick stories shift one's perspective toward growth and recovery (White & Epston, 1990).

People are selective about the stories they believe about themselves, and I am no exception. Through narrative practice, I have come to appreciate the stories of my childhood and my life. I am continually intrigued by how my mind chooses to remember certain stories and to bypass others. I ask myself: Why do I choose to remember specific events of my story? What sanctions do these remembrances hold? How do I bring them together to cohere for me at this point in my life? These questions, and more, continue to perplex me. One area of interest for me is the story that names carry.

## What Is in a Name?

I am an educator as well as a clinician. When I teach, I always start out by asking students to introduce themselves in multiple ways, like offering a statement that captures who they are at any select moment in time. They may choose to share a nickname, chosen name, or the significance of their name or contemplate why they did not really know. These introductions intrigue me because they elicit stories about complexity—What is in a name? I have also used this exercise with clients in the early stages of our work together. It is a simple means of connecting and learning a bit about each other.

Cora, a 30-year-old woman, told me about the transformational experience of hearing her young son call her mama for the very first time. The name affirmed her identity as a mother and gave her a new appreciation for her purpose and belonging:

> The first time my son called me "mama," I cried. In that two-syllable word was an invitation to belong, to be part of a family. My own mother passed away when I was just 16 years old, and my father was never really in the picture. My brothers and sisters were all many years older than me and had moved out of [our] home by the time I was old enough to form any meaningful relationship. I often felt untethered, bereft of a tribe, until that one day when "mama" changed my life, and I felt as if I had started my own. I had purpose, belonging, I was needed by someone. I've cherished the thousands of times my children have said that word since

> (exasperatedly, sometimes, when they forget to look for their socks before asking me where they are!) and I can't imagine what my life would have been like without this name and its meaning to me.

The storying of names is a conversation that opens doors for clients and therapists to work together. They remind us that everyone is an expert of their own life, carrying with them a host of stories. Stories reveal histories, contexts, traditions, and, sometimes, hidden identities. It is my experience that names begin the narrative therapy process by providing opportunities to explore clients' connections to various aspects of their stories. Like with Cora, names can evoke feelings of being loved and cared for. Others speak of their names as being historically grounded. Names remind some people of home and belonging, of finding their voice. Names can also signal a retaking of identity or found agency. People change their names to feel aligned with their identity.

In my culture, names are given to reflect various circumstances. They may reflect current events or connect to the past. When family members name a child after an ancestor, it is meant to carry the memory of that person into the future. A name may also represent wishes, hopes, dreams, and expectations in one's family. For example, among my ethnic group, the Baganda of Uganda, a name like Tusuubira (we hope) or Suubi (hope) signals a wish for hope. Among Swahili-speaking populations, Baraka (blessing) is a common name given to invoke blessings on families. Given names may also embody social harmony while others memorialize natural events. For example, among the Baganda, the name Musisi refers to earthquake. It is given when a child is born at or around the time of an earthquake. It is a traditional belief that in moments of such natural disasters, giving a child such a name will calm and perhaps prevent such occurrences.

Names may also be associated with special family events or milestones. For example, in my culture, there are names that are specifically reserved for twins as they are seen to carry special powers in the life of a family and society. Not only are twins given special names but the children born after the birth of twins are also given special names to reflect the power ascribed to twins. Even the children who preceded the twins have new names added to existing names to reflect the significance of the arrival of twins. The names are given according to the birth order preceding and following the twins. This highlights the power and significance of twins as well as the special cultural status of their parents.

## Clients as Experts of Their Own Story

Narrative therapy is a collaboration that acknowledges the client as the expert in their story. Narrative practitioners actively listen to stories using prompts and guides, enabling richer stories to emerge. It is not only the client who benefits from stories. Therapists, too, gain much from the stories told to them. Thus, we must be humble learners. KJay's story about his chosen name was one such learning experience for me.

KJay was a 22-year-old White trans youth when he first consulted me about his ongoing struggles with depression and countless hours of "always living in a funk." KJay was comfortable with his gender identity—however, his father could not find his way to accepting him. This relational struggle was especially difficult as KJay had a twin sister, and his father could not help but make unfavorable comparisons.

From the outset, I wanted to understand KJay's relationship to depression, including his sleeplessness, and to assess him for suicidal ideation. I asked him the standard questions to establish his level of depression. How you ask questions in the beginning of therapy is sensitive, especially in the initial stages of establishing trust. Will questions serve to open conversations, or will they shut the client down? Most people are not accustomed to exposing their inner lives and vulnerabilities. And yet, that is the function of the therapeutic connection. Campillo (2012) highlights the finesse that is needed when interviewing clients: "It is as if their alternative experiences of life remain locked behind solid doors. Our keys are questions. They are questions that can unlock doors to alternative memories" (p. 38).

Thankfully, KJay and I seamlessly moved through assessment and established a connection. Now that I understood what KJay saw as "the problem," I asked if he could help me to know him better outside of the story that everyone else (including himself) was telling. This is when KJay truly opened up. He was a twin—both of whom were identified as female at birth. Although KJay recognized his male gender identity in his early teen years, his father could not accept that his "twin children could be anything else but female." KJay's relationship with his father had always been fraught, but the rejection became even more pronounced when he selected his chosen name.

Through our work together, KJay became aware of how much his story was being written by his father—something he vehemently struggled against. In our sessions, KJay shared the meaning of his name and why he made that choice. The name was an act of defiance and self-definition, one through which he sought to regain his agency and power. Here's an excerpt from one of our sessions:

> THERAPIST: Tell me about your name.
>
> KJAY: My name means a lot of things. I like that it makes people stop and ask me about it. Just as you did. (*smiles*)
>
> THERAPIST: Tell me more about it.
>
> KJAY: It is my silent resistance that I, as a trans person, choose to do for myself. No one can question me about it. I am fighting back and taking this in my own hands. It is one place I can tell myself that I am okay. I need to tell that story as my story.

KJay is clearly the expert in his own story of identity, transformation, and empowerment. As a narrative practitioner, I listen to stories, help them emerge, and help them to become richer. The meaning of a name is just one story that offers insight into a client's perspectives and experiences. It is interesting to me how people's name stories will vary and shift in significance. This suggests that stories can serve both as gaps and openings. It also underscores the fact that authoring new stories is a continuous and evolving journey and that, as practitioners, we accompany them on that journey when they invite us along. KJay's name also reminded me of the importance of learning his name as he wished it to be known and storied.

## Hope and Complexity

Stories are multilayered, much like our lives. Some parts are known to us while others remain unknown, steeped deep in our unconscious. Stories can occur simultaneously, representing aspects of the past, present, and future.

Furthermore, different stories can be told about the same events, all of which are true. The complexity of stories makes it challenging for both the listener and the teller. This is especially the case when stories have been silenced or vilified, causing much pain and suffering for the person who has had to suppress their own truth. Narrative approaches seek to unravel and validate clients' stories, to move past the problem of saturation, and to locate the hope within them. With KJay, the story of his name moved the narrative from problem saturated to cultivating hope.

Like other clients, KJay's untold stories disconnected him from himself and from others. Here the words of Maya Angelou (1969/2010) ring true: "There is no greater agony than bearing an untold story inside you" (p. 98). Narrative therapists invite clients to share hidden stories and to hold hope for clients as they work through their meanings, experiences, and traumas. As a narrative practitioner, I have committed myself to witnessing and practicing hope, a process that fosters connection and resilience. Adopting a stance of hope is central to narrative practice, as it allows us to draw strength and direction from our personal stories. For me, hope often returns to a pivotal moment from my earlier years—a memory I refer to as the *crack in the window*. This serves as another entry point to my own story, representing a symbol of light and the possibilities of breaking through uncertainty.

## The Crack in the Window

I was 10 years old when a band of men stormed into our home that lay in the outskirts of Kampala, the capital city of Uganda. We were having dinner as a family in our tiny dining room. The intruders wore military uniforms and carried guns, which they brandished at us. They were very loud, demanding to see the man of the house: my father. We were terrified, hiding as best we could in the corners of the tiny room.

My father ran into the bedroom, the men not far behind him. The next thing I heard was a gunshot. It seemed like a long time before the men emerged from the bedroom, although it was probably only seconds. Stepping over the broken plates and other debris, they threatened us by saying that they would come back. We sat motionless, praying for courage. Then, quietly, one by one, we walked into the bedroom. There was a crack in the window, and a streak of blood on the floor. There was no sign of our father.

Since the brutal attack on my family, I have revisited the crack in the window story more times than I can count. Since the violent assault on my father and his subsequent disappearance nothing has symbolized the possibility of hope more than that memory. The crack in the window was a reminder of his presence, and the deep love and admiration that I felt for him. Though it was many years before my prayers were answered and my father returned to us, the crack in the window maintained my hope in his absence. Eventually, we learned that my father was captured by government forces, and he was detained for 5 years. During that time, we had no access to him, but the memory of the crack in the window somehow reassured me that he would come back to us. When my father was finally released, it was a monumental relief for everyone.

Now, years later, the crack in the window continues to be a symbol of hope in both my personal and professional life. It has been my silent companion, fueling passion for my work and finding ways to pass along the hope it represents to my clients. Holding on to hope has become a way of walking alongside the people who seek my therapeutic guidance. Every conversation I begin is rooted in an approach known as appreciative inquiry (AI) (Cooperrinder & Whitney, 2005). AI is a strength-based approach that elevates a person's capacities and positive characteristics that can be used to find solutions to problem. AI does not ignore problems or suffering but instead directs attention to qualities that can drive change within the context of connection. In my work, I use this practice to foster hope and build deep engagement with clients. I approach each person with a stance of curiosity, eager to learn and understand them beyond the challenges they bring.

This perspective allows me to see a more complex and multistoried view of their lives. I strive to understand not only how their experiences have shaped the issues they face but also how these issues, in turn, have shaped their lives. Through curious questioning, I explore the influence of these problems, mapping their effects and evaluating their impact. Additionally, I work to uncover any other forces that may be fueling these struggles, helping individuals gain new insights and perspectives on their experiences. And as for hope, I listen for the *crack in the window.*

## Conclusion

People's lives are filled with stories that are rich in meaning and complexity. Therapeutic conversations create opportunities for these stories to be told, heard, and honored. They also provide a space for more empowering, hopeful stories to be told that help clients assert their own agency. Narrative practitioners engage in deep listening—both to the stories shared by others as well as to the echoes of their own experiences. Storytelling forms the foundation of narrative practice, shaping the way individuals and communities make sense of their lives. Every person and every community carries unique stories waiting to be expressed, and through these narratives, new understandings and possibilities emerge. The next chapter explores some of the foundational principles for and approaches to narrative practice.

CHAPTER 2

# Setting the Stage

Conceptualizing narrative practice informs every aspect of how we formulate a treatment plan, determine the relational postures we embrace, and engage with clients. Understanding narrative theory and its philosophical tenets guides us every step of the way as therapist and client work together to deconstruct problem-saturated stories and reauthor them to make meaningful connection with alternative stories. Narrative practitioners appreciate that culture, context, and circumstance are interrelated as are their values, beliefs, and identities. My work with Mot crystalizes these key narrative theory concepts.

## THE STORY OF MOT

Mot, a 17-year-old, dark-skinned immigrant from Sudan, came to work with me shortly after he arrived in the United States. Mot and his family had been caught in the crossfire of the Sudanese civil war. He was deeply troubled and seeking my help to make sense of what had happened. His stories told of the many atrocities he had seen including family members being killed, others conscripted into the army by force to fight an enemy they did not know. Mot's own experience as a child was equally traumatic and dangerous.

> He served as a message runner for men involved in various factions of the Sudanese civil war. As a child, he was seen as posing little to no threat and was considered easily expendable. His role was to carry messages between groups, which exposed him to extreme violence. On several occasions, he witnessed other young boys like himself being forced to commit horrific acts.
>
> Once safely in the United States, Mot struggled desperately with traumatic memories that affected his health and well-being. His sleep was interrupted. He was angry with himself and with others. His anger appeared to stem from a sense of disappointment and frustration that he did not do more to protect his family, all of whom were killed off. He questioned why God would allow all these "bad things to happen." Raised as a Christian, he felt estranged from his religious upbringing. He was despondent and demoralized about life in general.

As I listened to this child's horrific stories, I wondered how we could possibly make meaning of all that he had endured. How might he make sense of the senseless? What fears, frustrations, hopes, strengths, and resilience would contribute to his alternative story? And how would these come together to allow him to dream of a better future?

Mot's story raised more questions than I had answers. What stories of pain and resilience did this self-portrait speak about? What other stories might Mot's experience tell? Does one narrative rise above the others in his collective storytelling? In what ways had larger forces such as war, dominance, justice, injustice, global politics, oppression, technology, global violence, power, and powerlessness influenced Mot's internal and external realities?

Mot's situation was highly challenging. To begin, I deployed narrative strategies using gentle questioning aimed at helping Mot embark upon the arduous process of unpacking his experiences and reflecting on how they had affected him. My questions exposed the multilayered ways that various discourses shaped his life. Mot's schooling had been repeatedly interrupted, leaving gaps in his education that fueled feelings of inadequacy and shame. He recounted losing close family members, describing a persistent numbness that blanketed his emotional world and made trusting others extraordinarily difficult. Mot also revealed subtler scars: how the narrative of survival had shaped his sense of self-worth, teaching him to suppress vulnerability and view emotional expression as dangerous.

These discourses underscored how cultural and broader social factors intersected with individual stories and emphasized how community plays a significant role in healing and well-being. Last, they surfaced webs of meaning that illuminated how together, clients like Mot and narrative practitioners can envision possibilities for positive change and a future.

This chapter presents core tenets of narrative practice and how they are culturally influenced and contextualized. Culture is a dynamic and evolving process that has deep roots in the philosophy of narrative practice. Dennis Saleebey (1994), one of the founders of the strengths perspective, believed in the power of narrative to unearth subjugated stories and the vital role clinicians can play to help clients bring them forward. "Practice is an intersection where the meanings of the worker (theories), the client (stories and narratives), and culture (myths, rituals, and themes) meet" (p. 351). He goes on to say that clinicians must be open to clients' truths and their constructions of a collective reality.

Narrative theory further considers the individual's relationship to sociopolitical factors as well as notions of liberation, power, and empowerment. Michael White and David Epston (1990) noted how individual stories never exist in isolation and are more often shaped by broader and dominant cultural narratives, including stereotypes, assumptions, and discriminatory myths. These concepts will be illustrated by examples from my clinical practice.

## Narrative Practice as an Approach

Narrative practice is informed by postmodern, feminist, empowerment, and liberation models that give primary importance to the everyday stories of people's lives, the social forces shaping personal narratives, and the ways in which these forces can marginalize, minimize, and obscure people's lived experiences. Narrative practitioners help clients articulate and identify multiple aspects of their lived experience and amplify indicators of strength and resiliency that often go unnoticed. It is also about understanding people's stories in sociopolitical contexts. Narrative practitioners describe this process as "thickening" the clients' descriptions (Morgan, 2000; White & Epston, 1990).

Narrative practice is distinguished by textual and narrative metaphors used as conduits through which people, events, organizations, groups, and communities make sense of lived experiences (Freedman & Combs, 1996; White & Epston, 1990). A text analogy helps to frame people's lives as part of a broader sociopolitical context embedded with power implications (White & Epston, 1990). Narrative practitioners seek to understand the complexity of these lived experiences through the uncovering of dominant and nondominant stories.

Dominant stories permeate what prevailing cultures consider knowledge and values while effectively keeping other truths in subjugated positions (White & Epston, 1990). In Mot's world, the dominant story was that survival meant silence. To show grief or admit fear was a sign of weakness and was seen as dangerous and even shameful.

These stories are powerful, and their impact is widespread. In some cultures, people are persecuted for challenging dominant discourse or living a life that does not conform to the "accepted" truth. White and Epston (1990) suggested that people who seek counseling often erroneously believe that their problems are associated with their nonconforming identity. As I listened to Mot, I began to sense that he had internalized a deep sense of defectiveness. He spoke about feeling "broken" and "wrong," not only of what he had survived but because he could not fit into his newfound community.

Narrative practice and language are inextricably connected. Language reflects people's culture, experience, values, and beliefs. It is the vehicle through which stories are told and heard. It is therefore requisite that therapy affords people a safe enough space to express themselves and construct their reality in their own words and vernacular.

It is sometimes the case, however, that clients may not possess the language to name their experiences. This was the situation with Mot. His war experiences overwhelmingly colored his sense of self and view of reality. In our early conversations he reported being fixated by images of war as he watched the news or social media feeds, all of which contributed to his deepening anger. He described spending long hours watching news reports and scrolling through stories online that depicted violence, injustice, and suffering—scenes that mirrored and amplified his own pain. Every image of destroyed homes, every headline about betrayal and cruelty, seemed to confirm what he already feared: that the world was dangerous, that people were untrustworthy, that survival meant staying angry and alert. Mot's anger was not only a personal reaction to his past but was continually reignited and reinforced by the narratives he absorbed daily.

Much of his rage was directed at the powers that funded war. Together we were able to name Mot's anger not as a problem within him but rather one precipitated by the external realities of geopolitical actions that were well beyond his control. We engaged in many discussions about power and powerlessness; we talked about how poor nations are misused in the global machinery of war. Redirecting Mot's legitimate anger away from himself and toward those who held the power helped to ease his internal suffering.

Through our interactions Mot's understanding of the mechanisms of warfare, its senselessness, and the conundrum people faced in its wake evolved. His anger as well as his insights were palpable:

MOT: (*clenching his teeth*) My country is very poor. We can't afford much. We are a very small country. Who is responsible for the weapons that are used against our people?

THERAPIST: You are raising an important question. Injustices played out in smaller poorer countries. How are you thinking about these concerns?

As part of his therapeutic journey, Mot named the global injustices he had witnessed and the havoc that senseless wars had wrought, often at the expense of poorer nations. By giving a name to these forces, he was able to externalize the source of much of his pain. With his anger now mobilized and purposefully directed, Mot began speaking of action rather than remaining trapped in rumination. He expressed a new aspiration: to become a human rights activist. Motivated by this goal, he now spends time researching social activist groups online and studying their strategies for creating change. Through this process, Mot began to transform his pain into purpose, reclaiming a sense of agency over both his story and his future.

### THE CASE OF BOB

Many clients begin therapy holding tightly to negative self-perceptions. Bob, age 30, was one of these individuals. He had just learned of his father's terminal illness when he came to me for consultation. His father had a history of substance use. His mother was living with dementia. An only child, Bob was the frequent target of his father's angry tantrums. Bob identified his parents' neglect and abuse as major sources of his debilitating anxiety beginning in early childhood. Now as an adult, taking care of his ailing parents had become his sole responsibility.

Making sense of his father's terminal illness and his mother's dementia was painstaking for Bob and formed the bulk of our early work together. He strongly believed that his parents were never going to recover. In this unfamiliar role he was confronted daily by his own fears of illness and dying. A critical element of the narrative process was to explore how Bob understood his relationship with his parents and their current predicaments rather than absorb what others told him to think and feel. Were there other ways for Bob to understand his parents so as not to unleash his own insecurities and fears? Could he decouple his experience of being parented from his present role as caregiver?

Narrative therapy invites clients to re-story past experiences, a process that many find painful and are afraid they will be unable to bear. Bob was no exception. Although he wished to form a bond with his father before he died, Bob worried about uncovering demons from the past that would reawaken his childhood fears, anger, and anxieties. He harbored unresolved anger toward both parents: his father for his substance-fueled abusiveness and his mother for not protecting him. I came to understand that Bob deeply feared becoming just like his father, a justification he used to explain his resistance to developing intimate relationships. He did not want to continue the legacy of intergenerational substance use nor replicate his parents' marital relationship.

Narrative theorists believe in the coexistence of stories. At any given time, people's lives are populated with multiple voices and accounts of their histories and lived experience. A consequence of this multistoriedness is the stance to "exoticize" the domestic (Michael White, personal communication, May 5, 2004). Seeing people's lives beyond what is ordinary or familiar opens one up to be curious.

A multistoried perspective moreover mitigates the tendency to stereotype or assume falsehoods about unfamiliar people or populations. Single stories perpetuate discrimination against others and unjustly disenfranchise communities. Author Chimamanda Ngozi Adichie (2009) writes: "The single story creates stereotypes, and the problem with stereotypes is not that they are untrue, but that they are incomplete. They make one story become the only story." As such, narrative practitioners are poised to invite people to shift from a single story, one that is necessarily incomplete, to a multistory perspective.

Bob's family appraisal evolved over time. We collaboratively examined his father's predicament from multiple lenses beyond popular views constructed about illness and suffering. We examined possible exceptions to what is often described as terminal illness. We sought out what narrative practice calls unique outcomes. "Unique outcomes are experiences that would not be predicted by the plot of the problem-saturated narrative" (Freedman & Combs, 1996, p. 67). Narrative practitioners seek to examine unique outcomes to allow for the emergence of other narratives that reflect local knowledges and alternative possibilities.

As time went on, Bob showed readiness to reauthor the story of his parents and their illnesses. Narrative practice opens the door for conscious "reauthoring" or "re-storying" conversations that detach from old and unhelpful narratives, though Morgan (2000) reminds us that

"No single story can be free of ambiguity or contradiction and no single story can encapsulate or handle all the contingencies of life" (p. 8).

Narrative practitioners pay attention to clients' storylines and as mentioned in Chapter 1, storylines can be thin or thick. Thin storylines are descriptions that do not allow space for people to articulate the complexity and particularity or meanings of actions within specific contexts. A thin description thus has the potential to leave one disconnected, powerless, and lacking any sense of agency.

Thick descriptions provide an alternative storyline with "rich descriptions" (Morgan, 2000, p. 15). They offer nuanced and multifaceted insights into understanding a particular situation, challenging a single or thin description of any event. In Bob's case, to achieve thick descriptions, it was crucial to take a multiperspectival approach. While a terminal diagnosis implies the end of a life, Bob was able to shift his belief to one that viewed his father's life as far from over. His ability to view his father as living with the illness, rather than dying from it, renewed a sense of hope for reenvisioning a better relationship. This alternative perspective strengthened Bob's support for his parents and also helped mitigate his relationship with anxiety as this exchange reveals:

THERAPIST: Do you remember what you told me about your parents' illnesses when we first started working together?

BOB: Yes, I do. I said they were dying. They had come to the end of their life.

THERAPIST: And do you recall the feeling that went along those beliefs?

BOB: I was angry, frustrated, and resentful about everyone, including the massive medical technology available to us in this country. What a fucking joke that no technology could save their lives.

THERAPIST: How do you feel about them now?

BOB: I have come to accept a few things. One, I do not see them as dying with their illnesses. Instead, I see them living with their illnesses. They have lived a good life and now I can concentrate on being here with them.

## A Story to Tell

Michael White was known to begin his lectures by asking the audience "What comes to mind when you think about narrative practice?" I happened to be at one of his lectures when, after posing this question, attendees simply pointed back at him, expecting White, the expert, to answer his own query. White refused. Turning to the audience, White pointed at those in attendance, imploring them "What about you, and you, and you? Each one of you has a story to tell." This was his way of fervently reminding us that we are constantly telling stories and seeking to make meaning of the events in our lives. Morgan (2000) writes:

> The stories we have about our lives are created through linking certain events together in a particular sequence across a time period and finding a way of explaining or making sense of them. This meaning forms the plot of the story. We give meanings to our experiences constantly as we live our lives. A narrative is like a thread that weaves the events together, forming a story (p. 5)

But meaning is constructed in relationship. Such relationship expands storylines in a multitude of ways, adding history, experiences, abilities, skills, interests, assumptions, achievements, fears, expectations, hopes, dreams, wishes, and values. In many cultures, it also includes relationship to ancestors, land, water, traditions, spirits, and spiritual beings. Storylines speak of power, domination, and language, each of which is associated with the past, the present, and the future. They represent the known and the unknown, the familiar and the unfamiliar.

## Meaning and Meaning Making

How we construct meaning matters. Meaning can be derived not only from what is seen but also what is unseen. In my teaching, I illustrate the idea of seen and unseen by asking students this common question:

"How are you?" I then tell them to pause a moment and then turn to another student and ask the same question. Person A asks Person B, then Person B answers. They interact for a few minutes, perhaps no more than two, when I announce that the exercise is over. I follow the activity with a few questions. How did they make meaning of what they were being asked? I wonder with them where does the meaning lie? Was it in the words that were used? Was it in some shared understanding of what was being asked? Who created and sanctioned that shared understanding? Did it shift at any point during the exercise?

Various responses emerge as students contemplate this question. Some believe that their answers depend on the relationship they have with the person they are paired with—for example, how different the answers are if the person is a classmate versus an anonymous person one would meet on the subway. Others indicate that as a casual question one might not give it too much thought. They may say it is a simple code to say hello.

The exercise introduces students to the many factors that affect how meaning is constructed in relationship. Where do meaning and meaning making lie? Do they lie with the encoder (the person who sends the message), the decoder (the one who receives and interprets meaning), or in the intersubjective space between them? One might ask whether both the encoder and the decoder have some mutually agreed-upon understanding of what the question seeks. Who holds the meaning in the moment the question is being asked? How is the meaning interpreted? Is it in the ensuing dialogue? If so, is it dialogical?

Meaning and dialogue are interrelated. According to Bakhtin (1981), meaning emerges from dialogical engagement among multiple speakers and listeners. Dialogue is relational. Meaning does not exist within the boundaries of the individual, "inside" either the speaker or listener, but appears to be shaped in the space between the speaker and the listener. The speaker's utterance finds its meaning in the listener's response, which turns the listener into the speaker and the speaker into the listener, and so it flows in an "unfinalizable" sequence. In Bakhtinian thought, while monologue tends toward conclusions, dialogue aims at developing possibilities.

Dialogue and its focus on possibilities is an important aspect of my work to engage people who become my clients. I use questions to help connect me with clients; we are in a continual process of seeking to construct meaning through dialogic connection. Each of us brings our own meaning to any interaction, but we also participate in collaborative meaning making that allows us to explore possibilities through dialogic connection.

## Core Principles of Narrative Practice

A core principle of narrative practice resonates with constructivist theory, which takes the view that realities are socially constructed, constituted through language, and organized and maintained through narratives (Freedman & Combs, 1996). Although each individual's life is uniquely authored, it is equally influenced by powerful dominant discourses that determine what stories are privileged or preferred, which are disenfranchised, and how each of these get told.

The function of a story is to convey a message and create meaning. Therefore, storytelling, especially the recounting of an event, is shaped by the frameworks to which the storyteller subscribes and will inherently reflect those perspectives. It is impossible to be purely objective without influence from certain respective positionality and context. Considering this, stories move from being a basic recounting of reality to a retelling that re-creates reality by creating parameters around experiences that then become written, shared, or internalized. This begs the questions, Who tells stories? What is taken for granted as listeners, and assumed to be truth? How can we engage with stories in a way that both acknowledges the value of creation, and the propensity of perpetuating messages that populate dominant discourses?

Michel Foucault (2002) examined the ways in which cultural discourses are internalized. According to Foucault, discourse refers to a collection of cultural assumptions taken for granted, unexamined daily habits, and the economic, political, and cultural institutions within which these assumptions and actions exist. Taken-for-granted cultural assumptions shape and maintain how people interact in a given society. Discourse represents "presumed truths" that are embedded in the fabric of everyday life, often becoming nearly invisible. Multiple, sometimes conflicting, discourses exist simultaneously, but over time, certain ones become dominant, occupying more space. These dominant discourses are often prescriptive, carrying cultural expectations about how people should behave, and serve as benchmarks for self-comparison. They both mirror and reinforce prevailing social and political structures.

According to Foucault (2002), people monitor and conduct themselves according to their interpretation of cultural norms. Through this process, discourse shapes our sense of who we are and who we "should" be. When cultural assumptions become the framework for making sense of our lives, alternative experiences may result in silent marginalization. People's own knowledge is obscured, and their life is interpreted through the lens of dominant discourses. Thus, discourse contributes to the construction of identity and in many cases—for example, transgender youth or immigrants—it constrains alternative possibilities contributing to social disenfranchisement, discrimination, and isolation.

Clients' stories may also reflect key cultural discourses that highlight strength, courage, and resilience. In my work with immigrant mothers, I have witnessed their remarkable determination to overcome challenges and survive. As I reflect on their stories and their ability to raise their families amid adversity and derision, I wonder where they find such courage. What cultural messages does society convey about their abilities, and how do they internalize those messages to persevere? How does silence give voice to their stories?

My mother's story is one of embraced silence. I often wonder whether this silence was a choice or if it was imposed upon her by the circumstances she faced. During my father's absence, she became the sole provider for our family. She worked tirelessly, cleaning rooms and performing daily chores for White missionaries. She struggled to feed and clothe us, yet she never gave up. Her life was a quiet struggle to keep her children alive in the face of adversity. Years later, she reflected that her silence was her prayer for survival. My mother's story resonates with the stories of other immigrant women I have encountered.

Did my mother merely survive, or did she thrive? How much did she learn over time, and what kept her going despite so many hardships? I wonder if she knew she was passing these strengths on to her children. What story sustained her? Was it the story of being a mother, or was it the story of staying strong through struggle, no matter what? What lessons did culture transmit to her?

Such questions reveal stories that highlight not only individual experiences but also the values held by communities. They uncover both dominant narratives and alternative stories, often those that may be silenced. Major plots coexist with subplots, reflecting a timeless collective activism and the resilience of women worldwide.

For my mother, her courage and determination provide a rich and detailed portrayal of herself as both a woman and a mother. She never needed to raise her voice to make her strength known. I remember how she worked long shifts while raising us, her exhaustion never outweighing her will to provide stability for us. Especially when my father was away, she maintained a silent resolve of someone who refused to let circumstances define her limits. Despite the physical and emotional toll, she remained steadfast in her goal to create a better life for her family.

Clients may enter therapy living in the shadow of silence, shaped by generations of unspoken pain and resilience. In this sense, therapy becomes an opportunity to break that silence. Silence itself can be generative: It creates space for reflection and the authorship of alternative stories. As it did with Mot, it offers clients a moment to reimagine their narratives, paving new paths toward healing and self-understanding.

## Unfinalizability and Double Listening

Cultivating curiosity around people's stories can open the door to new experiences. As Bob talked about his father's illness and his mother's dementia, I gently invited him to explore what he and his family understood about these illnesses. I also encouraged him to consider what other names or interpretations he might give to them. In doing so, I was inviting Bob to engage in what narrative practice calls a "double-listening" stance—where both the dominant narrative and its possible alternatives can be heard and considered simultaneously.

Guilfoyle (2015) explores the role of listening in narrative therapy. Therapists do not only listen to the content of the client's utterances but also pay attention to the subtext and unsaid aspects of the narrative. For Bob, not only did I listen to the content of what he said, I wondered about his expressed and unexpressed feelings. It was important to engage Bob at a pace he was willing to embrace rather than letting him assume positions that were not necessarily his own.

However, guiding clients toward alternative stories and reauthoring experiences is sometimes an approach taken in narrative practice, requiring the clinician to step away from a purely unknowing, client-centered stance. This is a useful strategy when the client may be on the verge of readiness to change but is not quite there. The clinician may choose to name alternative pathways, letting the client consider them at their own pace and time. Such empathic positioning is necessary to align with a client's readiness to engage. Clients can then feel understood while new ways of interpreting their stories and experiences are facilitated.

For Bob, to know and acknowledge his parents' impending deaths held a significant storyline. His view of his parents was that they were on a "downward spiral." The downward spiral represented a metaphor not to set his hopes high, to value what he had done for them, and his ability to care for them. It also lent appreciation for their accomplishments and their ability to take care of him when they could. It helped Bob to come to terms with his lifelong anger for the neglect he suffered at his parents' hands as a child.

Generation of unique outcomes originates from an understanding that no one story is ever enough to fully "capture a person's experience" (Guilfoyle, 2015, p. 44). A therapist does not need to take the lead in identifying unique outcomes or understanding that one story does not capture a person. This understanding is intrinsic in every person through the idea of "unfinalizability" in which "people overflow discursive constraints" because "people '*acutely sense*' that they cannot be fully captured and can use this sense to 'render *untrue*' stories that close them off to other possibilities" (Guifoyle, 2015, pp. 45–46).

In other words, making a person's position in a story visible, showing them in a stuck position, creates resistance against finalizability. Guilfoyle (2015) expands the concept of "double listening" to what he proposes to be "a kind of triple listening," involving "a three-stage journey: from constitution through resistance to agency" (p. 47). This means truly and openly listening to clients; reflecting upon what they are saying, or not saying; letting them resist their own position in the story, preferring that they create alternatives; and bearing witness to rather than guiding the process of reauthoring.

Mot's story echoes the idea that therapeutic engagement is about bearing witness to the pain and trauma in his life and allowing for uncertainty, resistance, and change. In Mot's case, the process is about not just hearing what he says but also attending to what remains unspoken. These moments become meaningful parts of his story. Bob's unfolding narrative also resists simplification, reminding us that healing often requires embracing complexity and holding space for multiple, coexisting truths.

## Conclusion

This chapter illustrated core principles and approaches to narrative practice. Culture and context are intrinsic to understanding clients' stories as well as their silences. Realities are socially constructed through language and organized and maintained through narrative. A stance of curiosity is instrumental to understanding people's stories and to facilitating dialogical encounters. Such curiosity invites practitioners to see people as multistoried and ever-evolving.

CHAPTER 3

# The Power of Questions

## TOWARD THE UNKNOWN

Questions unite people, answers divide them.
—ELIE WIESEL, 2006

There is a saying that the only dumb question is the one that does not get asked. The act of questioning is an invitation to show interest in what others have to say, and to explore what we do not know. Questions are used to pursue new learning, creating a tapestry of new knowledge. And while we may never acquire all the answers it is imperative to continue to ask questions and just as important to question answers.

Questions bring attention to what is known, to what is unknown, to what is spoken, and what is unspoken. The premise upon which questions are approached makes a difference; how questions are asked shapes the relational space where co-creation takes place. Questions encourage critical thinking, openness, and expansion of perspectives. They stimulate curiosity, encourage exploration, and deepen relationships. Questions launch a journey of discovery, innovation, and realization, helping us make sense of ourselves, others, and the world.

Questions are a form of intervention in narrative practice. They are used to probe what we do not understand and to enrich what we already know. Freedman and Combs (1996) note that we ask questions to "generate experience rather than to gather information" (p. 113). Questions are co-evolving and connect the questioner to the responder, and together they process experience, creating a conversational map that guides narrative conversations.

My grandfather always loved asking us questions whenever he told stories. One such story was about a turtle that ran faster than any other animal. He would start by asking the question, Why would a turtle run faster than an elephant? Such a question caused us to pause and think about the possibility of such a proposition. We imagined the race between the turtle and elephant trying to make sense of our grandfather's inquiry. Was it even possible for the turtle to win the race?

Like others, my grandfather's questions were shaped by his identity, positions, and views. They were intentional, designed to engage us in critical thinking or used as a device to impart his well-earned lived wisdom. In the case of the turtle story, wit, patience, and persistence were seen as crucial to life regardless of one's limitations. The turtle in its wisdom chose to sit at the tail of the elephant unbeknownst to the elephant, who took time to relax, assured that the turtle would not win the race. Hours later when Elephant started the race there was no site of Turtle, so Elephant ran fast to get to the finish line. When Elephant arrived at the finish line, exhausted and exasperated, Elephant sat down only to hear Turtle ask Elephant not to sit on Turtle. Our grandfather would then tell us to be as smart and wise like Turtle.

Questions might be factual, Socratic, probing, or reflective. Some invite people to remember events or facts. Others are aimed at creating evidence to be applied, analyzed, or evaluated to enhance understanding. Inevitably clients come to us with many unresolved questions. For example, the moment Pennie entered my office she let me know that she was seeking answers to many questions. Pennie was troubled by a midlife experience. She described it as "a journey into new territories," as she was about to turn 50:

PENNIE: I have many questions, and I am full of questions.

THERAPIST: This is a place where therapy can support you with your questions. I see questions as openings.

PENNIE: Yes, I just turned 50 and I feel like I'm beginning a journey into new territories. A journey that is questioning me about who I am and where I am going. I worry that I have lost so much time and there is no turning back.

With this response, Pennie introduced the metaphor of "journey." She was inviting me to embark with her on this journey by asking more questions and learning more about her struggles:

THERAPIST: So, there is a journey you have started on? Tell me about the journey. Where does this journey begin and where do you see it going? What does it say about you and your abilities?

PENNIE: At 50, I wonder if there is anything I have done in my life worth noting. I know I have had many missed opportunities with many people in my life. I realize how messed up my relationship is with my mother. How come she never sees me as I am? How come she treats me as a 12-year-old girl? How can I ever find a place in her heart? Why me? Why do I melt before her?

Pennie's rich and complex story came to life in those opening lines. They spoke boldly about the fraught relationship between her and her mother. As I sat with her, I wondered what questions to ask next. I checked my temptation to inquire only about the problem narratives. Instead, I kept myself from psychoanalyzing and formulated questions to elicit multivariate narratives that we would journey through together. As best as I could, I kept my mind open to possibilities but was simultaneously aware of biases that could impede the way.

## Therapeutic Postures

In narrative practice, a therapeutic posture refers to the therapist's attitude in relation to their client, one that embraces essential principles of respect, humility, collaboration, and a nonpathologizing stance. A therapeutic posture guides how one approaches unexpected events, influences therapeutic responses, and shapes the interactional tone of the therapeutic relationship (Beaudoin & Monk, 2024).

Beaudoin and Monk (2024) identify three therapeutic postures present in therapeutic relationship: centering, decentering, and co-centering. Primary to these postures is commitment to the bidirectional and collaborative nature of the therapeutic relationship. Postures are variably described as a relational stance involved—for example, in a cross-cultural negotiation (Madsen, 2007), a way of being in relationship and conversation (Anderson, 2007), and the art of bearing "witness" (Andersen, 1996; Hoffman, 2007). Both therapist and client bring something unique into the therapeutic exchange: The therapist contributes their theoretical and facilitation expertise, and the client brings their lived wisdom and is an expert in their life story.

Using a centering posture therapists apply their theoretical knowledge to the client's concerns while always positioning themselves around the client's beliefs, values, and experience. Using Pennie's metaphor, I decided to focus my questions on her childhood journey. I wondered about what positive memories she recalled as a 12-year-old. To her surprise, and mine, she told a story that she had not recalled in years. Her story went back to the time her older sister left for college. She described it as a moment that freed her up to be her "own person":

> PENNIE: My sister was 6 years older than me. She was the apple of my parents' eyes. They loved her and adored her. The day she left for college they all looked sad after dropping her off at college. Not a word was said as they drove back with me. Deep inside me, I felt a deep sense of relief. Now, I could be just me without having to measure up to my sister. Such a thought gave me a deep feeling of contentment. I kept those thoughts to myself.

THERAPIST: So, you experienced a sense of contentment?

PENNIE: Of course, I missed my sister too, but I was happy that I could just be me, my person, without my sister in the background. (*smiles*)

As Pennie shared her experience, I noticed how I was once again being drawn into the problematic narratives that had surrounded her 12-year-old self. I needed to co-center myself with Pennie and to deepen my understanding of her experience through mindful prompts and questions. According to Beaudoin and Monk (2024), "co-centering allows decentered practices to be influential, as it provides space for practitioners to honor the tradition of privileging clients' knowledge, while also integrating attention to affective, nonverbal, and embodied elements expressed by both therapist and client" (p. 46). Attending to Pennie's full expression I followed her words, feelings, behaviors, and sensations while concurrently attending to my own reactions.

## Types of Questions

Questions are an invaluable intervention tool meant to engage both the storyteller and the listener. Questions are designed to have specific intentions and directions—they may, for example, probe for deeper meaning or support curiosity about what a client has shared. They encourage reflection on the significance of issues, invite meaning making, or ponder other alternatives. Examples of such questions are Why do you think a particular moment stood out to you? What does this story reveal about what you care about most? What else might be true that you haven't considered?

Freedman and Combs (1996) propose five types of questions to help clinicians gain insight into clients' meaning making and fill gaps in storylines. The questions serve as interventions that generate the experience of re-storying. Question types include (1) deconstruction questions, (2) opening-space questions, (3) preference questions, (4) story development questions, and (5) meaning questions (p. 119).

## Five Types of Questions

1. Deconstruction
2. Opening space
3. Preference
4. Story development
5. Meaning

Freedman and Combs, 1996

Deconstruction questions prompt people to tell their stories in all their complexity. Therapist and client explore the story together using varying lenses to examine how it is told, unpack the storylines, and identify the client's preferred telling. Deconstruction questions examine held beliefs about such factors as gender, race, sexual orientation, religion, or class and intentionally raise power dynamics that are embedded in clients' narratives. For example, is racism playing a role in a Black middle schooler's isolation? A narrative therapist would carefully use deconstruction questioning to unearth whether discrimination was present in the youngster's storyline. Deconstruction questions seek to examine prevailing narratives and the power structures that are operative in maintaining those narratives that undermine a client's preferred story and inhibit their well-being. The kite story illustrates intentions of deconstructive questioning in raising assumptions and unpacking implicit issues of power.

## The Kite Story

The story goes like this:

> Walking along the seashore, a sage encountered a young person holding a kite. Intrigued by this young person, the sage asked, "What are you doing?" The young person looked at the sage, smiled, and replied, "Guess what I am doing." The sage paused in reflection, then smiled back and said, "I think you are playing with

> the kite." Gesturing in disagreement, the young person responded, "No, I am not playing with the kite—I am playing with the wind!"

One might ask many questions when analyzing this story. Who is the sage, and who is the young person? To some, the encounter suggests that the sage holds knowledge while the young person does not. Perhaps the sage simply seeks to engage in conversation, fostering a connection. After all, they are both at the seashore—an open, expansive space where casual exchanges naturally occur. One can imagine a lively beach setting with other people and various activities unfolding around them. The sage brings a particular worldview, however, one that may differ from the young person's perspective.

At first glance, the interaction suggests that the young person is merely playing with a kite—an assumption shaped by common expectations of youth. However, the young person challenges this view, offering a deeper perspective: They are not just playing with the kite but with the wind itself.

It is fascinating to hear the varied interpretations this particular story generates. Take a moment to reflect on your initial thoughts and images. Some people instinctively assign gender to both the sage and the young person. Often, the sage is perceived as male, reflecting underlying issues of patriarchy and the association of wisdom with masculinity. Similarly, many assume the young person is a boy. These gendered assumptions reveal how deeply embedded gender discourses are within cultural narratives, shaping the ways we perceive and interpret even the simplest of stories. Deconstructing stories reveals inherent biases and makes room for alternative narratives to emerge.

Opening-space questions uncover unique outcomes or small exceptions to the client's dominant, problematic story. They are meant to be expansive, revealing new insights, and they act to generate experience. By focusing on these revelatory moments, clients can recognize their agency and access opportunities for change. Freedman and Combs (1996) provide examples of such questions, including hypothetical ones, that serve as inquiries into alternative perspectives, or exceptions, with consideration for contexts or time frames. In what situations have you been able to make better judgments? Have there been times when complaining took a backstage? If you were to bring those moments to work on your behalf, what might that look like? Exploring unique outcomes using opening-space questions deepens both the client's and therapist's understanding of storied experiences.

When Bob (from Chapter 2) referred to his parents as living with dementia, as opposed to having dementia, he was suddenly able to see them beyond the confines of the problematic story. He focused on life, rather than death, as the key to understanding their situation. This simple use of language shifted his perspective, allowing him to appreciate the time they shared. Bob made a conscious effort to identify unique outcomes, no matter how small they might be. As Freedman and Combs (1996) note, a unique outcome does not need to be a grand triumph; even small shifts, acts of kindness, or resistance can be considered a potent unique outcome.

Preference questions encourage clients to articulate their choices and desires, and explore the values attached to them. This process helps them develop personal signature positions around their decisions and foster a deeper sense of ownership over their experiences and actions. Freedman and Combs (1996) suggest that therapists pose follow-up questions to better understand the reasons behind their clients' preferences. Such questions may look at details, contrasts, and nuances surrounding an issue. For example, Who stood by you as you made the decision to resist your partner's insults? How did you decide to stay engaged in the face of such behavior? Constructing preference questions is a mindful process as prompts can subtly reflect the clinician's underlying beliefs or implicit biases as opposed to the clients' wishes. Narrative therapists must remain cognizant to stay centered on the client's voice and not their own.

Story development questions encourage building a structured narrative, one that contextualizes a story within a time frame and to relationships that are significant to the story's meaning (Freedman & Combs, 1996). Through these questions, an event is examined in its complexities and allows ample space for the untold aspects of the story to emerge. Story development questions serve to anchor and solidify personal positions, helping individuals to connect with the deeper layers of their experiences. There are myriad ways to anchor a story, through the details, the texture of knowledge, or the broader context that surrounds it.

Meaning questions invite people to reflect on their stories from various perspectives, opening up new territories of self-understanding. These reflections reveal personal qualities, relationship dynamics, motivations, hopes, values, knowledge, and learnings (Freedman & Combs, 1996, p. 137). Meaning questions name and attribute significance to earlier questions, often leading to those "aha!" moments within the story. Such insights generate experience, deepening the client's understanding of themselves and their narrative.

There are also what I call out-of-the-box questions designed to disrupt automatic thinking, spark creativity, and open up new ways of seeing a story or identity. These questions help people break out of limiting narratives. They include metaphorical questions to encourage symbolic thinking, such as If your life were a book, what would this chapter be called? Time-travel questions invoke perspective shifting by imagining different time frames. For example, it is 10 years in the future, how might you tell this story to someone else? Outsider questions help to gain a distance from the narrative. For example, if a friend were in your situation, what advice would you give them? Playful questions can also spark spontaneous thinking or invite supportive perspectives from idealized figures. If you were a superhero in a movie, what would your strengths be? What would your favorite character do in this situation? Similarly, magical thinking questions help to explore hidden desires or reimagine possibilities. If you had a magic wand and could change one part of your story, what would it be? Working with children, I find these types of questions engaging. Connecting to children's imaginative world can have dramatic effects (Marsten et al., 2016).

Questions help make sense of the stories people bring to the therapeutic process. They create a structure through which problematizing narratives are deconstructed, re-storied, and an environment where people can be separated from their problems is forged. Questions build thicker, more nuanced understandings that reveal the inner and outer sources of problems as well as ways to address them. An example of the way questions opens possibilities is well demonstrated by the case of Jim below.

### JIM AND QUESTIONS FOR WORRY

Fifteen-year-old Jim had struggled with anxiety for years. His self-esteem was low, and he was plagued by self-doubt. His mother shared that Jim had begun skipping school over the past few months. Jim explained that it was too difficult for him to face his classmates day in and day out. He described the shame and scrutiny he felt at not measuring up to his peers. Our work began by identifying how he would name the problems in his life:

THERAPIST: Tell me what name or names you might give what you are experiencing.

JIM: Worry.

THERAPIST: Would it be okay to get to know some things about worry? When does worry come to you? What kind of things does worry do to you? What kind of thoughts does it put in your mind?

JIM: Well, worry is always there in my life. It is there when I wake up, just before I go to school, before I take a quiz. All the time. I . . . can't stand it. It is always whispering things to me.

THERAPIST: What kind of things is worry whispering to you?

JIM: Many things and it makes me do things. Things I would not like to do. I know I don't.

THERAPIST: What kind of behaviors or actions does it make you do or perform? What kind of things does it have you do that go against your best judgment?

JIM: Lot of things . . . I skip school . . . I make up excuses . . . I just do not trust myself.

THERAPIST: How long has worry been part of your life? In what ways has your life changed since worry became involved?

JIM: I have had worry all my life. As long as I can remember. I have

> not been able to be myself. I cannot trust anyone. I have these weird suspicions about any kid who tries to become my friend. Why would they want to?

My questions sought to help Jim build a thicker description of "worry" to understand the tactics and tricks worry deployed in his life. Equally important was to identify times when worry did not interfere, what happened when it was not disruptive. I also wanted to gain a sense of who Jim considered to be his supporters.

My exchange with Jim exemplifies questions used to lift the externalizing metaphor such that the client can better understand the function of the problem as well as the possibilities that could mitigate its influence. I typically inquire about the times when the problem is not around: "When is worry weaker or less bothersome?" "Are there times when you are able to ignore worry?" I also ask questions that thicken the story about personal agency: "How is it that you have managed to keep worry from completely taking over?" "What aspects of your life/yourself have kept worry at bay? The following dialogue illustrates how these types of questions were applied in practice:

THERAPIST: How does worry interfere in other parts of your life? When/where does worry show up?

JIM: I refuse to participate in sports . . . or even when I know the answer to the question, I will not raise my hand. I constantly put myself down.

THERAPIST: Does worry ever let up? What is it like when it lets go of your life? Does worry sometimes give you pause to enjoy your life, or does it always end up burdening you?

JIM: Hmm . . . (*pauses*) I don't know . . . I suppose when I play video games or watch videos.

THERAPIST: How come?

JIM: I guess I lose myself in the games. I get to talk to characters in the video games.

THERAPIST: What do you think worry wants for your life?

JIM: I do not know.

THERAPIST: What are you watching on TV or social media that supports worry in your life? What are you watching that goes against worry's intentions?

JIM: Sometimes, I watch videos of people who have beaten the odds. I see that they have made tremendous changes in their lives. I can see people like me who do not have as much as I have . . . but they persevere. They make it with so little. Like these videos of children in poor countries creating their own games and having fun. [He proceeded to show me a couple of videos of Ghanaian children who had turned old car tires into play toys.]

THERAPIST: What does that say to you about worry?

JIM: Worry . . . I do not know, maybe there is a plan for me . . .

THERAPIST: A plan? What kind of plan?

JIM: Yes, it's sending me messages.

THERAPIST: What messages from outside feed/strengthen worry?

JIM: That I am no good . . . that I will not succeed. That I am a fraud.

THERAPIST: So, worry is using every tactic in the book to get the better of you? Even when you see pictures of kids with so little but having fun worry continues to tell you other messages.

JIM: Yes, it berates . . . it makes me look at my failures all the time. It does not allow me to sleep or enjoy my life. It promises what it cannot deliver. It tells people to stay away from me when I get into these moments. I think it does the same to other people.

THERAPIST: Are there other people you know for whom worry inhabits their life? What tactics does worry use with other people your own age? How does worry operate in their lives?

JIM: I see it on social media. Kids. Dissing each other all the time.

THERAPIST: What do you see as worry's intentions, beliefs, and ideas? What do you think are worry's plans, likes, and dislikes? Do you think worry has a master plan? If so, is worry's master plan for you the same or different compared to that of other people you know?

JIM: I do not know but worry tells me many things. Some I believe, some I do not . . . I can see how much worry interferes in my life. I need to separate myself from worry and its plans.

THERAPIST: How do you see yourself doing that? Who might you call upon?

JIM: I need to tell myself that worry does not have a hold over me. I need to seek my own purposes in life.

THERAPIST: And how do you see yourself do that?

JIM: I need to separate myself from worry. You asking about worry is making realize that I can do things differently.

THERAPIST: Yes, you can do things differently. And you have already started. Our work together can support your efforts. In fact, you are making good observations. What do you see as worry's purposes, motives, wishes for you? And how might you choose differently?

JIM: Its wishes are not mine. I must see myself separate from this thing, which puts me down. I must find my own wishes and hold on to my dreams.

THERAPIST: What might those be? Who might be there standing next to you?

JIM: (*pauses briefly*) I guess my kindergarten teacher, who, years ago, noticed a kid teasing me and told him to stop it. She stood by me.

THERAPIST: So, your kindergarten teacher is an important ally in pushing worry aside.

JIM: She saw me . . . I like people to see me as I am.

Jim's responses revealed how much he already knew about "worry." Like many people, he was familiar with its tactics, motives, and intentions. Jim was also able to express what he considered to be possibilities. He was seeing himself as separate from worry, externalizing the problem. Externalizing questions help identify exceptions to the problem's control and also create opportunities to ask about the level of influence the person has over the problem. Externalizing creates dialogic space for clients to own their agency and see themselves as having power to change their lives.

Attending to sensory information in clients' lives is important. Together we contemplated if there might be sensory experiences Jim associated with worry. I asked Jim these questions: "Does worry show up when you open your eyes to something expected or unexpected? Is it instigated by a certain smell or sound?" "How does worry show up when you taste your food? Is it different for you if this happens in a familiar place or unfamiliar place?" Exploring sensory information was helpful to Jim. It connected him to moments of boredom and loneliness, which created anxiety and led to overeating to, as he put it, "fill the void." He had developed an insatiable interest in snacking.

Discovering exceptions to the problem's influence expands embedded storylines leading to meaningful results. I asked Jim these questions: "What does it say about you that you have resisted worry in this way, at this time?" "What does it mean that you have put your foot down to worry's demands?" "What would others think about you now that you have been able to stand up against worry?" People react to these prompts in diverse ways, but they always solicit details and move the narrative process along.

Establishing trust in relationship is prerequisite to asking about a client's moral beliefs and values. The questions I used were meant to open opportunities for reflection and promote agency and choice. With Jim, I was curious about both the beliefs that reinforced "worry" and the function that worry served in his life. I was hoping that Jim might discover ways to actively contribute to addressing it. Jim was nimble at naming actions and knowledges that he already used to manage worry. Putting these into words was transformational. It helped him deconstruct the problem narrative and re-story his experience:

THERAPIST: Would you say that the way you have engaged worry has been effective or not effective? Why would you say so?

JIM: In some ways, it has been effective. I have been able to stand up to worry. I refuse to begin my day by worrying about things as I used to do.

THERAPIST: What does standing up to worry say about what you believe in?

JIM: It means that I can do it. I know sometimes I fail. Worry wins but sometimes, I do . . . I can do it.

As our work progressed, Jim and I examined new possibilities to increase his influence on the problem:

THERAPIST: What would it do to worry in the long term if you were to continue to resist its influence in this way? What does it mean to you that you have been able to increase your resistance against worry?

JIM: Maybe worry will go away. I can become myself and not part of worry or worry's insidious plans and intentions. I can be myself. I can relax.

My work with Jim illuminates how identities are tightly entwined in the texture of people's problems. Externalizing conversations are an antidote to these internalized self-understandings. As White (2007) aptly notes, when engaging in externalizing conversations "the problem ceases to represent the "truth" about people's identities, and options for successful resolution suddenly become visible and accessible" (p. 9).

## Narrative Resistance

Narrative theory is committed to naming injustice; directly addressing issues of power, control, and oppression; and reinforcing counternarratives around such factors as gender, gender role expectations, earning power, class, and childcare, among others. Questioning may thus ask about matters of discrimination, racism, homophobia, and other encounters with dominant social narratives. McKenzie-Mohr and Lafrance (2017) introduced the concept of "narrative resistance," offering techniques used to identify and reauthor problem-saturated stories, create preferred narratives, and mitigate the power of master narratives (culturally shared stories that guide thoughts, feelings, values, and behavior). Master narratives perpetuate power imbalances, hierarchical structures, and oppressive narratives that have covert and explicit implications and influence on individuals' lives. Therapy engages people in finding and articulating counternarratives as a form of resistance.

Gender messages—for example, adherence to rigid and binary gender expectations—often arise in the stories clients share during therapeutic conversations. My work with heterosexual couples often uncovers core tensions around gender roles and expectations and how they get played out in daily life—for example, in financial and childcare responsibilities. Balancing questions, those that focus on the contributions of each party in the couple relationship, are helpful in clarifying unspoken issues. These questions can be challenging; couples often have quite different perspectives on the problem and how to solve it. My job is to invite each member of the couple to enter into dialogue, feel heard, and witness each other growing together.

Families, too, may be stuck in unnamed conflicts that are influenced by master narratives, such as those associated with gender, family violence, oppression, unrecognized grief, and other dominating stories. Jayson and his mother encountered many roadblocks in their individual and family stories. Their case offers a detailed example of questioning and its role in actualizing narrative resistance.

### JAYSON AND HIS MOTHER

Jayson's mother was distraught. Her 12-year-old son "terrorized" her, repeatedly shoving and acting in a threatening manner. He was clearly struggling with emotional regulation, especially anger. Jayson's father had abandoned the family early in his life. Jayson believed that no one cared about him. He harbored a lot of resentment toward his absent father but unleashed his anger and violent outbursts primarily toward his mother.

Jayson was diagnosed with attention and organizational difficulties. He had witnessed his parents engage in explosive fights. He worried a lot about what was going to happen to him, especially now that his father was out of the home and made no effort to keep

> in contact. Jayson struggled with learning and behavioral difficulties in school. His grades were falling. He had been suspended a few times for swearing at his teachers. Jayson also threatened his classmates and acted aggressively toward them. At home, he spent most of his time watching music videos, many of which communicated violent messages.

As a therapist, I am mandated to ask about abuse and violence in the home when I suspect it might be happening. Silence often accompanies family violence and so I was careful to balance my inquiry while simultaneously keeping Jayson and his mother engaged in the therapy. I assumed that there were many stories about Jayson other than his "terrorizing" behavior. I told Jayson and his mother that I was concerned and curious about violence and its presence in the home. I wondered with them about how violence was showing up in the home and when it mostly occurred. I was also curious about the times when violence or fighting was not happening.

I used questions that sought to bring out Jayson's "honorable self": positive aspects of his identity that were currently obscured by the overriding problem-saturated story. For example, I asked, "When you feel anger toward your mother, do you ever notice other feelings?" This question was asked to gauge aspects of his emotional or "feeling self" and whether he was capable of warmth or empathy toward his mother. I juxtaposed these questions with others about sensory experiences—for example, did he feel anger when he tasted the food his mother prepared for the family? I was hoping to generate inner contradictions about his feelings toward the woman whose food he tasted with the anger he held toward her.

Together, our work was directed toward bolstering the actions Jayson and his mother were taking to stop violence in the home. Questions were thoughtfully crafted but did not minimize the repercussions wrought by family violence. They were aimed at bringing out everyone's sense of agency, asking both to reflect on what they were doing to keep violence at bay—for instance, thinking back now, would you have done things differently? How would you begin to work against hitting? What allies might you call upon in the struggle against violence? How might you separate enjoyment of your mother's food from the anger you feel toward her?

Cultural myths and narratives about masculine power and violence intersected with Jayson's feelings of loss and the anger that arose from it. I inquired about where and how he had learned about hitting, a question that surprised him, and he momentarily became gripped by silence. This question, however, prompted a significant exchange about male role models, who he looked up to, and how they informed his actions. I learned that Jayson was watching many violent movies by himself, something that troubled his mother. This launched a curiosity-driven and client-centered interaction, referred to in narrative practice as a conversational map. In this case the conversational map explored how and why Jayson found allyship with despicable characters in the shows he watched.

One such character is Loki in the Marvel Cinematic Universe, a charismatic villain-turned-antihero known for trickery and inner conflict. Trickery and unpredictability seemed to appeal to Jayson. Together we debunked the unrealistic actions and false promises such characters portrayed. This discussion opened the possibility to consider role models with whom Jayson could honorably and reliably identify and dismiss the ones whose objectives were disconnection and harm.

Finding questions developmentally attuned to a 12-year-old that raise broader issues of power, gender, and master narratives in conversation is not easy. I asked Jayson whether he was more open to listen to his mom or to his impulses. "How might you push back on your impulses?" With this question I was trying to realign Jayson's agency, power, and knowledge and recognize his mother's contributions. That question was met with no result. However, the following one achieved the task at hand. I asked Jayson, "If a stranger came to your house and hit your mom, would that be okay?" After a pause, he said it would not be okay. I countered his answer by saying, "If it is not okay with a stranger, why would it be okay with you to hit your mother?"

I followed this exchange with related questions to prompt him to think about his values, intentions, and inner principles: "Do you think your mom has the right to be safe in her home?" "Do you think you have a right to be safe in your home?" "What kind of man/person would you like to be when you are older?"

My questions urged Jayson to unlock unsung moments in his life that led to new pathways and ways of being. The intention was to highlight Jayson's honorable self and root out exceptions, unique outcomes, and moments of difference in his experience. Exemplar questions might ask, "Who will notice first if you are trying to control your impulses? What clues might point you into noticing?" "If you were to brag about your efforts, to whom might you brag?" "Do you think your mom sees you differently when you are controlling your anger? How can you tell if she notices your efforts?"

Family engagement in narrative therapy is essential when working with young children. Jayson's mother was essential to co-creating the conversational map and I was curious about her family beliefs around gender roles and exercise of power in the family. "If an adult treated you the way your son does, would you put up with it?" This question aimed at bolstering her sense of agency.

Then, I asked Jayson's mom questions that sought to build a collaborative response to addressing the problem in the home: "How have you and your son worked together toward stopping the violence?" "What role do you think you might have had in hitting or yelling?" "Would you consider some continuing education, or a refresher course on hitting or yelling, the good, the bad, and the ugly?" Working side by side through curious questioning, Jayson, his mother, and I courageously moved forward to address violence in the home.

Roth and Epston (1996) differentiate between "problem-internalizing questions" and "problem-externalizing questions." Problem-internalizing questions create a situation in which "Seeing oneself as one with a problem implies that one's identity is the problem or includes the problem and therefore change requires the alteration of one's very being" (pp. 148–149). In other words, failing to separate clients from the problems creates a situation in which there is no way for clients to act against the problem without acting against the self.

Problem-externalizing questions explicitly separate the client from the problem allowing the client space to activate agency to shift their relationship with the problem (Roth & Epston, 1996). It is important to note that externalizing the problem focuses on developing a new relationship with the problem. It does not focus on destroying or killing the problem because the problem may not necessarily serve only as a problem. Problems serve specific functions and roles in the lives of people. For Jayson, he was eventually able to control his anger with his mother. However, after doing so, more problems with his peers ensued at school. Our work turned to finding ways he could transfer his newly honed regulatory skills in other contexts. However, the transfer of his anger from one space to another was a red flag that anger performed a greater function, and we needed to find its source.

Having established trust with Jayson and his mother, I believed it was time to address his abandonment and its impacts. I invited both Jayson and his mother to name the problem in their own words and express its unique meaning in their lives:

THERAPIST: I'm just wondering if there is a name each of you would give this problem.

JAYSON/MOM: (*total silence*)

I volunteered a few terms that had come up in earlier sessions:

THERAPIST: I was wondering about what you would call this problem, something like "being in charge," "depression," or the "worry" or the "guilt" or "self-doubt?" These are some of the things I was thinking of while you were speaking. What do you think?

MOM: Control.

JAYSON: (*shrugs shoulders*) Don't know.

Naming the problem was difficult for both Jayson and his mother. It involved externalizing the problem through questioning that traced the problem's history and influence, including its way of operating, its intentions, and its techniques. Naming the problem often generates difficult feelings, identifies tensions and conflicts between people, reveals cultural and social practices, and often raises more than one problem at any given time (Morgan, 2000, p. 21). Externalizing questions contextualize the problem, shining a light on the dynamic nature of problems and making space for alternative stories within the ebb and flow of the overall narrative (p. 36).

Because Jayson seemed to tense up when asked about his father, I was curious about the relationship between his anger and his father's absence. I used decentering and co-centering postures to elicit Jayson's agency by framing anger in a positive way. Co-centering invites therapists to tap into their own feelings and note parallel experiences with the intimacy of the therapeutic experience. Given our relationship, I felt I could share my feelings with him. I was careful not to assume that Jayson's anger was linked to his father's absence, nor did I want to assume that anger was the operative feeling for him. Tracing the history and influence of the problem includes attention to the wider plot and narratives beyond the problem itself:

THERAPIST: You know Jayson, I do not know about you, but I believe that most people would be furious at their fathers if they just left like that. I know I would be. Maybe you are, maybe you are not!

JAYSON: (*silence; shrugs shoulders*)

His silence spoke volumes, but I continued, asking Jayson if he had other feelings he wished to speak about. To my happy surprise, Jayson blurted out:

JAYSON: I am pissed at him. He has made me suffer. Does he care?

THERAPIST: I am very sorry that you have suffered from his absence, and you ask a very important question.

"Does he care?" was a powerful question, one that we would explore together.

## Exploring the Effects of the Problem

After naming the problem, its impacts, and historicizing the relative influence of the problem, the next step is to address their effects. This involves questions that explore how the problem has affected a person's sense of self; their self-perceptions as a parent, partner, mother, wife, sister, son, brother, worker; and their hopes, dreams, and dreams for the future:

THERAPIST: Tell me what anger has you do that goes against your better self.

JAYSON: (*silence*)

THERAPIST: Does your better you [self] give you some sense of calm about your abilities?

Asking questions about the consequence of the problem is important in demonstrating to clients that their distress is taken seriously. It is important to do this with externalizing language that sheds light on the way the problem operates in real time and avoids reinforcing oppressive or pathologizing narratives. With Jayson and his mother, it was important to evaluate the effects of the problem vis-à-vis their relationship. How would they prefer to relate to each other given the lessons they had learned about hitting and shoving? In one exchange, I asked Jayson and his mom the following:

THERAPIST: How have you both taken steps to work side by side in taking on hitting? What other lessons are you learning about yourselves? What might you tell others about your abilities to keep away from hitting?

The question recognized the skills and abilities both had acquired in managing hitting and shoving. It was now important to explore how master narratives had reinforced the performance of violence in their home. Both identified that violent movies were one of the cultural supports that heroized the violence that occurred in their home. Together, we addressed the myths, falsehoods, and gendered narratives that upheld these beliefs and deconstructed them through questioning, listening, and re-storying.

According to Bruner (1986), stories are both "transformed and transformative" (p. 146). There are no fixed meanings. These "narratives are not only structures of meaning but structures of power as well" (p. 144). Maintaining attention to the collaborative, unknowing, curious stance of narrative therapy promotes change in ways that are meaningful and purposeful to clients. However, as Bruner points out, stories are not static. Being alert to their evolving meaning without judgment requires that the therapist check in to make sure they're attuned to whatever version is in progress.

## Crafting Questions

Crafting questions is an art. In narrative therapy questions prompt clients to re-story how problems both effect and contribute to their lives. Well-crafted questions inform the conversational map that guides useful and change-making interactions. Questions are used as guides to unpack pathologizing stories, opening up opportunities for clients to discover alternative or preferred stories more aligned with their identities and goals.

Tracing the roots of problem narratives offers new pathways to consider and enact one's identity and move past pathologizing stories that have inhabited people's lives. Stories have timelines that reveal how problem narratives have dictated who one was in the past, who they are in the present, and who they might become in the future if not recognized or addressed. For Jayson and his mom, it was a herculean effort to redefine the problem of "hitting in the home" and moreover, to work collaboratively to assign a different identity for how they would manage "hitting" in a re-storied life.

So, how does one craft questions that trace individual, family, or community problems, debunk the standing-problem narrative, and formulate an alternative story inclusive of abilities, talents, ingenuity, and resilience? As we have discussed, problem stories are thinly described and typically made up of single narratives that often focus on dysfunction. Questions therefore probe for details that enrich clients' storytelling, adding content about the nature of their abilities, their talents, and personal qualities. For Jayson and his mom, there was clearly more to their relationship than the problem of "hitting." The problem survived and thrived in isolation and unspoken feelings of loss and sadness. To instigate change, mother and son needed to enhance the relational storyline by acknowledging the positive aspects of their bond, their resilience as a family, and form a partnership of friendship:

> THERAPIST: I notice that you and your mom enjoy a closeness that often gets interrupted by hitting. What else might you call upon if hitting were to take a break from you? How might you find special moments for yourselves? In fact, do you imagine it might make your time together more enjoyable?

The above questions seek to understand the nature and source of Jayson's actions, raise alternative relational possibilities, and ask him to imagine how such changes might improve his life story. Defining the problem as "hitting" and not something wrong with Jayson, stems reactivity. Jayson can analyze the problem from a safe distance making it possible to consider different feelings and actions. For Jayson, his life was marred by his father's absence, though his feelings about abandonment were unspoken.

Fighting and hitting took control of his life, and anger wrote the script of his story. Fighting was the story he heard about himself and "hitting" was how he expressed his relationship with others, especially his mother. He shared with me that no matter how abandoned he felt by his father he could not help but blame his mother. His mother was an easy target for his anger because in his eyes, she had not protected him. Jayson did not trust that anyone could protect him, leaving him feeling alone and vulnerable. Left to his own devices and bolstered by the pervasive masculine images of violence, he attached his identity to hitting and fighting.

With growing awareness and the motivation to construct an alternative version of his story, Jayson and I focused on generating an asset-saturated story, one that identified strengths and ways to imagine a different future. Well-crafted questions guide the transition from problem-saturated stories where the problem controls the byline to asset stories that elevate qualities of resilience and hope.

## Using Questions to Raise Alternative and Asset-Saturated Stories

Questions designed to explore alternative stories seek to identify unique outcomes, times when clients have resisted impulses or avoided resorting to problematic actions or thoughts. For example, when was Jayson able to resist "hitting" in his interactions with his mother? What factors were present at times when "hitting" did not show up in his relationships? I was trying to generate an alternative story when I asked Jayson whether it was okay for a stranger to hit his mother. How might this direct his thinking to an alternative story about his own "hitting"? Might there be another version of the problem story that Jayson could tell? What would that look like? What details would shift the narrative and what support might be needed to maintain an alternative story?

Genre in narrative therapy refers to the style, structure, and emotional tone of how a story is told. Examining the genre of storytelling aids in understanding its content and is necessary to create an alternative story. Genre reveals the tenor of a narrative—for example, is it viewed as tragic, humorous; is it filled with hope for change or riddled with impenetrable despair? Questions track the problem story moving it toward the unfamiliar, looking for irregularities, thinking "outside the box" for something different from what is typically predicted. It is about listening with a third ear and seeing with new eyes noticing what aspects of the story may be strange, anomalous, irregular, or out of the ordinary, contributing to a counterstory that contradicts the problem.

To help create a counternarrative to Jayson's problem story, I asked him where he learned about "hitting" or what academy certified him as a "hitter." I was hoping the use of humor would engage Jayson in seeing the senselessness of his aggressive actions toward his mother. Linking hitting and being certified as a "hitter" made him chuckle. He mused about such an academy, and he appreciated the suggestion to take a refresher course in hitting. The genre of the question as comedy set a new pathway through which Jayson and I began to craft new stories and counternarratives.

The potency of questions depends on their context and purpose. A thoughtful question can open doors, challenge norms, and create direction. Questions can also have various endpoints. For example, externalizing questions can bring forth people's problems as well as their strengths and appreciations and explore their bidirectional influences.

Naming what people appreciate about themselves is one way to elevate and externalize positive elements of stories. Jayson appreciated his ability to stand strong when he was bullied, what he initially named resilience and later changed to "stick-to-itiveness." Together we tracked the history of stick-to-itiveness; mapping and evaluating its positive effects on Jayson, his mom, and their relationship. Questions such as these spotlighted its impacts: When did you first notice resilience in you? How does resilience interact with other people around you? How has resilience brought you to unexpected places? How did you know that this was a positive force in your life? Who supported you in your resolve? Such self-appreciation provided Jayson with the opportunity to talk about his honorable self and identify supports that solidified it.

Questions that led Jayson to identify how he influenced positive aspects of self were critical to reinforcing his agency and highlighting how he had choice in deciding his words and actions. We discussed how stick-to-itiveness added to small ways of valuing himself, which we later called micro-appreciations in his life. As much as he hated school, Jayson continued to attend school. He later added that watching videos made him appreciate the art of filmmaking and hoped to explore that skill.

We also explored ways Jayson nurtured his story of influence, how his values and their meaning contributed to maintaining a sense of self-appreciation, and how they fit with his evolving self-perception. Jayson named resilience as an important value in his life. He noted how much he and his mother had endured the absence of his father in his life. Although he fought his mother many times, he also knew that his mother had his back and identified with the commitment she brought to their relationship. He valued people who cared in his life, including teachers who had high expectations for him at school. He also internalized values of integrity, honesty, and accountability, all of which helped improve not only his relationships with teachers and peers at school but also his grades.

I have often asked myself questions about my questions. I have wondered whether and how the questions I use in narrative practice are effective in what they are supposed to do or achieve. How genuine is the question I am posing? What is the purpose of the question and what do I want it to achieve? Who is the question serving? How do I engage the tone, the affect, and the structure of this question? Does this question require a response, or is it engaging fresh thinking or feeling? Is it provoking insight, or prompting a more complex way of understanding? Am I using it to focus on the relational world outside therapy, or am I calling into question some cultural givens? Does the question generate hope, imagination, creativity, or taking charge? Is it about creating a sense of fit or expansion? Is it asking for facts or is it a relational question?

For Jayson and his mother, like many clients, some questions worked well while others did not. I was always careful not to ask misleading questions although I was aware that my own biases could not be avoided. We can never be completely neutral. While some questions fostered connection, there were questions that did not make sense to Jayson and may have temporarily caused disconnection. The use of metaphors sometimes helped move our work along, and at other times, they slowed us down. Overall, our work together was a delicate dance; I walked a fine line—inviting but also challenging Jayson and his mother to stay engaged in the complexity and paradoxical nature of our work.

## Conclusion

Questions provide a conversational map to guide narrative conversations. Crafting and asking attuned questions are key to advancing storytelling, moving it from thin to thick narratives, away from problem-saturated stories to ones that propose positive alternatives. Narrative therapy prioritizes coauthorships, which therapists and clients use to explore pathways to understanding, meaning making, and re-storying lived experience. Achieving coauthorship requires that the therapist carefully positions themselves from centering or active guidance to decentering, becoming more of a collaborator or witness, to co-centering, attending to the therapist's and the client's affective embodied states, which represent a true partnership in conducting the therapeutic process. Language plays a significant role in storytelling. In the next chapter we explore the power of language.

CHAPTER 4

# Standing Up to Silence

## LANGUAGE, POWER, AND POWERLESSNESS

Human experience is deeply influenced by the stories we tell about ourselves, and the stories others tell about us. As Siegel (2012) notes: "A story is created by both the teller and the listener" (p. 84), who each contribute to the narrative, and by society, which brings cultural biases and norms to its content. Stories rely on language. Stories evolve throughout our lifetime as we navigate myriad experiences, discovering and affirming our identities along the way. Over time, dominant stories are framed and reinforced, influencing how we understand ourselves and our world.

Language is a powerful tool that profoundly shapes how we perceive, interpret, and make meaning of struggles, joys, transitions, and other life-affecting events. Every society possesses some form of language to facilitate communication (Pagel, 2017). Language evolved from drawings and hand signals to vocal sounds and complex spoken words (Donald, 2017). Merriam-Webster (n.d.) defines language as

> words, their pronunciation, and the methods of combining them used and understood by a community . . . a systematic means of communicating ideas or feelings by the use . . . of gestures, sounds,

> or marks having understood meanings. (Merriam-Webster, n.d., Definition 1a & 1b[2])

Language is at the heart of communication; it is how human beings connect and share ideas and is the hallmark of human civilization.

Narrative theorists view language as much more than a mechanism for conveying messages. As an expressive tool, it shapes thought, creates realities, and influences meaning making and ways of being. On a broader scale, language influences cultural beliefs and norms carrying messages beyond their literal meanings to take on cultural significance and sway. Thomas and McDonagh (2013) observe that language produces identities that foster both connection and disconnection across individuals, communities, and populations. Words hold great power and are elevated by the context in which they are spoken and the authority of those who speak them.

The role of language as an oppressive agent is best understood within the context of history. Language suppression by the powerful is one example of such oppression. The eradication of a spoken language for certain populations has been likened to linguistic genocide (Shaw, 2013). Indigenous peoples have endured systematic language suppression throughout history, and its oppressive impacts remain evident as noted in intergenerational trauma, health disparities, and mental health issues, including depression, anxiety, and substance use resulting in impairment of self-identity, well-being, and self-esteem.

Similarly, many colonized peoples around the world have been forced into suppressing their native languages, restricting their ability to maintain cultural connections, uphold values, and create meaning. Such acts erase ancestral stories, traditions, cultures, and identities embedded in those languages and for some, extinguish lives altogether. The sanctioning of specific languages as "legitimate" in education, politics, and media reflects and perpetuates existing power imbalances and marginalization (de Varennes & Kuzborska, 2016).

In this context, the preservation and reclamation of suppressed languages become acts of resistance and empowerment. Decolonizing language serves as a unifying force, enabling marginalized communities to reclaim their stories, assert their identities, relinquish their invisibility, and resist systemic oppression. Language in this context is much more than communication: It is a medium for cultural resilience and collective liberation. As clients use language to tell their stories, they reclaim their lives, self-identity, well-being, self-esteem, and empowerment.

## Other Forms of Storytelling

Storytelling goes beyond written and verbal language. Langer (1957) compares language to "pieces of clothing . . . strung side by side on the clothesline" (p. 81), illustrating how words alone do not create a story but serve as a vehicle for storytelling. Storytelling takes place in nature, at the water cooler, or by lecture. It can be performed in films, social media, and theater. It can be nonverbal, expressed by body language or art. A symbol can convey multiple meanings depending upon how the observer interprets them. Storytelling can also intermix expressive modalities—for instance, combining narrative, digital audio, and visual content to produce both process and product, resulting in a dynamic, memorable, and compelling way to share stories. For example, the sounds a storyteller uses with the words can communicate deep meanings.

Visual images are rich with multivariate interpretations as the observer's positionality determines their meaning. They constitute forms of narration, used to raise specific messages such as those depicting violence, political unrest, inequality, and environmental degradation (Schutz & Luckmann, 1974). Public art is a powerful universal storytelling tool that transcends spoken language and mitigates cultural barriers. It provides a visual language for understanding different cultures and perspectives, fostering cross-cultural dialogue and appreciation. Copes and Ragland (2016) caution that in some instances, image-based storytelling, especially in the sociopolitical arena, can be guilty of presenting partial or single-story narratives through curated visuals (Copes & Ragland, 2016; Sandberg, 2016). Selective representation can also be coercive, aimed at upholding dominant, repressive narratives. As such, they reinforce oppressive messaging and perpetuate dominant, one-dimensional narratives that target certain groups and populations.

Meaning making in storytelling is inherently dialogical, shaped by context, including such factors as age, development, culture, experience, and circumstance. It can easily be misconstrued, misrepresented, or interpreted in an entirely different way than intended depending upon the storyteller and the audience. Children's storytelling is a good example of how context matters. Some of my youngest clients have conveyed profound messages through artwork, demonstrating the diverse ways in which meaning can be expressed and understood. The therapist's role in decoding what the art conveys requires curiosity, astute questioning, and avoiding assumptions.

Five-year-old Kayla took her time scanning my office as her mother and I discussed concerns. She seemed particularly drawn to the Play-Doh on my shelf, so I was surprised when she chose a different medium to use in her artwork:

THERAPIST: Kayla, I see you looking at the Play-Doh. Would you like to play with it?

KAYLA: (*shrugs shoulders*)

THERAPIST: There are different colors. You can choose any colors you would like to use.

KAYLA: I like to draw.

THERAPIST: Sure . . . [hands her paper and crayons] Here are some paper and crayons.

I was humbled as I sought to understand what Kayla was communicating to me. Kayla drew two lines, which she proceeded to show me and her mother, saying, "Look, look, it is a house." She made elaborate pictures with her drawings. There were people, houses, clouds, and many more things that she alone could name. The pictures of people often had missing limbs.

For children, artwork is a form of language. It provides a window into children's perceptions and feelings (Cohen Konrad, 2019). Young children especially do not have the language to convey emotions or analyze complex thoughts. Their worldviews are based on their limited life experience.

With two lines across the page, Kayla instructed me that she had drawn a house. The drawing was a language symbol that we both mutually understood. If I had insisted that Kayla put the meaning of the house in words only, our communication would have been constrained and our relationship hampered. Her excitement to show me the house was an invitation to engage:

THERAPIST: Tell me about the house.
KAYLA: Hmm, this is my house.
THERAPIST: Where is your room?
KAYLA: Here . . . [points to the end of the scribbled line with a dot] This is my mom's room. Here is the fridge. Here are my toys.

Curiosity and interest in Kayla's drawing prompted questions that both revealed and masked important clues to Kayla's inner life. There were also questions that I might have asked: Why did she not draw her room? Did she have a room of her own? How did she conceptualize home? In storytelling, language helps to link events in sequence. Two or more things linked together begin to form patterns of meaning that are enhanced by interaction and dialogue. How language and performance cohere, however, is a perplexing question, particularly when working with children or when using art as a medium for language with children.

With Kayla, I wondered if she would draw a similar picture of home for her mother. How would she elaborate on the drawing? How did the therapy space and timing help define the drawing? Would it be the same display if Kayla were among her peers, or with her kindergarten teacher? Indeed, how is drawing a performance of one's identity?

Marsten et al. (2016) outline the power of connecting with children's voices through imaginative play, words, and actions. For children, imagination is the vehicle for storytelling. Children personify problems through imagination and in so doing they affirm their identities. Children's fantasies invite therapists to think outside the box as the children think inside the box. Indeed, "Children often express what they cannot yet say in words through images. When they draw the problem, they begin to see it as something that can be studied, understood, and outwitted" (p. 77). Kayla's drawings became a narrative medium through which she told her stories, revised them, and made them visible.

Drawings bridge verbal and nonverbal worlds and open children to engage creatively in the therapy process. My work with Kayla was greatly enhanced through our drawings. Over time, she invited me to draw with her in co-creating new stories. In effect, "our task is to listen carefully, to help them name their skills and knowledge, and to join them in imagining new possibilities" (Marsten et al., 2016, p. 52). Our drawings became the avenue for her to "talk about" or language some tragic events she had witnessed in her home.

## Reframing

Reframing, a technique used in narrative practice, fosters client agency and the promotion of positive change. Reframing encourages clients to reevaluate problem-saturated narratives with the goal of assigning new, less judgmental meaning to their experiences. It concentrates on re-storying experience in a way that explains rather than blames the individual for the problem.

A case illustrating the use of reframing involves three young men who arrived in the United States as refugees. They were among a group of unaccompanied minors who had escaped the killing fields of the Sudanese civil war. They witnessed atrocities committed by both sides as they fled. When conscripted, they were forced to commit terrible acts. Their escape was harrowing; they had to cross dangerous rivers and escape predatory crocodiles and animals. Life did not become much easier in the refugee camps, and it remained challenging after their arrival in the United States. As refugees they had to make major adjustments in an unfamiliar country—for example, living in foster families, navigating school while managing language barriers, finding employment, and many other transitions.

In our work together, we addressed the trauma of displacement and the many adjustments that had to be made. The young men often spoke longingly about home. They longed for employment and the means to support themselves. While they desperately wanted to work and succeed in their new country, no one would hire them. They lost confidence in their abilities and became mired in a sense of hopelessness. Cultural and language barriers complicated their situation. For instance, when asked about skills, they reported they had none. For them, "skills" were interpreted as computer and software knowledge, a miscommunication that reinforced a deficit-focused narrative.

In our sessions we examined the young men's day-to-day lives, identifying many important job-worthy skills they could put on job applications. We reframed an array of household chores, such as setting tables and carrying out trash as organizational skills. Acts of valor used to escape the war and survive were reframed as crisis management skills. These reframes highlighted agency allowing the young men to see themselves as capable, not powerless.

Reframing is a communal practice that broadens clients' abilities to imagine new possibilities. Reframing is achieved in different ways depending on where clients are in their process of change. Therapists are influential partners as they collaborate with clients to reframe storylines (White & Morgan, 2006). In narrative practice reframing invites relational accountability and honors clients' resourcefulness as they harness and activate agency to reauthor and positively shift their lives.

## Language and Relational Accountability

Language, thoughts, and memory are inextricably linked, affecting both current and past cognition. Loftus and colleagues (1978) studied the *misinformation effect*, described as when accurate memory of an event becomes less reliable due to being told false or misleading information over time. Their study had participants view an event, such as a car crash or crime, then asked them questions that purposely included misinformation. Researchers found that the accuracy of participants' recollections was partially influenced by the misinformation that they were provided (Loftus et al., 1978). The language used in the questions posed by the researchers further affected the acuity of their memories (Loftus et al., 1978).

In a similar manner, the words and actions we use to communicate with clients shape their responses to our inquiries and the relationships that we form. Words and actions expressed within the therapeutic encounter no matter how intended have influence, and as therapists we are ethically accountable to their effects. "Relational and accountable presence" in narrative practice acknowledges the mutual responsibility between client and therapist to respectfully navigate the process of co-storying and meaning making. This reciprocal process inevitably has transformational impact on both client and therapist.

A therapist's commitment to relational accountability includes continuous self-reflection and heightened attunement to how one's language and actions may, intentionally or not, reinforce impoverished and problem-saturated stories (Carlson & Haire, 2014). Such scrutiny is especially salient when clients' narratives parallel our own. There is no doubt that my relationship to change has been influenced by the therapeutic work I have done with refugees. Listening to the language of war and escape can easily trigger my own vulnerability—their journeys were not unlike my own. As I bear witness to my clients' stories, I must be vigilant and separate them from my experiences and the emotions connected to them. This requires an ongoing pursuit of self-understanding and adherence to relational accountability.

## Protesting Powerlessness

Clients typically seek out therapy in a state of heightened vulnerability. It is our distinctive role to accompany them when they are feeling powerless to face the problems that inhabit their lives. Active listening is requisite to narrative practice, and it is our job to ". . . invite the people who become our clients to tell their truths openly, without constraint" and without reservation (Browning, 2003, p. 335). We hear their struggles and self-doubts. Some painfully grapple with a sense of isolation, a feeling of not belonging anywhere or to anyone. Many feel invisible and question their sense of self. Totalizing gazes surround them; they feel controlled by the looks, opinions, and judgments of others, not knowing how to address them, real or not. Problems tell them stories about the kind of person they are and who they should be. Like with Maria, feelings of inadequacy, failure, and powerlessness were at the root of self-doubt and shame.

### THE CASE OF MARIA

> Maria, 55, was haunted by what she named as the "many demons" from her past. She became a single mother after leaving an abusive relationship. Maria was devoted to her two boys and two girls working long hours to support them with little rest for herself. She struggled with depression and persistent anxiety. As a devout Catholic, Maria felt a strong affinity to the church with its rituals, worship, and practices. Unfortunately, she was betrayed by a priest who abused her soon after disclosing her experience of intimate partner violence to him. In the aftermath, she wrestled with her faith and her relationship to the church.

Despite her strong affinity to her faith, Maria would not talk with me about the church. She was devastated by what the priest had done to her during such a vulnerable time. She questioned whether there was a God and if this God cared at all about her.

Maria described extensive neglect in her own family of origin. While she longed for meaningful relationships with men, these relationships inevitably ended up as disappointments. She sought spiritual connection and comfort in relationships, which she described in her own words as "something I never had." As a child she comforted herself by withdrawing and isolating. She told me:

> I would spend a lot of time with myself, daydream and fantasize about things. I would read, knit, and practice playing the piano.

> My parents did not notice. My mother would have me and my siblings compete against each other. She often sought to invalidate us. She also had a lot of resentment towards me because I was very close to my father.

Maria also described the extent of mental illness in her family, with a deep sense of despair:

> I am surrounded by mental illness all around me. My father struggled with mental illness. My husband did, my daughter and her boyfriend all did. I am also surrounded by a world of drugs. My daughter has been dealing drugs even with her mental illness. Her boyfriend has also been caught up with drugs. People in my life leave me, be it family or lovers. Winters often bring up those feelings of abandonment either from the men I have known or from the people around me. I feel lost. I feel helpless and powerless.

Maria named her story as one of powerlessness. She saw herself as ineffectual in relationships. A discourse of helplessness wholly consumed the way she viewed life. The following therapeutic exchange illustrates her perceptions and an approach to deconstruct their powerful grip:

THERAPIST: You often speak about lacking a say in anything. Where does that view come from? Who has given you those messages about yourself?

MARIA: I do not know. [She went on to describe herself as inadequate, and ineffectual. Most of the terms she used revealed strong negative self-beliefs.]

THERAPIST: It seems there are many messages and beliefs you have about yourself. Have there been other messages alongside these messages?

MARIA: Well, I know I have been strong as a single mother. I have made good decisions for myself and my children. I threw my husband out and decided to live my own life.

THERAPIST: How did you get that sense of power to act on your behalf? Who was there for you in your corner as you made those choices?

MARIA: I often hear the voices of my grandmother. She was a no-nonsense kind of woman. She would not put up with any crap.

THERAPIST: No nonsense?

MARIA: Yes.

THERAPIST: How have you embraced this no-nonsense woman in your life?

MARIA: I carry a picture of her in my purse. You know some people carry the picture of the Virgin Mary. I carry the picture of my grandmother. [She went on to pull out the photo of her grandmother.]

The photo revealed a beautiful woman whose resemblance to Maria was unmistakable. I took hold of Maria's connection to her grandmother's image, exploring it as a significant artifact in her life. Maria talked about the sense of power and presence she got from her grandmother. She described that having the photo in her purse always made her feel valued, a feeling she wanted desperately to maintain. Her grandmother's constant presence was protective and a reminder of her own inner strengths, especially in the face of oppressive power.

### THE CASE OF LYNN

There are many reasons that clients feel powerless. For Lynn, 55, illness and loss rendered her helpless to face the many problems that flooded her life. Hers was a sad and painful story that at first sight, seemed to have no happy ending.

Lynn presented with a complicated medical history, including a recent diagnosis of Stage 3 kidney disease. Other medical conditions included high blood pressure, diabetes, and limited mobility. She was referred to me by her medical doctor who was concerned about depressed mood and suicidal ideation. Lynn had

> also recently experienced the loss of her father due to heart failure. She described life as unfair and senseless. She felt powerless to impact the circumstances of her life.
>
> Early exploration revealed a significant trauma history in Lynn's family. Lynn's brother was seriously abusive, one time pouring boiling water over her in a fit of rage leaving her skin irreparably scarred; another time raping her as a teenager. Lynn was again a victim of rape as a young adult by another man. Lynn's filial abuse was glossed over by her parents who entreated her to be silent, especially when confronted by state authorities. Such experiences reinforced Lynn's burgeoning sense of powerlessness, which often left her unable to accomplish even the simplest tasks.

It was critical that Lynn and I explore moments of power and agency early in our work together. It was the second week we met that Lynn began sharing what she saw as her strengths, abilities, and skills. Importantly, she also exhibited a desire to push back on powerlessness and find a capable sense of self. Doing so was difficult as she did not trust herself enough to sustain her newfound strength and courage. From week to week, we reviewed and reinforced her progress:

> LYNN: This week was a good one. I went to a concert. I loved it.
>
> THERAPIST: Tell me more. What did you like about it?
>
> LYNN: Well, my friend said it was nice going to the concert with me.
>
> THERAPIST: How did that make you feel?
>
> LYNN: Not good because those things are unsustainable . . . I do not know if we will ever do it [go to the concert] again. It is a lot of work to get ready. Oh . . . I only took a shower twice this week. . . . The shower is painful. [Lynn struggles with incontinency. She wears a diaper, and she struggles with weight issues. It takes a lot of energy to clean herself.]
>
> LYNN: I felt embarrassed after disclosing to my friends about my distress. They encouraged me to speak more about my problems with them. . . . They were concerned I did not tell them earlier about my challenges. Then I asked them, what would

you have done if you learned about this sooner? And then, they asked me what I need from them . . .

THERAPIST: Oh . . . you asked them? What did they say?

LYNN: They could not answer because what I need, they are not able to give.

THERAPIST: And what is that?

LYNN: A cure . . . of my kidney disease.

There was a long silence as Lynn appeared occupied by feelings that she later described as "feelings of powerlessness." She berated her inability to do anything, asking herself if life would ever get better. But then she surprisingly changed course, reflecting on what was going well in her life, saying that she "did not feel totally defeated." She recounted some of her blessings and achievements in life:

LYNN: Well, I know I have had a good education. I can think clearly even with all the medical issues in my life. My friends value my humor and wit.

Narrative practice helps clients separate themselves from their problem narratives. Reauthoring encourages them to push back powerlessness and reveal inherent agency that opens opportunities for self-expression. Lynn found spaces in her new story where she felt powerful and accomplished.

Lynn's story also highlights the power of silence as a crucial aspect of relational accountability. Clients often share deeply personal experiences, yet there may be no words to fully capture their pain and hurt. Pauses create space for therapists and clients to navigate new dimensions of relational accountability, and to acknowledge meaning in the absence of words.

### THE CASE OF ARMENA

In our early work together, I often ask clients to describe themselves to begin the process of storying. Such descriptions are like cover stories that over time bloom into a tapestry of narratives. Armena's cover story, like Maria's and Lynn's, told of her unique battle against powerlessness. Armena, 28, was an immigrant woman from the Dominican Republic. Her struggle to find a place to call home highlights the transition from powerlessness to belonging:

THERAPIST: So, Armena . . . tell me about you. How would you describe yourself?

ARMENA: (*long pause*) . . . I can begin my story in one of two ways: "As a child of immigrant parents, responsibilities and expectations placed upon me robbed me of my childhood" or "As a child of immigrant parents, I learned skills that have prepared me for the real world."

This self-introduction was particularly meaningful to our work. For one, no one else in my experience had begun by offering two possible self-descriptions. I found this approach both intriguing and an invitation to delve deeper into the stories being shared. As a graduate student, Armena had spent a significant time reflecting on her immigrant story and observing her classmates from diverse backgrounds struggle to adapt to a foreign culture.

Armena described her parents, who emigrated from the Dominican Republic to the United States as hardworking and determined to make the best of their lives. Like many immigrants, they sought better opportunities for themselves and their families. Armena spoke fondly of visiting her parents' childhood home, a place she described as "paradise"—while also acknowledging it was the site of some of their greatest challenges. She described how her parents had no running water in their home. The family had to travel long distances to fetch water for their daily use. Armena emphasized the immense sacrifices her parents made to ensure that their children could access opportunities for themselves in the United States.

Growing up in the United States, Armena lived in an inner-city community marked by poverty, unemployment, and crime, often depicted in the daily news. She lacked role models to look up to. As her family's cultural broker, she bore significant responsibilities, acting as a bridge between two worlds. Armena recalled the pressure of translating for her parents during life's crucial moments, such as doctor visits or grocery store trips. This responsibility often came at the cost of her own childhood, leaving her to assume the role of "parenting her parents" instead of fully enjoying her youth.

Armena described how her father attempted to attend high school but had to drop out to work and support his family. Armena stated that her parents did not have opportunities, so she channeled their aspirations into her own, especially to pursue higher education. Before entering college, Armena worried that she might not be smart enough, but she soon learned to trust her abilities.

In college, Armena navigated between two or more worlds. She often found herself living in predominantly White spaces, where she had to write, speak, and behave "White," dismissing her own culture in order to fit in. She described the tremendous pressure and resulting exhaustion of constantly code-switching between the dominant discourse and her own cultural identity.

Experiences of marginalization made Armena believe that she was not good enough, that she did not belong, and that she did not have adequate education to be sitting in the same classrooms as her peers. These experiences authored a story of powerlessness that engulfed her life. They reinforced a lie of incompetence as the lens through which to see herself. Away from college and back at home, Armena still struggled with not belonging. Her friends at home had no concept of her college experiences and could not understand why she had changed. Armena was distressed, discomforted, and unable to make sense of the life she now lived.

Over time, Armena, like many immigrants, was able to transform her disenfranchisement into opportunities for growth and empowerment. She pursued advocacy work for immigrants and refugees, amplifying their voices and striving to create meaningful change. In so doing, she found a new language to name her reality.

> Armena describes her experience of living between two worlds as an expansion of her cultural and social capital.

Guarnaccia (2019) explains that immigrant children build cultural capital both within their families and through their interactions with the broader society. Armena's journey mirrors that of many immigrants who navigate the complexities of their cultures of origin alongside those of the host culture. By engaging with multiple languages and cultural contexts, immigrant populations develop the ability to be bicultural and transition fluidly between diverse worlds. In doing so, they challenge and overturn discourses of powerlessness.

## Conclusion

Narrative therapists play a pivotal role in helping clients reauthor stories of powerlessness. To do so, they holistically embrace the lives of their clients by noticing and witnessing a wide range of sensations, reactions, thoughts, and emotions. Bird (2004) describes this process as "the attention to thoughts, feelings, sensations, visions, body responses, smells, the said, the partially said, the struggle for words, the emotional quality of the words spoken, the look, the presence, the absence and much more" (p. 35). In the next chapter, I explore working with the story of trauma as a relationally accountable practice of witnessing.

CHAPTER 5

# Trauma and Resilience Narratives

Meeting a new client is like opening a book for the first time. The first pages may seem obscure, even incomprehensible, but with each chapter another discovery awaits. A client's narrative is like the language in a book never studied, unaccounted for among other predominant volumes that have crowded it out. With great care and reserving judgment, narrative practitioners start by opening the cover to a text that may have been unopened for years. Then, like anthropologists, they enter unchartered territory, embracing a stance of humility as they gather artifacts of a life that has been hidden, encumbered by pain, shame, and losses. It is a difficult exploration because there are often no words to describe the content—at first listen, the narrative may sound like a foreign language or be indecipherable.

What I have just described using metaphor characterizes the experience of working with a trauma story. There is no typical trauma story and the discourses that surround trauma are equally variable and unique. Narrative techniques approach trauma work through the lens of meaning making. For most trauma survivors a sense of meaning has been lost; the exigencies of trauma have rendered aspects of experience senseless and daring to hope again, to believe in possibilities, feels like the riskiest of pursuits.

This chapter explores approaches to healing psychological trauma through story and storytelling. Intrinsic to this work is the art of witnessing and the role of hope in working with people who have experienced trauma.

## Narrative Practice and Trauma

Narrative practice is a dynamic approach to clinical work informed by postmodern, feminist, empowerment, and liberation models, all of which give primary importance to the stories of people's lives, the special forces shaping personal and collective narratives, and the ways in which these forces can marginalize, minimize, and obscure lived experience. Narrative practitioners work with clients to de-pathologize problem-saturated narratives and instead help them identify and amplify indicators of strength and resiliency that go unrecognized and unacknowledged when telling their stories. Trauma is one of many storylines in people's lives, not the only one.

Narrative techniques and practices lend themselves well to many aspects of the therapeutic process when working with trauma, including conducting interviews; assessing its impacts; and contextualizing their social, cultural, historical, and spiritual influences. The trauma story, personal or collective, is always complex and multivariate, complicated by pervasive shame, suppressed memories, and uncertainty. Narrative practitioners walk with trauma survivors as they reauthor their stories, replete with the horrors they experienced, the guilt and self-loathing they feel, burdened by ambivalence toward the perpetrator(s), and filled with desire for revenge, all of which make up a plot linked in a sequence of experiences across time (Morgan, 2000). The narrative, then, becomes the thread that weaves these elements together by engaging new perspectives and self-perceptions that seek to mitigate debilitating storylines. As Morgan points out, stories are never free of contradiction or ambiguity nor can they "encapsulate or handle all the contingencies of life" (p. 8). However, if successful, the trauma story can take on a richer description, one that doesn't negate trauma and its ramifications but adds content that brings healing, hope, and possibility to the client's self-belief and their world.

I have had the honor of working with several young persons whose lives have been displaced by war, and I have come to appreciate both the individual and collective significance of their trauma stories. As individuals, each in their own way has been profoundly affected by trauma, experiencing enduring psychological symptoms. Collectively, even combined as they are into composite case studies, their stories reveal shared historical trauma as a consequence of the civil wars that shattered lives, populations, and communities.

## THE STORY OF CHET

I first encountered Chet when he was 17 years old. Early in our work together, he told me about his refugee journey and his many losses. Before escaping to Ethiopia his father was killed, and he lost contact with his mother. Chet and his sister, along with an uncle, subsequently crossed over into Sudan where he suffered severe chest trauma from being hit by a large rock. Soon after, Chet found himself in a Kenyan refugee camp but has no memory of how he got there. He describes conditions as "horrendous" with only one meal a day subsidized by a biweekly allotment of cornmeal, which frequently ran out before the next distribution. Sometimes Chet's rations were stolen, or his family had to sell them to get other necessities. On some days, he simply went without food.

Hunger was a daily struggle for Chet, his family, and mates. On one occasion, Chet, along with three other boys, acquired five shillings (equivalent to a dime), which they had to decide how to spend. Would they buy a piece of bread, or would it be better to purchase corn that would fill their bellies? Deciding when to eat was a daily quandary. Should they eat during the day and go to bed with empty bellies or save their ration of food for the evening and have a good night's sleep? Even more traumatic were the actions of the peacekeepers who Chet describes as "protecting us during the day but coming into our huts to rape us at night. It was bad; very bad indeed."

The details of Chet's story are chilling. They expose a depth of unimaginable feelings as Chet made sense of these experiences. They also reveal the brutality of war. Chet was a victim of political violence, the effects of which transcended what any presentation in therapy reveals. But Chet's story also embodies hope and resilience.

In listening to stories such as Chet's, narrative practitioners serve as key witnesses. By telling these stories, these children reclaim a path toward healing. In the telling, they also experience a type of healing from all the years of indoctrination, fear, and confusion that characterized so much of their lives. In the telling, they are also weaving together a new tapestry of existence.

What does it mean to share these stories? Invariably, Chet and other children I have worked with have answered this question by saying, "so that you can tell others about these stories." Extending the telling expands the circle of witnesses to their lives. To me, the desire to share their stories represents the deep human need for relational connection. It also emphasizes the importance of relational accountability to witnessing. Weingarten (2000) grounds such witnessing experiences in the principle of *ubuntu* and the way in which "Ubuntu creates persons simultaneously as participants and witnesses to everyone else in one's community" (p. 400). *Ubuntu* further highlights the collective responsibility to foster a "community of caring" such that no one person should "bear her pain alone" (p. 400).

## Witnessing as a Narrative Technique

"We are all always witnesses. People speak, we hear, whether we choose to or not" (Weingarten, 2000, p. 392). For therapists, witnessing is an especially powerful role, particularly meaningful to those who have previously been silenced by humiliation and disenfranchisement or have painful stories to tell. As witnesses we occupy different positions that are influenced by our understanding of the narratives being told and by how empowered we feel to affect them. Weingarten designed a witnessing schema inclusive of four dynamic positions relative to the witnesses' relationship to awareness, unawareness, empowerment, and disempowerment. The interrelationship of these four witness positions has consequences for the witness and for the witnessed who might include individuals, families, communities, and society. They are as follows:

*Witness Position 1* provides the most desirable position for an individual/community and most constructive for others. In this position, the person is aware, cognizant, and mindful of the implications, and has an idea about how to take effective action in relation to that which is observed. This position commands a sense of competence and effectiveness.

*Witness Position 2* represents the most toxic situation for others since a person in this position is unaware of the meaning and significance to the victim of what is being witnessed but is empowered in relation to it. A person in this witness position is most likely to do harm, where "do" refers to omissions as well as commissions. Weingarten has likened this position to one in which powerful world leaders find themselves (K. Weingarten, personal communication, May 4, 2004). Such persons fail to see the plight of another, yet they command so much power in these very situations.

*Witness Position 3* depicts persons who are unaware of the meaning and significance of what they are witnessing and therefore cannot act in relation to that to which they are exposed. The effects of such unawareness and passivity can be very harmful to those affected.

*Witness Position 4* represents the position that people experience with the most evident distress. Persons are aware of what they are witnessing but feel helpless or ineffective in relation to it. One knows that another has suffered trauma but feels powerless to comfort that person. Practitioners may have a keen awareness of the issues affecting people but lack the ability to attend to them.

Witnessing positions change over time—for example, a witness can move from not knowing to awareness as they enter into a client's story details. A client can transition from feeling despair to experiencing hope as they feel known. In the case of traumatized persons, the experience of trauma presents challenging positions as those persons negotiate their own self-understanding. Narrative practice through relational and accountable engagement offers opportunities to explore these witness positions. Indeed, witnessing is an imperative if the work of therapy is to be successful.

Kaethe Weingarten founded the Witness to Witness (W2W) Program in July 2018. W2W has two primary goals: (a) to make people aware of themselves as everyday witnesses to violence and violation, and (b) to provide people with the tools to cope with the biological, psychological, interpersonal, and societal effects of witnessing. Reflecting on her practice, Weingarten (2000) documents the complexity, compassion, and dilemmas of witnessing. Here she comments on her supervisees' application of these concepts when working with trauma:

> They made a commitment to listen with open minds and hearts to the stories of those who have been physically, emotionally, and spiritually assaulted. They have made a commitment to feel in the cells of their bodies what it is like to be touched against one's will, to be penetrated beyond one's ability to imagine a way to make it stop. And, they have made a commitment to try to render that experience to others on behalf of their clients. (p. 394)

Weingarten's work has been instrumental in shaping my practice as a narrative practitioner. I have spent countless hours listening to my clients' stories of abuse suffered at the hands of powerful entities, whether through senseless wars that force children into combat or the exploitation of women, girls, and young boys by men in positions of power.

Like Weingarten, I have also listened to supervisees share harrowing accounts of clients who have endured such exploitation. We have sat together in deep contemplation, grappling with the complexities of our clients' struggles often bereft of language. Indeed, the lack of language to name some of these experiences highlights the complexity of trauma narratives as well as the challenge in navigating through these witness positions.

Weingarten (2010) views witnessing as a transformative act of being fully attentive to others and of enabling hope. For Weingarten (2010) ". . . how we think about hope has all to do with whether we can cocreate hopefulness with our clients and whether we can maintain our own" (p. 5). Weingarten developed the concept of "reasonable hope" as a "variant of hope . . . suggest[ing] something both sensible and moderate, directing our attention to what is within reach more than what may be desired but unattainable" (p. 7). She underscores hope as relational and as a practice we do with others; witnessing, she believes, is a critical relationship in fostering reasonable hope. For Weingarten (2010, 2022), reasonable hope seeks goals and pathways and accommodates doubt, contradictions, and despair.

Cognition plays a role in helping people hold on to hope to reach their goals (Snyder, 2000). Agentic thinking, believing one can achieve something, and pathway thinking, thinking that guides action to develop plans to reach one's goals, are cognitive processes reinforced by hope (Weis & Speridakos, 2011).

Hope is also understood as an emotional state that balances both confidence and uncertainty (Miller, 2007). Comprising relational dimensions, hope encompasses sharing, feelings of care, and a sense of belonging (Miller, 2007). Feeling accepted and understood by another person additionally fosters hope, something that practitioners are well equipped to do as compassionate witnesses. Farran et al.'s (1995) multidimensional conceptualization expands the construct of hope, viewing human life as inherently challenging, incorporating a spiritual component rooted in faith, engaging in thought processes that consider goals in relation to available resources, and experiencing relational processes in which hope is shaped through interactions with others.

Paulo Freire (2014), an influential educator and philosopher, coined the term "critical hopefulness," which he refers to as the need for hope in the struggle for social justice. When all seems hopeless, critical hopefulness serves as its antidote. He writes:

> Hopelessness paralyzes us, immobilizes us. We succumb to fatalism, and then it becomes impossible to muster the strength . . . for a fierce struggle that will re-create the world. I am hopeful . . . out of an existential, concrete imperative . . . my hope is

> necessary . . . without it, my struggle will be weak and wobbly. We need critical hope the way a fish needs unpolluted water. (p. 2)

Freire understood suffering as a shared human experience. When viewed from this perspective, hope becomes a collective component of healing from the pain of trauma.

Freire (2016) likened hope to love, trust, peace, humility, courage, and patience that could be individually held or situated in social and political contexts. He associated hope with moral goodness directed toward an ethical and better world. Hope is ever evolving, a dynamic process that is unfinalizable according to Weingarten (2000).

Hope has been conceptualized by some as an essential virtue, that "becomes a necessary component of one's existential experience, of one's radically being a presence in the world" (Freire, 2004, p. 100). It is a constant companion in therapeutic work, something we continuously practice doing (Freire, 2014; hooks, 2003; Van Hooft, 2014; Weingarten, 2000). Hope is a transformational force not just for individuals but for the community and the world at large.

## WITNESSING, AGENCY, AND CHOICE

Choice and agency are additional boons to survival and posttraumatic resilience (Beaudoin, 2005). Beaudoin highlights the narrative practitioner's role in emphasizing agency and incorporating choice to amplify its impact. She further underscores the importance of recognizing the diversity of responses to trauma and the ways in which individuals variably cope in its aftermath. She proposes a reauthoring map (see Chapter 9, Figure 9.1) that examines actions taken or not taken and the way they may be storied or not storied toward choice and agency.

## SILENCE AND WITNESSING

We witness with our presence, our bodies, and our senses engaging in meta-conversations with clients that explore all depths of experience. Silence is part of witnessing; it leaves space for meaning and understanding to take shape. My work with Chet and Mou vividly illustrated this reality. Words could not capture Chet's horrifying experience of escape. So instead, he and I sat in silence. Silence is difficult to interpret and can mean many different things. It can communicate a moment of deep connection. It can also indicate disconnection, disinterest, fear, or worry. It might convey helplessness in the face of horror and pain or waiting to embrace the inevitable. On the other hand, silence may convey intimacy, like lovers in each other's presence, or the calm of a sleeping baby in a mother's arms. In other contexts, however, silence may signify the absence of answers in the face of big questions—for instance, the silence of a political prisoner or the anticipatory calm before a storm.

Making room for silence in clinical conversations is not always easy but is an essential skill to unlock unfolding narratives. Sitting with silence has been helpful in my work with clients who have endured traumatic experiences. Sometimes, such silence has been the occasion to enter new territories as this interaction with Chet illustrates:

THERAPIST: (*silence*) You shared with me quite a lot about your experiences. What was it like for you to talk about these experiences?

CHET: (*long silence*)

THERAPIST: I notice you are thinking and feeling silently.

CHET: (*sigh*) I do not know. I wanted to tell my story. We all do. And we hope someone will listen.

THERAPIST: Who else would you want to tell your story?

CHET: (*silence*) Tell everyone. People need to know how much suffering is out there.

The details of stories intrigue therapists. However, it is often the case that exclusive focus on details without attentiveness to their meaning or impact fails to shift the narrative in any substantial way or aid clients in reauthoring their trauma stories. Meta-conversations occur when therapist and client observe and reflect upon their interactions, noticing how they evolve and the emotions they evoke. When I asked Chet what it was like to share his experiences with me it advanced insight into how his narratives were being constructed and subsequently felt.

Such interactions promote storyline development and bolster thicker descriptions. They prompt meta-disclosures, or discussions about the conversation at hand that lend insight to clients' narratives.

In the next section, the composite case study I offer is the story of Tasha and her therapist, Meg, who I supervise.

## TASHA'S STORY

Tasha was 24 when she graduated from law school. As a young Muslim woman, she struggled to fit into a mostly male-dominated professional culture. The youngest child of her father's first wife, she was one of 18 children, and one of three who shared the same mother and father. Tasha described her biological brother as towering and intimidating. Although they spoke little, she looked up to him.

Tasha had moved from the village she grew up in to live with her brother and sister in the city. Her brother benefited from Tasha's help in raising his own children. She did the bulk of child-care and in exchange, he paid for Tasha's tuition at the university for which she was grateful and in turn, made every effort to do well. Tasha's sister, who had dropped out of school, had started her own business as a cosmetologist.

After graduation, Tasha was hired by a law firm that supported her in preparing for the bar exam. Eventually she distinguished herself in the specialty of construction law. Tasha's passion for learning propelled her to educate herself on family and immigration law, though her ultimate dream was to become a corporate lawyer.

Tasha spoke about what it was like living in a patriarchal society. She felt great pressure from her family to carry on the traditions of Muslim women. Her parents and brother, a successful businessman, questioned her career choice. As a result, Tasha felt unsupported by her family. Her life choices were devalued, and this made her feel less safe and secure about herself and estranged from her family except for her mother with whom she shared warm moments.

Now an adult woman, Tasha's father was pressuring her to marry. He was obsessed with getting a dowry, but Tasha was not ready for marriage. That said, she was burdened and conflicted about her family's cultural expectations. She would ask herself whether getting married and appeasing her father would open opportunities or whether it would be the "nail in the coffin" in finding her freedom.

Tasha described herself as a very private person. Her daily life revolved around work, caring for the home, and spending time with her nieces and nephews. She had no social life, spending her weekends cleaning and doing household chores. Although she was motivated in her career, she was a junior member of the firm and was paid very little. She did not have any clients. Despite the meager salary, she worked hard and described herself as one of the "worker bees of the law firm." Tasha loved her job, but her family's disapproval was stifling and she felt "hemmed in."

A breakthrough came when her law firm commissioned Tasha to manage a satellite office in a small town away from the city. Though it was designated as a "hardship location," Tasha embraced the opportunity. She was intent on making the best of this assignment regardless of its challenges as it freed her from the watchful eye of her family. Away from them, she could be her own person and pursue her own dreams. Tasha felt some trepidation about stepping into the unfamiliar, but she was ready for this new challenge.

The people in the little town she moved to were friendly and she noticed that for the first time she was thinking on her own and making her own decisions, even as basic as what and when to eat. Her preoccupation with pleasing everyone was no longer holding her down. She visited surrounding villages and began to learn the local language. The villagers took to her and even gave her one of the local names. She felt welcomed, and a sense of belonging.

Unfortunately, barely a month after she relocated, Tasha contracted COVID-19. She developed severe symptoms leading to hospitalization and quarantine for 2 weeks. She lost her sense of taste and appetite; suffered from debilitating fatigue and brain fog;

and experienced shortness of breath, heart palpitations, and chest pain. During her illness, no one in the family reached out to her. For the first time since coming to the village, she felt very alone.

Post-illness, Tasha found herself mired in resentment. She resented her family and their expectations. She resented her firm and all it represented. When diagnosed with COVID she had been told to "ride it out." But most of all, she resented herself. She ruminated about her plight, cried, and ultimately fell into a depression. As much as she loved to be on her own, she also knew that returning to the small town was not viable. Tasha could have died from the virus, and she fully believed that her family would not have cared. She was bereft of any dreams for herself and increasingly overwhelmed by debilitating anxiety.

## SELECTING MOMENTS OF WITNESSING

One might ask where to begin with Tasha, her story is rich with detail and full of seemingly irresolvable conundrums. Narrative practitioners address such complexity by developing maps of externalizing conversations. Externalizing conversations provide antidotes to people's deficit-saturated stories (White, 2007). Paying close attention to Tasha's words to unlock internal meaning and identity was critical to the therapeutic conversation:

TASHA: I do not know if anyone cares. (*silence*)

MEG: I am glad you are here. Therapy is here to support you.

TASHA: I could have died. I was alone in a remote village. I knew practically no one. I lived alone in a small room. No one would check on me. How do I know that I even matter?

MEG: Mattering is what therapy is about. You matter here. And I want to accompany you on this journey. Tell me more about what matters for you. What has mattering been like for you?

For Tasha, mattering became a tagline as she spoke about how her life was unfolding. Like most clients, she began the therapeutic encounter with a serious question: "How do I know that I even matter?" Meg acknowledged and legitimized her query by giving it voice and letting her know that in the therapeutic space she mattered, "You matter here," and she was not alone, "I want to accompany you on this journey."

Being witness to what mattering means to clients leads to connection and the development of storylines that serve as entry points to understanding. In Tasha's case, Meg could have reacted to her fears of dying: "I could have died." Instead, she chose to enter from a place of mattering as a way of privileging Tasha's choice and agency. What happened next in Tasha's story underscored her sense of agency.

Tasha convalesced for no more than a week before she got called back to the office. She still felt weak and not nearly recovered from her illness. Instead of passively complying, Tasha told her boss that she needed more time; she simply was not ready to return to work. On reflection, Tasha felt a sense of agency at standing up for herself and feeling that her life mattered. This was an important first step in shifting the course of her narrative from doing what others expected of her to doing what she needed for herself.

Themes of agency, choice, and mattering threaded through Tasha's subsequent storylines. For example, she requested more professional development opportunities to advance her career. To her great surprise, she was selected to represent her law firm at an international law training institute (LTI) for corporate lawyers. Tasha was equally ecstatic and daunted by this opportunity. She was getting a second chance to find her voice, leave home, and succeed at her chosen field. She wrote in her journal: "Allah is giving me a new opportunity at finding my life." Tasha also believed that she had earned this opportunity through diligence and hard work, a sign of a newly forming identity. Later, she reframed finding her voice as using her voice.

During her time at LTI Tasha gained comfort with her identity and found purpose. She wore the hijab without worrying about how she might be perceived. She easily established camaraderie with the woman with whom she shared an apartment. She had prepared well for the institute, having done research on corporate law, mergers, and acquisitions. There she attended meetings and for the first time she experienced feelings of belonging.

These feelings were unfortunately disrupted by two traumatic events. First, after 2 weeks at LTI, Tasha suddenly became ill. Her symptoms caused both bodily and mental distress. She was ultimately diagnosed with a bacterial infection, but she later learned that her boss had ordered bloodwork to rule out HIV and sickle cell disease. Tasha interpreted the tests as a violation of her medical privacy information and replete with bias. She had been singled out for this test while her colleagues were not. Tasha was intent on having a discussion with her boss about his actions once she recovered.

### THE NIGHT EVERYTHING CHANGED

It was New Year's Eve, just a month into her time at LTI. The institute was closed for a month and Tasha could not afford to go home for the holiday. She anticipated spending time alone in her apartment—watching movies, catching up on sleep, and enjoying her independence—as well as waiting for her brother's promised visit.

Tasha's memory of what took place that New Year's Eve remains foggy. She recalls her boss unexpectedly entering her apartment and sexually assaulting her. She woke up naked the next morning, bruised and in shock. She felt utterly isolated. For 2 days, she struggled alone, unable to eat, and constantly vomiting. When her brother arrived for a visit, he brought news of their father's grave illness, which significantly compounded Tasha's distress.

When Tasha disclosed the assault to her brother, his response of blame and anger—rather than support and comfort—intensified her feelings of shame, guilt, and betrayal. He insisted that she return home. At home, Tasha's brother monitored her every behavior, cutting her off from friends, and adding to her trauma by keeping her secluded and disconnected from potential supports. Tragically, after Tasha's return, her father died, deepening her anguish, sorrow, and isolation.

## "WITH-NESS"

Being present with clients in their suffering is a key element of any therapeutic practice. Andersen (1996) describes "with-ness" as an act where listener (therapist) follows talker (client) not only in hearing the words but also seeing how the words are being uttered and how those words are bodily expressed. Siegel (2010) describes this similarly, as a process of "feeling felt" by the other person or attunement with another's needs.

Tasha's determination to overcome trauma and adversity was met by her therapist's commitment to be fully present through all phases of their work together. Meg, my supervisee, listened attentively to Tasha's story, sharing deeply felt moments of silent connection and with-ness. She was there for Tasha at times of self-blame and discouragement, holding her hope while fostering her agency and resilience to rewrite the problem-saturated narratives of failure and unmet expectations. Tasha was "determined to beat the odds," defying her brother's desire to isolate and shame her. Meg kept her focused on a healing journey, one that supported Tasha's inherent agency and drive. At times Meg and Tasha paralleled each other's frustration, not an uncommon occurrence when facing the challenges of trauma work.

The next story speaks to the therapeutic function of witnessing and transformation from trauma narratives to ones of agency and choice. Layla's experiences open doors for re-storying into a quest for new causes.

### LAYLA'S STORY

Layla, 18, was experiencing newfound freedom as a college freshman. Without reservation, she delved into college culture, experimenting with drinking and socializing with older students, some of whom were men from off campus.

Layla worked diligently to achieve academic success while navigating the challenges of being biracial in a predominantly White community. As the daughter of a White mother and a Black father, she often struggled with a sense of belonging. During high school, she emerged as a strong advocate for diversity and inclusion and played a leadership role in advancing efforts to decolonize the curriculum. She waged a wellness campaign for smoking cessation. Despite her strong academics and support from sympathetic teachers and friends, Layla felt isolated among her predominantly White schoolmates and in her neighborhood. Balancing her identity and values with the pressures of social acceptance was an ongoing struggle.

Layla chose to attend a Jesuit institution known for its social justice mission. She was eager to continue her dedicated advocacy work, determined to become a community organizer. Layla was committed to her principles, refusing to compromise despite the inevitable challenges from those whose priorities differed, particularly classmates from affluent backgrounds.

Layla's delight at being a college student and young activist was abruptly shattered early in her time at the university. She was sexually assaulted by one of the men who frequented dorm parties, plunging Layla into a crippling depression and anxiety. Overwhelmed by shame and guilt, she grappled with intrusive memories and flashbacks and plagued by suicidal thoughts. She avoided certain campus locations not wanting to confront memories of the assault. It became increasingly difficult for Layla to concentrate and regulate her emotions. For the first time in her life, she experienced emotional, often angry outbursts. She blamed everyone but mostly herself. Why did the world not protect her?

In therapy, Layla was overwhelmed by confusion, anger, and self-blame, as she struggled to tearfully recall details of the assault. Flashbacks and nightmares constantly brought the trauma of the assault back to consciousness. Exacerbating her distress, Layla was forced to recount details of the trauma events to inform legal proceedings. A cycle of repeated questioning by an array of professionals was retraumatizing, intensifying her emotional turmoil and causing her to socially withdraw and avoid school activities.

## Retraumatization Versus Agency, Choice, and Justice

Retraumatization occurs when memories of traumatic events resurface, evoking reactions and emotions that replicate those experienced during the original trauma. They can be activated by sensory, auditory, or visual stimuli that the survivor associates with the trauma. Reliving aspects of trauma can reinforce the negative conclusions that people hold about their identity and about their lives.

Beaudoin and Monk (2024) view retraumatizing and retelling as distinctive in the therapeutic setting. They propose that retelling shifts the focus away from past struggles toward clients' abilities and accomplishments, protecting integrity and agency in the here and now. The authors contend that "the retelling is more likely to be helpful if clients are positioned as active agents, who engage in self-protective efforts aligned with values held before, during, and after the disturbing event (p. 97). It is a therapist's challenge to not focus on the deficit-saturated aspects of people's stories. As such, therapists need to be open to the many aspects of people's lives, including those that have not yet been storied.

In Layla's case, questioning by professionals, both therapeutic and legal, provoked memories and escalated her feelings of shame, hopelessness, and futility. Such reactions further reinforced her negative identity, rekindling earlier self-perceptions that she was somehow unacceptable and did not belong. The trauma had left Layla with thin narratives about herself that contributed to feelings of vulnerability.

It took time for Layla to see herself beyond what had happened to her. But she did. Narrative work helped her reflect on aspects of her identity separate from trauma. She found comfort in naming the parts of herself that represented strength, agency, and the ability to manage the trauma and regain her vitality and dignity. Fortunately, Layla had done previous work using internal family systems (IFS) therapy (Schwartz & Sweezy, 2020), a practice that promotes healing through acceptance of different parts of the self, including the mind. This exchange illustrates how she used IFS language to advance her self-discovery and recovery:

LAYLA: I feel like I have many things going on inside me. There are different parts. I need to name the different parts going on in me.

THERAPIST: What different parts?

LAYLA: I am recognizing what I am feeling. I have a perfectionist in me, which I call my work bee part. And when it comes up, I know what it wants to communicate to me. I do not push it away. I like to sit with that part. I like to listen to it. I feel like it protects me. It makes me feel good.

THERAPIST: It makes you feel good about what you can do.

LAYLA: Yes, and my other part is the critic. It is super loud. As you can see, I am a very loud person (*lowers her voice*). But I am also very self-critical. I say to myself: "What does the critic want of me?" Can we tell this critic that we know we can handle these things? That we can make mistakes. Understanding where I am feeling it in my body. Like, there is this thing that I feel in my shoulders. It leaves me with a lot of shame. Doing a lot of work with shame.

THERAPIST: Shame around what?

LAYLA: About a bunch of things. But, shame sometimes serves a purpose. It wishes things never happened again. It kind of burns you. Learning that things will be better. Making you feel strong. A *can-do* feeling.

THERAPIST: A *can-do* feeling . . . sounds like a sense of agency. . . . Does it give you a sense of agency?

LAYLA: I feel empowered because I know more. I think it is like another story. I feel much more than that. I am also proud of all that I have done. I feel strong and empowered in myself. I could go through all of that and I am alive and am better. I feel grounded

THERAPIST: Grounded. . . . What makes you grounded?

LAYLA: For me what really works is journaling. You start with nothing on paper and you finish with something. It is an empowering act. It makes me realize things take time to happen. I can see what I can create. When I paint and do something it makes me see that at any point, I can create something. I say, "I did that." So, art and journaling have been very good to me. I imagine something and I produce. It helps me around social media.

THERAPIST: What about social media?

LAYLA: I do not like social media. I think it is bad. It is something I am working on. I can feel a little shame because I feel I have wasted my day. It gives me a false sense of grounding, some kind of dopamine. And because I have dopamine it feels good because I have ADHD. It feels like I have wasted my day. Doing it every day is unhealthy. I need to find a different activity.

THERAPIST: That is good to know about oneself.

LAYLA: Social media really affects people's mental health.

THERAPIST: What about keeping up with social connections?

LAYLA: Yes, I always call friends. I love calling friends. I like to be in touch. Especially with people who share my passion for certain causes, social justice causes.

Layla's commitment to social justice and its healing properties emerged in our work. She built on her passion for community organization and her calling for advocacy:

THERAPIST: What about seeking justice? What does that look like for you?

LAYLA: When the anniversary [of the assault] comes up, I think about it often. You recall I had to give a victim impact statement. It also related to my love for organizing. That was the first time I put my skills of organizing a community of friends to be there and support me. I found it cool to have people come out and support me. Since my mom could not be there with me, I organized to have a circle of friends to be there with me. It was a small win for all of us. People came and supported me. I feel I could help to organize for other people. And being able to stand up and speak my truth. A sense of empowerment

> to stand up and speak my truth. It was going to go to trial, but I decided not to press charges and not go through a grueling trial, not to re-traumatize myself. A great decision. I feel I had a choice in my decision. To make that choice I was so happy. And so, I believe that whatever survivors choose to do is important as long as they have their choice. That, in itself, is so empowering. That is a small win for all of us. That is justice.
>
> THERAPIST: The choice part is key.
>
> LAYLA: Yes.

After 2 years of therapy, Layla joined a women's group focused on survivors of violence. There she found connection and camaraderie with women her age. Some members were newly married or had become mothers, reflecting diverse experiences but shared values. Layla found solace and a sense of belonging in the group, describing it as a place of "homeness" where stories of survival were shared, and collective hopes for the future were nurtured. The stories of group members offered an array of experiences that helped to ground her.

Layla has regained trust in herself, taken ownership of her journey, and continues to explore her identity. Inspired by her experiences, she has honed her skills as a community organizer and advocate for women and marginalized communities. She dedicates herself to the pursuit of justice in solidarity with groups and individuals who suffer abuse and discrimination. Layla's commitment to seek justice has been a rallying force in her re-storying her life narratives.

## Moments of Witnessing

Clients entrust us with their stories and by doing so, we become aware and empowered witnesses to the work that needs to be done. We actively listen to their narratives and walk with them as they relinquish desperation and embrace an aware and empowered witness position. Our listening and willingness to go into the emotional abyss alongside clients sets a pathway for hope.

The stories of Tasha and Layla speak to different moments of witnessing and the imperative of hope. Witnessing is a complex and dynamic process influenced by the positions of both client and therapist and the stories that unfold. Narrative practitioners share an important role in accompanying clients as they navigate these witness positions.

Tasha was a victim and a witness. She vacillated between awareness and unawareness, empowerment and disempowerment. Her story illustrates how family expectations, scrutiny, and devaluing of life choices can negatively impact one's identity. Tasha felt trapped by her family's deficit-saturated narratives that dismissed and derided her chances of succeeding as a lawyer. Their cultural beliefs and actions created ambivalence that inhibited Tasha's pursuit of her dreams. Tasha was also a victim of her boss's demands and ultimately, his sexual violation. She did not feel empowered to confront her boss about the assault, but she found awareness that helped her acknowledge the violation and do what she needed to heal.

For Layla, recounting traumatic events challenged her witness positions. She was deeply aware that as a Black woman there was a lot going against her—she worried that no one would believe her. When Layla fell into deep depression, her narratives were ones of helplessness and hopelessness, and she could not visualize what she could do about her situation. She could not access awareness of what it meant to seek justice not just for herself but on behalf of all women who are assaulted every day. She felt disempowered by society's complicity surrounding sexual assault.

In our narrative practice, it was Layla's commitment to justice that empowered her to advocate for herself as she would for others in her position. Passion for justice transitioned Layla from desperation to healing. Her recognition and lifting of her strong "parts" in retelling her trauma story speak to being self-protective after her assault and in the journey of self-discovery. Layla began a journey by redressing the harm done to her, slowly reconstructing her stories from depression narratives to those that elevated her abilities, her hopes, and dreams for the future.

Layla's emerging witness position propelled her to embrace a stance for justice and a commitment to community organizing. Her determination to pursue justice reflects Freire's (2014) notion of *critical hope*, conceived as a necessary struggle that integrates both cognition and affect. Grounded in the pursuit of humanization and fueled by the passion and rage required to confront oppression (Freire, 2014), Layla embodied this commitment with resolve. For example, she advocated with Muslim women to find safe and respectful spaces to breastfeed their babies. Such small acts of kindness became mini acts of resistance for Layla and helped transform the lives of many women. Her zest for justice led her to pursue a legal career committed to seeking justice for those who desperately need it. While clients witness to the depth of feeling associated with their experiences, therapy also provides the containment for that witness. As therapists assess, listen, and intervene in the lives of clients they play an active role as co-witnesses to those stories.

## Narrative Practice and Restoration of Meaning

Narrative therapy is well suited to explore ways in which clients can reauthor trauma and restore meaning in their lives. Steger and Park (2012) suggest that following traumatic events, people seek to reconcile situational meaning (trauma) with their previously held beliefs, goals, and understanding of the world. They posit that one's level of distress posttrauma is related to the discrepancy between the situational meaning of the event and a person's prior worldview. As such, reconciliation of trauma ". . . can be incorporated into a person's global meaning but can also lead to a shattering of that meaning" (p. 173). For example, if one lived by the belief that good things happen to good people, a traumatic event would be terribly incongruent and destructive to their previously held worldview. For those who take the position that life is fraught with difficulties to overcome, trauma is still painful but aligns with their essential philosophy.

The trauma story is personal, complex, and multivaried. Tasha's and Layla's stories illustrate this complexity. There are always gaps and openings in trauma stories, places to unfold meaning beyond constraining discourses. There are also ways for clinicians to genuinely listen without reifying dominant structures (Kamya, 2012). This work involves clinicians maintaining a collaboratively curious stance and listening through a

> dialogical discourse with another . . . listening not only for the story of trauma but also for what the person holds precious, the person's response to trauma and times when the effects of the trauma may not be total. (p. 235)

Just as lives are multistoried, trauma is not just about stories of pain but also involves stories of resilience, resistance, and people holding tight to their preferred values (Ncube, 2010).

Exploring clients' preferred identities even while engaged in trauma narratives creates a context to recognize and restore personal agency and avert being trapped by negative discourse alone (Beaudoin, 2005; Ncube, 2010; Shachar, 2010). Such preferred narratives can be found, even within the distress and pain that a person is experiencing due to the trauma.

Responses to trauma have a "foundation . . . based on what the [person] gives value to: this might be a dream, or a hope, or some vision of what life could be about" (Ncube, 2010, p. 4). Such responses are ever present and witnessing them sheds light on possibilities for surmounting pain, assimilating the trauma story, and moving forward. People are actors in their own healing not merely . . . passive recipients of the traumas they are subject to" (Shachar, 2010, p. 52). Even when feeling powerless to influence or change their circumstances it is a testimony to resilience that people ". . . still take what steps are available to them to modify what they are being subject to in some small way . . ." (p. 52).

## Small Acts of Resistance

Witnessing gives voice to what Wade (1997) calls "small acts of living," a form of resistance to violence and oppression seen as evidence of health in people subjected to trauma. Rather than focus on pathology, Wade uses a therapeutic approach that views survivors' coping mechanisms and management strategies as resistance. Doing so helps them to reconceptualize their experience and "begin to experience themselves as stronger, more insightful, and more capable of responding effectively to the difficulties that occasioned therapy" (p. 24).

Wade (1997) also gives examples of the ways in which dissociation during sexual abuse, such as mentally making shopping lists, can be seen as an act of resistance. "Any act of resistance in such circumstances is inherently and profoundly significant, regardless of what it may appear to have accomplished" (p. 32). The important therapeutic task is to recognize and honor these acts of resistance and to explore what it means to the client to recognize one's "history of resistance" (p. 37).

Meg and Tasha explored the small acts of resistance she enacted following the sexual assault. Together they reclaimed the mutism that immediately followed as a form of resistance, a coping mechanism that Tasha needed to emotionally recalibrate and recoup from her trauma experience. Trained in mindfulness techniques, Meg engaged Tasha in a three-step awareness process, which involved slowly broadening an awareness from self, to space, to person(s).

In supervision, Meg and I discussed the importance of grounding oneself to enter the sacred spaces with our clients as they moved through trauma narratives. When relaxed and aware of what is going on in our bodies and minds, we are then able to extend this awareness to our therapy spaces—including the furniture, the books, the lighting, the noise, sound, stillness, and colors—we are ready to invite clients into the awareness of their state of being. Beaudoin and Monk (2024) emphasize that such awareness is foundational to co-centering. This grounding self-awareness exercise can be helpful, and Meg used variations of it with Tasha:

MEG: Keep eyes open, light on, look around the room and name the objects and colors, feel the chair and your feet touching, feel your hands, wiggle your toes, notice your body, and describe how it feels. Clench and grab on to an object and release it. Notice how your body feels. Touch and name all the objects around you.

At other times, Meg used this exercise:

> MEG: Describe the room in detail using all senses. Name all categories of [food types, TV shows, plant types, colors]. Count or say the alphabet out loud forward and backward. Say or repeat a coping statement: "I can . . ." Think about and describe a safe place or person. Now return to present-moment planning for immediate needs: safe place, call someone, eat.

Tasha's hypervigilance following the assault made her very sensitive to noise, sounds, and lighting. Over time, she converted this to a healthy respect and appreciation for stillness. The awareness exercise gave Tasha a means to center herself in therapy when she was flooded by memories of the assault and it was also transferable outside of therapy where she worked hard to keep intrusive thoughts at bay. Self-blame and doubt, however, continued to plague Tasha. Meg sought to spotlight "acts of resistance" that she used to fend off these feelings that were no small acts at all:

> TASHA: Maybe I did not lock the door. But I heard the key turn. Maybe I should have gone home to be with my family. But I wanted to have time by myself. Maybe I should have screamed louder. But it was deep into the night, and I knew no one was around.
>
> MEG: So, there is a lot of second-guessing of self (SGS) about what you should have done.
>
> TASHA: And I still hear the voice of my brother blaming me for what I did and what I should have done.
>
> MEG: You were resolute. You resisted him, you tried to fight back. How did you get the courage in that moment?
>
> TASHA: I do not know. But I felt I had nothing to lose.

In the context of trauma, narrative techniques are about strengthening stories of resistance, healing, and reclamation. Reclamation refers to repossession of one's own life, which the trauma story takes away.

Such an effort may, for example, involve finding new meanings and self-understandings in the context of the old and the new. Stories of resistance and healing also help to create directions for community trauma response, which collectively begins with working toward social justice and social change. As such, communities serve as witnesses and engage in "doing hope" (Weingarten, 2000) with those who have experienced trauma. Ultimately, it is about seeking the preservation of life and rebuilding those fragmented parts of oneself.

Meg was ever aware that Tasha's trauma story pervaded the room even when it was not the overt topic of discussion. Tasha needed a safe and nurturing space to manage the dysregulation caused by the trauma. Meg and Tasha worked diligently to deconstruct the SGS positions that often told her that she was not enough or that she could have done more to protect herself. It was a therapeutic necessity to normalize the adaptations she made posttrauma, build a sense of empowerment, and renew her identity to decrease her sense of shame and isolation.

I encouraged Meg to stay close to Tasha's feelings and invited her to do the same. They each explored and evaluated the effects of SGS as well as mapping how SGS permeated their lives. Tracking affective responses helps not only the individual but also attends to how emotions generated by recovery may affect the relational systems to which they belong (Beaudoin & Monk, 2024). This was especially important for Tasha as she navigated the harsh responses of family members to her taking hold of agency and independence. For example, Tasha's brother was unsympathetic to the impacts of the assault. She believed that his resentment and anger toward lawyers were now projected on to her. Tasha had initially internalized a problematic identity as she, too, was a lawyer:

TASHA: All he [Tasha's brother] cared about is that he had wasted all this money sending me to law school. And I had nothing to show for it. He would say to me: "How can you trust lawyers? Why would you want to be one?" (*silence*)

MEG: So, your brother was blaming you for taking charge of your life?

TASHA: (*thinking*) Well . . . I guess so but he has always pushed me to go to school . . . One can never be right. I hear conflicting messages . . . I still worry about what the rest of my family thinks and what he is going to tell them. I need to worry about me.

MEG: Yes, who determines who you are or the choices you make? Which decisions were yours and which decisions were beyond your control?

TASHA: (*pauses, smiling*) Me.

MEG: Yes, you need to worry about you.

Tasha's revelation that "I need to worry about me" was a touchstone, launching her agency and belief in her right to have choice. Meg encouraged Tasha to notice how attending to herself connected to her body, her choices, and other moments in her life.

Meg also suggested that Tasha think about how women's stories are frequently constructed by others, mostly by the men in their lives. Tasha's story was being dictated by her brother and Meg urged Tasha to interrogate these messages, or "truths," to understand their rootedness in patriarchy. Stories about women guided by dominant cultural ideas are assumptive, producing thin narratives and erroneous conclusions (Weedon, 1997). Meg wanted Tasha to form an identity determined by her own choice of action rather than by others' responses or presumed knowledges.

## Survival and Coping

While Tasha's therapeutic work continues to bear witness to the pain and harm she suffered, it has also allowed her to explore ways to honor her survival and coping efforts as wise and strong. Such therapeutic conversations can best take place in a nonjudgmental environment and within a relationship that is respectful, dignified, and imbued with trust. The therapist creates a psychologically safe space where emotions are expressed and contained, reconnections are formed, spirituality grows, and where clients are permitted to grieve and mourn for as long as it takes. White (2007) describes these as remembering conversations that "provide an opportunity for people to revise the memberships of their association of life" (p. 129).

For Tasha, therapy was also a space to reconnect with her body and regain a sense of control. Body integrity tells an important story. Meg listened empathically as Tasha shared her body story, letting her lead the way and helping her manage the affect associated with the telling. Throughout, Meg offered Tasha education about sexual assault, normalizing her responses as the body's/mind's way of coping with overwhelming stress. Using a narrative practice approach, Meg bore witness to hope without diminishing the depth of Tasha's pain, suffering, and loss.

## Conclusion

Narrative practice invites people who have experienced trauma, who are vulnerable and alone, into daring to hope again. Witnessing is a form of storytelling that builds connection. Narrative practitioners act as key witnesses accompanying clients on the journey to agency, choice, and justice.

Narrative practices acknowledge the plurality of stories, some of which are hidden or untold for different reasons. Some stories have no words to express them. Others are intentionally silenced, because the privileged do not want them to be written. The language of such stories may be best represented in body movement, through artwork, or emotional expression. It is therefore crucial for practitioners to be open to a variety of contexts for listening, witnessing, grounding, and speaking.

Narrative is an approach that fosters and invites witnessing in community. As Weingarten (2000) contends, "Hope is something we do with others. Hope is too important—its effect on body and soul too significant—to be left to individuals alone. Hope must be the responsibility of the community" (p. 400). In the next chapter, I reflect on my encounter with people from Rwanda whose lives were deeply affected by the 1994 genocide. The Rwandan people's experiences of trauma and their efforts to find hope and rebuild a sense of connection tell important stories. The chapter also illustrates how narrative methods articulate growth, reconstruct shattered assumptions, and locate the words to voice experience.

CHAPTER 6

# Listening to Stories of Hope

People's problems are so often sustained and reinforced by problem-saturated interpretations of experience (White & Epston, 1990). As Riessman (2008) states, "individuals turn to narratives to excavate and reassess memories that may have been fragmented, chaotic, unbearable, and/or scarcely visible before narrating them" (p. 8). Through stories, clients identify, externalize, and deconstruct problematic narratives that present seemingly insurmountable obstacles. Reauthoring stories facilitates new preferred narratives that elevate resilience and reinforce preferred outcomes (White & Epston, 1990).

Stories are embedded in traumas of the past and the present. Narrative practitioners strive to gain deeper insight into people's experiences through active listening and being fully present. Practitioners focus on meaning making, understanding that narrative content is contextual and situational, and influenced by power relations and factors such as gender, life cycle, and relational processes. Narratives exist within global, cultural, and historical contexts. For individuals and communities, re-storying is both personal and collective.

## Trauma and the Rwandan Experience

In my travels across Africa, I have been honored to listen to people's stories. Some speak to joy and resilience, while all too many tell of pain, suffering, and trauma. I have come to appreciate the universality of trauma stories through my work. In many countries, historical traumas linger in people's memories and play out in their everyday lives. In South Africa for example, people continue to experience the lasting impacts of apartheid. In Uganda, the enduring trauma from tyrannical dictatorial wars continues to profoundly affect large segments of the population. In Rwanda, the devastating effects of the genocide haunt generations.

This chapter is grounded in the narratives and traumatic experiences of survivors of the Rwandan genocide. I spent considerable time talking to the Rwandan people about their experiences before, during, and after the 1994 genocide. Whatever wisdom I share originates from what I learned from survivors' stories and from those of their offspring who experience generational trauma. Trauma and response to trauma varies. Guilt, grief, alienation, recovery, and peace are expressed in diverse ways. Though many survived the Rwandan genocide, nobody was spared its horrors. It impacted people regardless of economic status, background, gender, age, or religion. To this day, survivors carry its enduring wounds and devastation.

People find ways to make sense of their lives through stories. Storytelling is a way of fostering narrative integration, a process that is critical to developing an integrated identity in the face of turmoil. Narrative integration interprets meaning from life experience or autobiography, forming a coherent and integrated sense of self and community. Such integration can help reframe negative experiences into positive ones or are used to cope with life's challenges. Randall (2011) explores how individuals use narrative to make sense of their experiences, suggesting that life stories function as metaphors that help people understand their lives and identities. They create pathways to self-understanding.

Stories are multifaceted and too complex to be reduced to binary categories. The Rwandan genocide narrative is often framed in binary terms, as a conflict caused by ethnic tensions between the Tutsi and Hutu, and as a story of victims and perpetrators. Such reductionism does not nearly capture the brutal experience for Rwandans. In 1994 members of the Hutu ethnic majority in Rwanda murdered as many as 800,000 people, mostly of the Tutsi minority. The war lasted 100 days and by the time it ended, hundreds of thousands of Rwandans were dead and an estimated 2 million people fled the country, causing a humanitarian crisis.

What is less known is that the racialization of Rwanda also devastated a third group, the Twa, an indigenous people, who are rarely mentioned in discussions of the genocide. The Twa people faced fierce discrimination in Rwanda, were denied access to essential resources by the government, and experienced violent victimization before and during the genocide. Knowing this brief history offers insight into the sweeping historical trauma experienced by the Rwandan people that is alive within them to this day.

The stories that follow illustrate the wounds endured by genocide survivors and their offspring and the adaptive reprocessing of traumatic memories they work to achieve. These stories highlight the resilience of the human spirit and the need to tell and retell stories. In Beaudoin and Monk's (2024) book, Nathalie-Marie Beaudoin offers an apt analogy. She states that "just as fish can swim through rough waters but not ice, people can move through trauma but not frozen stories" (p. 96). Survivor experiences speak to a deep yearning for belonging, resistance to being labeled as victims, and to the ravages of spirit that take place when people are disenfranchised and Othered.

Rudeka's story has great significance for me as a clinician. It is a story of how deeply held values, agency, and choices can pave the way for autobiographical continuity, the feeling that one holds on to their identity despite the myriad circumstances that befall them (Beaudoin, 2005; White, 2004). Rudeka helped me understand how therapy is a daring and humbling experience. Entering intimate space with another requires the mutual willingness of both client and therapist to be open, fostering vulnerability for each. First encounters matter. How we greet clients, maintain eye contact, and listen to their words influence relational connection. Rudeka reminded me that every word, every action, how we move, and every gesture in that initial meeting counts.

### THE STORY OF RUDEKA

I met Rudeka, 75, at a spiritual center where we were both staying. I noticed him at breakfast every morning before we formally met. His 7-foot stature and gray hair made him difficult to ignore. He wore distinctive glasses that made him look pensive and contemplative. Rudeka sat alone silently eating, scanning the dining room. One morning I decided to approach him. I asked if I might join him for breakfast. I vividly recall our first conversation. He told me that he was at the center for a few weeks to "reflect about life." It was at that moment that our friendship and intimate connection began.

Rudeka told me he did not speak much English and was more comfortable speaking in French. I told him I could understand his English and had enough knowledge of French to aid our communication. Periodically, he used Google Translate to find the right words to explain himself; he was very particular about his chosen words. Rudeka had been at the spiritual center for a month, and he "so much wished to speak to someone." The desire for connection is a human yearning, and Rudeka, as a relational being, yearned for connection and communion with others.

Rudeka told me that he had lived most of his life as refugee. He was planning a return to Rwanda 30 years after the 1994 Genocide, under the "Come and See" program. This governmental program was designed to welcome back war refugees to Rwanda.

Rudeka spoke softly and pensively as he recounted his story. He described escaping the genocide and living in refugee camps with his wife and children after his parents were murdered by neighbors who showed up at his house armed with machetes. He escaped through the back door, though he has no memory of how he did it. "I did it, I do not know how it all happened," he says. Following his escape, he moved from one refugee camp to another, leaving his pregnant wife and family behind, traveling to Tanzania, Kenya, and Cameroon, before finally settling in France. There he awaited the arrival of his family. Rudeka talked about how some countries were welcoming while others shunned him. At times, he felt deeply betrayed by his country and its people.

Once in France, Rudeka drove trucks for a living and wrote about the politics of his country. Writing helped him escape from what he called "the demons of life." Writing also allowed him to imagine a better future. He described feeling a deep sense of anger directed at the colonists who exploited Africa's resources for their own interests, leaving countries impoverished and causing divisiveness among nations. "Most of Africa was plundered in the name of development by European powers who sought its resources for their own enrichment," he once said at one of our breakfast meetings. Rudeka believed that the genocide in Rwanda was an outgrowth of this exploitation.

Rudeka interspersed philosophical musing throughout the telling of his escape and resettlement. He fervently believed that "it is humanity that binds us all together," adding, "humanity helps us tell our story." He described the power of thought and imagination as something that travels faster than the speed of light. He noted that thought and imagination were essential to his life, sustaining him even during times when "life was not easy."

Rudeka recalled emotional confusion during his time in the refugee camps. He felt caught between feeling a sense of safety after his miraculous escape from the genocide but simultaneously being in constant fear for his life. He had no respect for the United Nations peacekeepers, who offered some measure of safety but also committed atrocities in the camps. In addition, people in the camp stole from one another and there were some people that Rudeka was afraid to approach. "We constantly feared for our lives. There was little we could do." Each day there was the possibility that anyone could be moved to another country without warning. There was too much uncertainty to rely on anything.

But Rudeka also spoke of moments of generosity and kindness that took place during and after his traumatic escape. He described what he called "small acts of kindness" from some people and places that received him well. There were people who gave him shelter for the night or a hot meal before he set out again. Rudeka recalled with deep appreciation a neighbor who lied about harboring escapees, saving his life while he hid in a back room.

As Rudeka spoke, he paused a few times looking for the right word to describe his experience. At times words eluded him and he would do a quick search in his Google Scholar dictionary: "Intruder . . . that is the word I am looking for," he exclaimed, to explain his struggles with belonging. No matter where he lives, Rudeka says that he feels like an intruder. He asks, "What does belonging mean?"

Rudeka reminisced about the changes he has undergone in his life. Despite the horrific personal and philosophical consequences of genocide, he now feels a glimmer of hope, which he translates into his writing. Rudeka writes children's comic books. He uses this creative outlet to send subliminal messages to his readers. While the comics are aimed at children, he believes they also reach parents, delivering meaningful lessons. Through writing and storytelling, he has found a way to imagine and create alternative possibilities, offering both himself and his audience a chance to envision something different, something better.

## Metaphor and Storytelling

Metaphor is central to storytelling and Rudeka liberally used it in his narratives. At one of our meetings, he told me a story about two dogs sitting by a fireplace, silently sharing each other's company. The dogs struggled to find the right words to say, much like Rudeka did when he turned to Google Translate. Both dogs were aware that one of them must gather the courage to speak. Rudeka continued: "But neither dog does. Finally, one dog barks, and in so doing, it breaks the silence." A long, deep stillness follows the tale of the dogs, then Rudeka continues: "Breaking the silence is the gateway to hope."

Rudeka's story of the two dogs speaks to the burden of silence and the courage it takes to break it. For Rudeka, writing is a courageous act, breaking the silence surrounding the pain he has endured and witnessed. Speaking and writing are ways of seeking hope and finding purpose amid his grief. The great author Maya Angelou (2010) understood this well when she wrote that there is no greater agony than bearing an untold story. Rudeka had borne such agony until writing created an opening to give voice to his sadness over the loss of his parents and the survivor guilt that left him with lingering questions: "Why did I survive the ordeal? Why me? What did my parents do to deserve this?" Rudeka continued to ponder unanswerable questions but now he could express them and simultaneously imagine a brighter future.

## Harnessing Threads of Hope

As I reflect on Rudeka's story, I marvel at the creative and courageous ways he chose to generate threads of hope. Rudeka's silence masked a life of suffering and challenges. Breaking the silence announced hope and opportunity. In many ways, the beauty of therapy lives within the ability to sit with a person's silence and work with them to announce hope.

During another one of our conversations, Rudeka told me the story of a little bird that sees a big brush fire burning. The bird contemplates what to do as everyone is fleeing. The bird decides to go to a pond, suck up as much water as it can, and fly back to the brush fire spitting on the fire with the hope of extinguishing it. The little bird flies back and forth several times trying to put out the fire. Rudeka was in awe of the little bird's courage and perseverance to make a difference. For him, the little bird embodied what it means to engender hope. Like the little bird, Rudeka's mission is to bring a bit of hope to whatever he can in life, writing being one avenue to make that happen.

Rudeka's story, albeit briefly represented here, underscores the vital role of individual and collective storytelling posttrauma. His story encapsulates those of other ordinary people seeking to make meaning of their lives. Narratives articulate growth, reconstruct shattered assumptions, and have the potential to express what has previously been silenced. For those who experienced the genocide, it is imperative to listen to the rawness of their voices. The ability to narrate accounts that took place before, during, and after the genocide helps restore coherence and meaning to those whose lives and communities sustained irreparable harm.

Rudeka, unlike other genocide survivors, did not wish to meet his perpetrators. Instead, writing gave him "comfort and solace toward a sense of hope." Writing became the opportunity to generate counter-narratives and to imagine future possibilities.

## Expanding the Audience

An important technique of narrative practice is expanding the audience through retelling stories. Stories may be retold to family, friends, or significant people in a person's life. They may be shared with others who have struggled with problem-saturated stories. Powerful supporters may also bear witness to an individual's emerging preferred stories (Monk, 1997; White, 2007). Expanding the audience also facilitates reauthoring conversations in which practitioner and client become coauthors in the storying process.

Retelling stories is an important way to keep them alive for future generations so that they are not misrepresented or vanish in reframed histories. I have often wondered about the impact of Rudeka's story on the next generation. What will his story mean to them years later? How does a generation, who did not experience the genocide firsthand, make sense of it? Will their bodies carry the echoes of trauma from so long ago?

## We Are All Rwandans

To explore these questions, I enlisted stories from young adults in their late 20s and 30s, many of whom were not even born during the 1994 genocide. I was curious about the significant moments in their lives, their memories, and what they had been taught about the genocide, whether in school or by the adults around them. I asked about their most difficult challenges, their greatest concerns, and what has caused them the most pain. At the same time, I wondered with them about what gave them hope and what made their "soul dance."

Despite their varied backgrounds, all participants expressed that the trauma of the genocide continues to affect their lives. They strongly identify as Rwandans, reflecting the inclusive national identity promoted by the current government. They rejected ethnic divisiveness moving instead toward an inclusive national identity. The impacts of the Rwandan genocide, however, continue to cast dark shadows over the international community's complicity of silence during the horrors of the ethnic war.

Like all the case studies in this book, the following interview vignettes are composites.

> PARTICIPANT 1: I identify myself as a person who belongs in a community. A community of believers. Accordingly, I do not identify as a Hutu or Tutsi. But as a person. Being a religious person . . . once you give your life to Jesus, you are a special human being because at the end of the day you do not identify yourself as one person or another but as a Rwandan person.

Some participants spoke about "the struggle to belong" as bi-ethnic children of Hutu and Tutsi parentage. One participant described being asked to choose an ethnicity rather than acknowledge their mixed heritage. Over time, when choosing was no longer required, they found that identifying as being human sustained meaning and belonging.

> PARTICIPANT 2: If I can recall from my high school experience, it was very hard. You had to identify as either a Hutu or a Tutsi. You were forced to . . . like me who came from both sides. It was hard . . . to identify as one tribe. We often identified ourselves as Tutsi because after the trauma, we got more privileges. It was a

> struggle to belong. Now, we do not need to identify with any clan or group because at the end of the day we are all humans.

Participants' reflections inspired me to ask more questions. I was curious about where they shared or heard stories about their families' genocide experiences. Where did they originate and whose stories brought them knowledge of their history? I understood that my curiosity could be triggering for these young people even after so much time had passed. Creating safe space for such difficult conversations would be essential. To my surprise, my questions sparked significant interest within the group.

Cultural humility, sensitivity, and willingness to listen attentively are hallmarks of narrative practice. As practitioners, we can never be sure how clients will respond to our questions. I approached questioning the participants with caution, aware of the heavy silence that surrounded the genocidal trauma. Like Rudeka, the young adults emphasized the need to break the silence searching for the words to give voice to their experiences and those of their families. Breaking the silence was the only way to forge healing. As one participant expressed:

> PARTICIPANT 3: Before . . . in high school, people were not talking about being a Hutu or Tutsi. But you would know who a Tutsi was and who was not. All children whose tuition was paid for belonged to the Tutsi. So, if you were not in that group, you would be able to know that you are Hutu. There was no speaking about it publicly. I would go to my parents and ask which tribe we belonged to. My parents would not say.
>
> But now with the healing of the wounds people are talking about it. During the month of April, the period of *Kweyibuka* [Commemoration Remembrance], we are talking about it more. We are talking about these atrocities. People come together and they become friends. They are asking for forgiveness in the *Gacaca* [Restorative Justice Commission] courts.

Some participants spoke to the complexity of the issues that fueled silence. This included the reality that some children were born as a consequence of sexual assault. Perpetration of such horrific violence against the community was made worse by the complicity of different groups, including extremist groups; Rwandan Armed Forces; and administrative, military, and political leaders at both national and local levels. While reports indicate one group over another in the perpetration of violence, there were also individuals among those groups who risked their lives to protect and hide victims. But these young people wanted to acknowledge and speak out about the atrocities their families endured:

> PARTICIPANT 3: Rwandan culture is a quiet culture. People are encouraged to listen or be seen, not to be heard. From a very young age you are told not to speak. So, a lot is unspoken. Even parents wait for triggers to speak about it. Parents do not like to tell children about their own experience of genocide. I think that has its problems. Triggers may or may not lead to healing. I have seen people from either side, including people who were born out of rape and their mothers hate them. They were born as children of crime. It is a hard conversation to bring out. When these conversations take place, it brings out what happened, and it gives you a sense of community. If you are a survivor, you are more likely to be accepted by other survivors. When people begin to open up then we realize that we are all victims, and it gives you a sense of acceptance. Opening up is very hard even in close families. In families, there is a lot of silence. I wish we could talk more.

Some participants were angry and blamed their parents for conspiring with silence, even though it was motivated by a desire to protect their children from knowledge of past horrors.

> PARTICIPANT 1: Our parents are hurt and are hurting. Talking about what happened helps the healing. Our parents think they are protecting us by holding on to pain. They say: "For your safety, we cannot talk about it especially if it is going to cause harm to the child, the product of rape." I think our parents should find a good way to share it with us. So that it helps in the healing process. For

> me, I am Christian. We say the devil is a liar. He tells you there is more suffering. More than the other. We forget that there are other people suffering. Children are always trying to understand what happened to their parents. I did not choose to belong to this tribe. Biologically, we are all the same. This one is tall, this one is short. Parents should tell their children what happened. They need to break the silence.

Listening to these stories made me reflect on where these young people found hope. I was pleased to learn that nearly everyone in the group had something that kept their hope alive. Sources of hope included faith in God and reading scriptures, as well as sharing conversations and tears with others. They found solace in connecting with family members, remembering, and recounting experiences through music, dance, laughter, and prayer. Others enacted their hope through seeking justice, speaking out, learning new skills, and honoring the memories of the victims by telling stories. Telling and retelling stories had a profound effect on them.

Spirituality was a common source of hope and rootedness. Studies with refugee and migrant children find that strong faith fosters resilience in the aftermath of traumatic, life-changing events (Bronstein & Montgomery, 2011; Yohani & Larsen, 2009). Many of these young people were members of faith communities where belonging was engendered and offered as inspiration for a better future. Support from significant others—for example, parents, pastors, and traditional and civic leaders—also gave them the direction they needed (Huemer & Vostanis, 2010).

> PARTICIPANT 4: Being a Christian, my hope is in God. God has good plans for us no matter what is happening to us. This gives me hope as a child of God. I feel a sense of unity that is bringing us together. Our country has become a country of unity. This gives us hope. In the years to come, something good is happening.

> PARTICIPANT 2: Also, our president. His stand offers us hope. We have a good leader pushing us forward. He is pushing us into

health, education, and politics. He is the one and only president. It is not a perfect country but there is hope that things will get better. We are acquiring new skills, and we want to bring those skills to our people, to do something for our community, to support the survivors, and find new families to belong.

Some participants shared how telling stories had become a personal pathway to healing and reconciliation, helping reduce feelings of isolation. By opening up and discussing their experiences, they found connection, which fostered both individual healing and a sense of community.

PARTICIPANT 3: People are sharing . . . and people are friends. In my school, I have encountered people who come from two different groups and are seeking ways of belonging. Intermarriage has resumed and our country is reaching again in those spaces. It is going to get better when we, young people, grow up. The process of reconciliation is helping. Things are changing.

Interviewees clearly acknowledged that there was still much work to be done to heal from the past. Some participants spoke philosophically about hope and the human experience recognizing that finding hope plays out differently with individuals and across communities and nations.

PARTICIPANT 2: I realize that hope is not facilitated. Hope is individual hope, hope for the community and hope for the nation. . . . Hope is multilayered. There is shared hope for the nation in terms of laws. The government has done a lot. There is a lot of healing done and a lot more needs to be done. We are going to see different expressions of trauma. There is still unchartered territory. The foundation of healing has been done. But there is a lot of hope. This shapes individual hope. In general, hope keeps changing depending on where you are.

For these young adults, given the historical trauma of genocide, life is never taken for granted. Being alive has become a call to activism.

Collectively they expressed a deep sense of responsibility rooted in giving back to their communities. This sense of personal responsibility to alleviate suffering was captured by several participants including this:

> PARTICIPANT 3: I like that question (*how are you giving back?*) . . . I love community, and the pain of my community hurts a lot. I want to contribute to the health care promotion. Because at the hospital I focus on a few people. But if I could work to improve the well-being of my community, this would be a great achievement. Being a medical doctor is biased. My happiness is seeing other people happy. I will give away 75% of what I have to others. I want to see that I contribute to reducing suffering in the lives of people.

This participant described how becoming a physician was her way of giving back:

> PARTICIPANT 3: When you finish university . . . the Ministry of Health assigns you randomly to a hospital in a rural or urban area. When I got there [my assignment] it was in the village, it was a new experience. There were a lot of challenges. I tried to start a social movement to pay the money for the patients who could not afford their medical care. What I did, and I am happy for, is because we started a social movement and used it to help those who came to the hospital . . . I realized that there were people with no insurance. I started to help people without insurance and recruited doctors to help. I work with an association where we can provide medication and food. I like that . . . this is creating a sustainable project in the hospital. It is one way of giving back, and an important story in my life.

Asked what makes her smile in doing the work, she refers to her smile as a "soul dance":

> PARTICIPANT 3: (*laughs*) What makes me smile is what makes my soul dance. I know I am going to help someone. Like today, I heard a patient who said she was having abdominal pain. I have

> cancer. . . . I did some tests, and I told her not to worry, there was nothing to worry about. That puts a smile on my face. But it worries me today because we give so many prescriptions. I need to change so I can teach people, and not have to be giving medication all the time. I need to give them a sense of hope. That is my prescription. That's my soul dance.

## Rebuilding Trust as Doing and Telling Hope

I have learned a great deal from the different groups that have honored me by sharing their stories. Their words have brought into sharp focus the power of doing, telling, and witnessing stories of hope. Stories need to be told and listened to in order to facilitate healing. Therapy creates space to weave these collective memories together to restore balance and recovery.

Trust is essential to relational safety. Gaining trust is a formidable process for most Rwandan people, whose trust was breached and betrayed by so many. It must be formed and rebuilt repeatedly to assure that it is real. Betrayal was fomented by decades of colonialism and ethnic divisionism, sowed by European imperialism and conquest. Communities that had lived together for generations were pitted against each other. Their stories of survival and resilience were turned into stories of violence and competition. Families were ripped apart. Even the church, whose paramount responsibility is caring across communities, failed to honor their charge. A culture of silence, secrecy, and suspicion permeated people's sense of belonging.

Story and storytelling aim to rebuild trust. One interviewee interpreted silence as both a form of self-preservation and a protection that masks the anger and distress people feel. She went on to describe the experience of a friend whose silence was manifested in her sensory response to certain foods:

> We do not normally talk about things except when we are angry. A friend of mine lost her family and she would not talk about it.

> One day in the market, we were going to buy greens. But she would not want to buy the greens. She would not want to buy them. So, I kept asking why not buy the greens, and finally, she said in 1994 [the year of the genocide] I was eating grass for 4 months and I cannot stand the smell of greens.

Trauma consciously and unconsciously affects the brain's sensory systems. Beaudoin and Monk (2024) draw attention to the benefits of using stories to bring sensory information to awareness. Smells can be comforting, evoking positive memories, but they can also be unsettling, as in the young woman's recollection of eating grass. In a similar way, the river's waters conveyed conflicting feelings. For some, the flow of the river offered a sense of calm, while for others it was a haunting reminder of its role as a dumping ground for the dead during the genocide.

## Stories of Belonging

Questions surrounding identity weighed heavily on these Rwandan young adults. They faced challenges navigating belonging as a consequence of the complex ethnic identity issues that precipitated the 1994 genocide. For some, the mantra "We are Rwandans" provided motivation to redefine themselves with a new sense of self-understanding. Their nation's history and its profound aftermath complicated their quest, adding layers of complexity to their personal and collective search for identity.

One woman, the child of Hutu and Tutsi parents, spoke of the hypervigilance she developed because of her mixed ethnic background. She struggled to find a place where she belonged. She told of the progress being made in how ethnic groups are now opening up to each other, which fills her with hope for the future. She reflected on her life:

> So, depending on triggers, one can open up. Life forces you to open up. The country today is different from 10 years ago. People are sharing and people are friends. In my school, I have

> encountered people who come from two different groups and are seeking ways of belonging. Intermarriage has resumed and our country is reaching again in those spaces. It is going to get better when we, young people, grow up. The process of reconciliation is helping. Things are changing.

## Listening to Other Stories

Narrative practice is about giving voice to alternative stories of unspoken trauma. The 1994 genocide was a brutal wave of organized violence in which almost 1 million Tutsi lost their lives (Nikuze, 2014). The Rwandan genocide, unlike those that took place in Armenia, Turkey, and Cambodia, was primarily carried out by people victims knew (Jansen et al., 2022), amplifying its horror. Rape was a tool of humiliation, aimed at ethnic cleansing and eradicating the Tutsi culture (Mukamana & Brysiewicz, 2008). Tutsi women and girls were subjected to systematic and gang rape, and many gave birth to children as a result (Banyanga et al., 2017; Hogwood et al., 2018; Straus, 2004).

It was not surprising that the young people I interviewed spoke of the profound and complex challenges faced by mothers who had been violated and the children born of genocidal rape. In Rwandan culture, rape violated female identity and defied ideals of sexual purity. Women were blamed for their assault, ashamed and excluded from their own families and community. Years later, these mothers continue to grapple with stigma, posttraumatic stress disorder (PTSD), depression, anxiety, and relational ambivalence fluctuating back and forth between rejecting and accepting their children. Writers on the Rwandan genocide suggest that these mothers projected their negative associations with violence on to their children because they are painful reminders of their perpetrators (Denov et al., 2020; Denov & Piolanti, 2019; Kahn & Denov, 2019).

Children conceived under these traumatic conditions grapple with societal rejection, family maltreatment, and struggles with identity and self-perception. Maternal and familial rejection is common. One participant reported how he struggled to form a bond with his mother but could not achieve a relational connection. Other interviewees told similar stories about friends who felt rejected by their mothers and by their community.

One participant was born to a mother who had been a victim of genocidal rape. He shared how difficult it was to talk with his mother and how she bitterly wept when she told him what had happened. Another participant spoke about a friend who expressed feelings of guilt for being the child of his mother's rapist. He loathed being a daily reminder of his mother's worst nightmare. One participant spoke about the challenge a peer faced juggling relationships with both his father's and mother's families:

> PARTICIPANT 2: It troubles me to live unwanted by either my mother's side or my father's side. I realize that people, my agemates, are not interested in building friendships with me because of my birth conditions. My mother's family stigmatizes me as I am a son of a rapist and killer. My father's family rejects me because my mother's family accused him of having committed the rape. I do not know where I belong.

Even with the determination to find some peace with both families this participant noted rejection with feelings of shame, self-hate, and guilt:

> PARTICIPANT 2: I did everything to maintain a good relationship with both sides of my family. My mother did not want it, but I did! I tried several times to visit my father's family to familiarize myself with them, but they reject me because I represent a source of conflict between the two families.

Another participant spoke about challenges in developing relationships:

> PARTICIPANT 4: Of course, conversations would come up about who your father and mother are. You cannot keep explaining to friends where you came from. You are damned if you do, damned if you don't. You just give up on making friends. Questions will

> always come up about you. You try to avoid them. You feel guilty and ashamed. You just do not like yourself.

This participant expressed concerns of having children of his own in the future. He feared bringing a curse on his progeny due to unresolved stigma and discrimination. His story among others reflects enduring feelings of guilt even as these young adults bear no responsibility for the genocide or its impacts. That said, feelings of self-blame, self-hate, and anger abound as do struggles with forming and maintaining relationships. Such disconnections contribute to emotional and social isolation.

## Double Listening Revisited

Stories of survival, healing, and reclamation inextricably coexist with those of loss and pain. In Chapter 2, *double listening* was defined as when both the dominant narrative and its possible alternatives can be heard and considered simultaneously. Narrative practitioners seek to know the whole person, both within and outside problem-saturated storylines. In my interviews I wanted to learn about the full lives of these young Rwandan adults, including positive and hopeful aspects of their lived experience. One young man talked about his sense of connection with his peers:

> Being with my peers with whom I share the same story, I feel happy. When I'm with them, I feel free because I know they don't judge me. I can laugh with them, and I can share with them as much as possible. I am not selecting what I share with them.

Another participant shared a newfound activity that gave him purpose and replenished his spirit:

> Every time I wake up in the morning, I keep myself very busy because I do not like to have enough time to think about myself.

> For this, I invest myself in tending my small poultry farm and when I am done, I go to church. Prayers allow me to remain calm. The chanting in church is also very calming. I can think of positive things in my life.

## Developing Support Teams: Bottom-Line Exercise

Senseless acts of violence and dehumanization produce hopelessness and helplessness for clients and for therapists. Engendering hope can be daunting in light of the pervasiveness of trauma and sorrow. Support teams can play an important role in addressing trauma. In my work with clients, I have used the *bottom-line exercise* to assist clients in developing a support team.

In the business world, the term "bottom line" refers to the net income or net profit of a business. It gives businesses an overall appreciation of their valued earnings—what businesses primarily care about. I use the term "bottom line" to reveal through stories what people truly care about. What do they most value? What drives them to achieve worth? What elements support what really matters to them? Often, such valuing has been unspoken, perhaps disenfranchised by societal discourses. My role is to invite people to tell these hidden stories of value.

To begin, I invite people to develop a virtual support team. A support team is conceived broadly. It consists of people, dead or alive, ideas, organizations, moments, experiences, circumstances, or events that coalesce to offer support. I ask people to bring to consciousness the fullness of this support team and to visualize it. Acknowledging the team members and entities is crucial. Once established, I ask clients to tell me what the team looks like. How does it feel? What tastes, sounds, and smells welcome the team?

Support teams serve to revive hope. Often, in organizations, people's morale waxes and wanes due to a variety of factors. These may include poor organizational practices, such as unaccountability, disrespect, lack of voice, or simply, no recognition for people's time and contributions. Support teams help people connect to the issues that matter and motivate them to seek further connections. They serve as valuable consultants to people as they are visualized and brought forward.

As part of the exercise, I ask people to choose a significant time in their life and reflect on what helped sustain them during that period. I then invite them to consider how they maintain hope relative to their work or relationships. Can they talk about a time when they were able to work from the heart? What sensory experiences are associated with such work? What does working from the heart feel, look, taste, smell, and sound like? From there, we further assess factors that enhance the experience of work, and alternatively, what constrains it. Last, I ask what was needed to benefit the client's experience. What do people care about most in their daily lives? How can that be accessed? The development of the support team and the accompanying stories elevate the bottom line in people's lives. I invite people to hold on to those bottom lines.

## Applying the Bottom-Line Exercise

For Rudeka and the young adults who shared their experiences of the Rwandan genocide, the bottom-line exercise tapped into new territories. There were persons, circumstances, events, and moments that grounded these experiences. They included people like members of the clergy who offered a place of refuge during the genocide, or neighbors who opened their homes to strangers. There were also survivors whose courage in the face of senseless acts of violence never waned.

Rudeka's support team included his father and grandfather. Words such as "integrity," "courage," "determination," "stick-to-itiveness," "trust," "hope," and "possibility" were recorded. He most valued integrity, and he vowed to prioritize it throughout the rest of his life. He described it as "the hallmark of life, my north star." This bottom line gave Rudeka confidence and permitted self-forgiveness. Remarkably it also allowed him to forgive those who hurt his family, a humanizing life effect.

Rudeka described integrity as a warm blanket that gives him hope for the future. Writing is an aspect of that blanketing comfort. Rudeka expands his stories using metaphor and incorporates sights, smells, tastes, and sounds into his comic books. For instance, the tiny bird struggling to put out a brush fire reminds him of the duty to do what is needful. Like Rudeka, the bird seeks integrity and accountability to make a difference notwithstanding the challenges of dire circumstances. Rudeka described the stench of the fire with vivid imagery, reminiscent of the burning of fields at harvest time during his childhood. His embrace of integrity called him not to turn away from the stench, but to go toward it. As he put it, "behind the stench lies a scent," brimming with possibilities of connection to moments and stories that will be sustaining.

Rudeka also reflected on his choice to eat breakfast alone. He talked about how living a fast-paced life does not allow people to savor their food. He prefers to enjoy food. Taking time to eat his breakfast provides him with a sense of calm and appreciation of his food. As he reflects on his sense of taste, he finds food nurturing, sustaining his sense of integrity, and engaging his sense of mindfulness.

## Expanding Stories Through Mindful Practices

Narrative practitioners use mindfulness to expand stories. Mindful practices can be found among most religious and spiritual traditions and are readily taught and learned. Mindful practices—grounding, cultivation of presence, attuned listening, compassion, and clarity—benefit therapists (Beaudoin & Monk, 2024). For clients, mindfulness offers new perspectives on problems, improves regulation, and increases awareness and embodied experiences (p. 165).

The integration of narrative therapy and eye movement desensitization and reprocessing (EMDR) can be advantageous as "new learning and new neural connections are made when new information is consolidated and integrated into other memories" (Beaudoin & Monk, 2024, p. 174). EMDR is a method that focuses a client on a specific traumatic memory while the therapist uses bilateral stimulation (commonly guided eye movements) to decrease the power generated by the original event. By repeated exposures to the memory accompanied by sensory stimulation, the client is eventually able to reprocess and integrate the trauma so that its impacts are no longer disruptive to functioning.

### THE STORY OF MUREMA

EMDR was instrumental for helping Murema re-story trauma. Murema, a 35-year-old Rwandan man, came to therapy to deal with his anger, shame, and anxiety. As a genocide survivor, his life was consumed by anger and anxiety that often left him incapable of completing his tasks. When his parents were killed in the genocide a neighbor raised him. Growing up, he hoped to find some answers about his parents. In those early days of the genocide, his foster family would visit the rivers to look for family members. The stench and the sight of the dead left an indelible mark on him. His anger intensified during those visits. Over the years, he has had a painful relationship with water, especially bodies of water, as in a pool, river, or lake.

Murema was often triggered by flashbacks of dead bodies in the river. He vehemently refused to learn how to swim as water reminded him of the horrors of the genocide. His anxiety around water affected his personal grooming as he would avoid taking showers or baths. His fears surfaced as anger outbursts in his interactions with others.

Murema was overwhelmed by emotions when we first started working together. EMDR helped him to reprocess traumatic memories associated with water bodies. As Murema visualized his body touching water the bilateral tapping gradually helped him associate a new narrative for that experience. The ability to process these early memories greatly helped Murema address the shame associated with grooming issues among other issues. In turn, his anger subsided.

## Conclusion

I have been immeasurably moved by the stories immigrants tell about themselves. Their experiences are rich with sensory detail highlighting the memories of touch, sight, taste, smell, and sound. Descriptions of their journeys are vivid, filled with remarkable and poignant detail.

To listen is to submit oneself to a dialogical encounter. It is an invitation to enter the complex stories of people's lives and gain deeper understanding of their experiences. Exploring how people make meaning of life experiences has broad implications for identity, regulation, relational trust, and capacity to live a hopeful life. The next chapter explores the role of narrative practices in holding and valuing different stories when working with couples.

CHAPTER 7

# Couples

## WITNESSING EACH OTHER THROUGH COMPLEX STORIES

Couples inhabit many stories. Some of them are shared and others are individual, while many comingle in the couple's relational stories. Each member of a couple brings stories that shape the relationship and facilitate a process in which more stories are expressed and experienced. Like with individual therapy, couple therapy identifies and externalizes problem-saturated narratives, so that partners can work together to develop a relational understanding of themselves and each other. Practitioners facilitate a reflective process that helps partners bear witness to each other's stories to facilitate small acts of connection. Engagement in relational practices is meant to raise awareness of how words and actions shape the couple's individual and collective lives, thoughts, and actions.

In this chapter, I illustrate the concepts of witnessing, relational accountability, and empathy as foundational elements of couple therapy from a narrative standpoint. I offer the following definitions to explain how each of these themes is used in narrative practice.

## Theme 1: Witnessing

Witnessing is about telling and listening. A witnessing and positioning structure facilitates opportunities for partners to alternately tell their stories and then reflect upon the stories they've heard with consideration for different viewpoints (Freedman, 2014). The structure also enables the practitioner to gain insight into each partner's perspectives and gauge openings for co-creation of mutually preferred narratives. The structure allows for the deconstruction of problematic stories and contributes to understanding and meaning making. When couples witness each other in their struggles and triumphs, it opens the door for healing connection and empathy that has potential to reconcile conflict, increase understanding, and generate new, preferred stories.

## Theme 2: Relational Accountability

Relational accountability promotes heightened attunement to how one's language and actions can reciprocally reinforce problem-saturated stories (Carlson & Haire, 2014). As relational beings, we are responsive to and influenced by other people's narratives (Weingarten, 1991). As witnesses, partners are held accountable for how their actions, words, and nonverbal messages, intended or not, shape each other's stories and inform their relationships. Goals of relational accountability include developing a shared understanding of each other's stories, identifying unique outcomes, and mutually reflecting on how to actualize accountability to each other for the purposes of improving communication and enhancing more functional relationships.

## Theme 3: Empathy

Relational accountability requires entering into the experience of the other through acknowledging and developing empathic attunement. When attuned to another, one responds in a way that makes them feel understood, validated, and valued. Listening closely is essential to attunement and is a hallmark of empathy. Empathy is the capacity to experience another's feeling state, even if it is different from one's own. When partners are empathic, they are continually involved in affectively bringing their stories to the relationship. They strive to be emotionally connected to their partner, engaged in self–other awareness, and willing to honor their partner's perspectives and experiences without judgment.

## Many Stories, Many Realities

Therapy with couples is multifaceted and thus challenging for therapists. Couples bring many, often conflicting stories to therapy and understanding and honoring them is critical to effective intervention. I begin with couples by asking about whose idea it was to pursue therapy. This question helps me gain a sense of each partner's motivation to engage in the therapeutic process and reveals their perspectives on therapy overall. Knowing where each person stands at the start contextualizes their stories—for example, what are the origins of the issues they face? What beliefs and messages do the partners bring to their stories? These may include conflicts around gender roles, power dynamics, future goals, and political views. Sociocultural factors can amplify conflict, especially with mixed-status couples, partners from different racial groups, faiths, or cultural backgrounds and ethnicities. Overall, differences are at the heart of relational stories that couples bring to therapy.

Couple therapists pay attention to verbal and nonverbal cues. For example, who speaks first in a session? How do they express themselves? Where do they look while speaking? Which stories do they emphasize and why? Narratives shared in therapy offer insights into each partner's commitment to the relationship. Their words reveal vulnerability, often expressed by anger, fear, loneliness, disappointment, hurt, or despair. Observing how each person reacts to naming these issues also provides important information about how to attend to, and improve, patterns of communication.

Most often couples come to therapy when they are at an impasse due to unresolved conflict, distancing, or mutual withdrawal (Fraenkel, 2011, 2019; Scheinkman & Fishbane, 2004). These impasses may manifest as "polarized reactivity and power struggles that make them feel increasingly disconnected" (Scheinkman & Fishbane, 2004, p. 281). The literature on couple therapy is vast and offers a broad range of approaches to address impasses and help couples resolve them (Doherty et al., 2015; Fraenkel, 2009, 2023; Gottman, 2011; Scheinkman, 2017; Scheinkman & Fishbane, 2004).

In my couple's work, I find the concepts of the vulnerability cycle and multicultural "intimacies" helpful (Scheinkman, 2017, p. 1). The vulnerability cycle occurs when one partner's ability to self-reflect or appreciate the other's perspective becomes obstructed, thus inhibiting their willingness and capacity to solve problems and maintain relational connection. Understanding how the cycle plays out helps therapists understand and address reactive moments in a couple's relationship. According to Scheinkman:

> Vulnerabilities may stem from our existential condition; we are all susceptible to loss, rejection, abandonment, and betrayal. They can arise from traumatic experiences or contextual stresses such as poverty, stigma, physical limitations, dislocation, or deprivation. They can also emanate from power differentials where one person feels subordinate due to gender, class, race, age, or earning potential. When vulnerabilities are triggered, they activate defensive positions designed to protect the self. (p. 2)

The vulnerability cycle integrates systemic, relational, and intrapsychic perspectives to guide therapy. Stories are personal, interactional, communal, and located in systemic and historical contexts. Therapy seeks to give voice to the multiplicity of stories that arise in couple therapy. It also assists couples in moving from impasses to intimacies.

Intimacy encompasses a range of experiences, including relational connection, feeling known, sharing, togetherness, and belonging (Scheinkman, 2019). The need for intimacy and how it is expressed varies from person to person and across cultures. Partners' expectations for intimacy are influenced by variable contexts, activities, priorities, and relational processes. The multicultural concept of "intimacies" offers a versatile definition. It considers diverse priorities and meanings shaped by an array of issues, including life cycle stages, gender, race, class, culture, personal and collective histories, fears, longings, previous love relationships, trauma, family dynamics, and gender and cultural legacies (Scheinkman, 2019). Viewing intimacy from a multicultural viewpoint allows therapists to be responsive to couples whose stories hold diverse priorities and meanings.

## Conceptualizing Couples

Gauging a couple's mutual commitment to the therapeutic process sets the stage for making things work. Some theorists have found creating a typology for a couple's therapeutic commitment helpful in choosing effective intervention strategies. For example, Fraenkel (2023) distinguishes between two types of couples that enter therapy: *non-last-chance couples* and *last-chance couples*. Non-last-chance couples are characterized by both partners' systemic or relational understanding of the problem, willingness to strengthen their relationship, optimism for therapeutic success, and openness to examining their strengths and challenges. The role of the therapist working with non-last-chance couples is to build therapeutic credibility, foster a commitment to change, and increase hope.

Last-chance couples as defined by Fraenkel (2023) consist of partners with differing motivations—for example, one who is motivated to stay in the relationship while the other might be ready to leave. In such cases, there is no common relational understanding, rather one partner may enter therapy with skepticism, be unenthusiastic, and in some instances, may seek to sabotage the process. Fraenkel notes that last-chance couples begin therapy with significant ambivalence, making it crucial to prioritize the voice of the ambivalent partner and avoid assuming they will want to continue therapy.

Doherty (2002) also categorizes couples seeking therapy as those committed to the process of strengthening relationship and those uncertain about whether they should remain together. For both classifications of couples, the ideal outcome of therapy is to establish a sense of relational possibility, therapeutic credibility, and existential safety, which can foster increased hope. For the therapist, successful engagement requires navigating the complexity of individual, collective, and societal narratives that couples carry. Ultimately, the goal is to reignite the relationship in a preferred direction.

Both Fraenkel and Doherty propose binary views of couple relationships, a limitation that does not fully appreciate the fluid and diverse nature of intimate partnerships. Although it is true that many couples present with these themes, there are many more that come to therapy to seek help with situations that are complicated by traumatic circumstances, loss, sudden illness, family crises, and other disruptive life-affecting situations. Scheinkman's (2019) multicultural concept of intimacies offers a nonbinary conceptualization of what couples bring to therapy, one that avoids assumption and is open to the diversity of stories that couples communicate.

Couples may be trapped in their individualized stories and narratives. Such traps may include attributional errors: the tendency to explain human behavior in terms of the traits of individual actors, leading to finger-pointing or seeing the wrong in the other when a mistake is made. It may also be an attribution bias: the tendency to explain the behavior of others with dispositional attributes, but use situational attributes to explain one's own behavior.

Regardless of their reasons for seeking help, understanding the stories couples bring to therapy is essential. Listening for gaps and openings in their narratives is key. Couple therapy involves showing interest and curiosity by asking questions that invite people to retell, reexperience, and expand their stories into richer, more meaningful narratives. In the next part of this chapter, I discuss two cases to illustrate narrative approaches using witnessing, relational accountability, and empathy.

## CASE VIGNETTE: ALARI AND STELLA

Alari and Stella could be categorized as a last-chance couple whose narrative journey focused on cultivating empathy through the mutual act of witnessing. The partners had known each other for nearly a decade and had been married for 8 years. When Alari, 59, and Stella, 43, arrived at my office, the acrimony between them was unmistakable. Seated on the love seat, their body language told a story of discord: They had their backs turned toward each other and hardly maintained eye contact. Both were grappling with significant questions about their relationship and wondered if there was a future for them as a couple. They were both ambivalent about therapy and acknowledged significant differences in their relationship.

Alari, who was originally from an East Asian country, was passionate about politics and international affairs. He aspired to build a career in conflict management and resolution. Stella, a White American, had spent several years traveling the world and had recently secured a position at an international peacekeeping organization. Shortly after meeting, they discovered a shared passion for global travel.

During the first 2 years of their relationship, they traveled extensively. Despite a significant age difference, they felt a strong connection. Stella eventually joined Alari's company in his home country—a small, start-up movie business in which Alari devoted time to writing and editing short films. She moved in with him, and their romantic relationship began. They spent most of their time together, but during this period Alari's company failed to thrive and he experienced bouts of anxiety and writer's block. Though he had hoped his work would provide financial support, its limited success only deepened his frustration and disappointment.

The couple mutually decided to make a fresh start and relocated to the United States. After the move, however, Alari struggled to adapt. He felt alienated and invisible in his new environment. He yearned for the familiar comforts of his home country. In addition, he could not reconcile his past professional achievements with his present circumstances, leaving him uncertain about his identity and future. His lack of income and dependence on Stella's earnings contributed to feelings of emasculation. In many ways, he felt like a failure.

Stella grew increasingly worried about Alari's emotional state as well as his lack of stable employment. She became resentful of being the sole breadwinner. As a hardworking only child who had the support of doting parents, she had hoped for a partner who matched her ambition and drive. She initially thought Alari was that partner, but now she believed he was not making sufficient effort to find a "real job."

Stella, however, struggled to express her frustration without making things worse between them. Their communication followed a troubling pattern: Stella would state her concerns, Alari would respond defensively, Stella would withdraw and become anxious, and then they would go for days without speaking to each other. Over time, their communication, emotional connectedness, and intimacy deteriorated. They described a "cold spell" in their sexual relationship. Alari perceived the absence of intimacy as both a blow to his masculinity and another personal failure.

## Beginning Therapy: Weaving and Listening to Different Stories

During our first session, Alari pronounced that therapy was either their "last chance to rebuild the relationship or let it fall apart." As he saw it, their problems stemmed from poor communication; whereas he was open about his feelings and eager to share his emotions, Stella kept her feelings to herself, which left him in a constant state of frustration. Alari described himself as a "thinker," criticizing Stella for not engaging in thoughtful reflection. I observed that Alari intellectualized his thoughts and feelings, which made it difficult for Stella to respond.

When Stella felt belittled by Alari, she would withdraw. To cope, she channeled her energy into exercise and spending time with friends. The couple agreed that their differing approaches to conflict, along with Stella's demanding work schedule and Alari's preoccupation with writing, left them with little time to spend together or enjoy each other's company. I observed that during our sessions neither Stella nor Alari addressed each other directly. Instead, each spoke about the other in the third person.

### Understanding the Dynamics of Communication

We are always communicating, either by design or by default. It is important to understand the dynamics of a couple's communication. Alari was quick to point out (and critique) the couple's differing styles and views. This early exchange, which took place shortly after brief introductions, highlights their contrasting perspectives. It also illustrates their reactive and existential impasses, as well as their cultural differences, especially Alari's frustration with Western worldviews and gender norms:

> ALARI: As I mentioned to you over the phone, I am from [an East Asian country]. I have always spoken my mind since arriving here. I am tired of having to sit back and listen to what I see as the feminist progressive neoliberal thinking that I believe will ultimately undermine this country. . . . I consider myself a thinker. My wife does not. I wish she would engage in intellectual discussions with me or at least show some interest in my work.
>
> THERAPIST: (*turning to Stella*) Tell me about how you see what is going on for you.
>
> STELLA: (*clearly angry*) I like to think about things too. He often won't entertain any perspective other than his own. Yes, this may be our last chance.

Providing opportunities for couples to tell their stories from different entry points is an important aspect of the narrative process. Entry points may convey stories of pain and hurt in the relationship, or they may represent aspects of relational pride. With Alari and Stella, I needed to better understand how they positioned themselves in their commitment to the therapeutic process. I had already witnessed them enact conflict. I asked the following question: "Before we delve into the issues that brought you to therapy, I'm curious to know whose idea it was to seek therapy." Stella quickly responded saying that she really wanted to have another person help them look at their process, so she had reached out. Alari simply shrugged his shoulders and said he was generally skeptical about therapy.

My early questions were intentionally designed to uncover Alari's and Stella's individual stories. I wanted to learn how they shaped the couple's current relationship. Individual stories inform broader narratives—for example, how a couple may feel about themselves, about each other, and/or stories society might have constructed about them. Curious questioning shows interest in all aspects of the couple relationship, not just the problematic story. It is an invaluable tool for assessing the status of the couple's current and historical relationship. I am mindful that each partner comes to therapy with their own strengths, even if those are obscured beneath stories of struggle. My questions are meant to invite alternative stories, especially alternatives to the stories that may have guided them toward seeking therapy.

I used a conversational map for the couple to do an initial relationship assessment. A conversational map names the problem or problems, traces the history of the problem, charts and evaluates the effects of the problem on the person or couple, explores each person's influence on the problem, the problem's influence on the person, and identifies sociocultural factors that reinforce the problem. The map also identifies exceptions to the problem. Last, mapping helps to clarify a person's preferences and values and offers possibilities for change. The goal is to shift away from a problem identity to a new preferred self (Beaudoin & Monk, 2024). Early on in our work together we had an exchange like this:

THERAPIST: Help me to understand how each of you understands what is going on. What names might you give the concerns between you?

STELLA: Alari does not care at all.

ALARI: She worries too much.

THERAPIST: [I noted the fact that Alari did not call Stella by her name] So, it sounds like "not caring at all" and "worrying too much." (*turning to Alari*) Would you say worrying too much is caring at all? How long have you noticed this as part of your lives?

Alari and Stella had different recollections about their relationship, especially when things began to deteriorate. Listening to the naming of perceptions was important. I juxtaposed worry and caring to highlight how each storied their experience. They held different perceptions of the relationship. They were wrapped in a strong blame/attack–defense cycle. Alari blamed Stella for her strong feminist independent approach to life and Stella blamed Alari for his cerebral intellectual approach to living.

Alari and Stella agreed that although they lived together, they were like "ships in the night." Together, we explored this metaphor. Metaphors both mask and reveal informative aspects of people's experiences. I used the "ship" metaphor to gain insight into the couple's relationship. I asked questions such as these in our session, curious about what they would elicit:

- What is it like to be "ships in the night"?
- What is it like to have a night of such experience?
- What effects does being "ships in the night" have on your life? On your relationship with each other?
- What does it make you imagine about your partner?
- How does it make you feel about your own relationship with your partner?
- What effect does "ships in the night" have on other relationships for you?
- How does "ships in the night" clarify your wishes, hopes, and expectations for yourself?

- What unspoken stories does "ships in the night" leave out about you, your partner, and your relationship?
- How has "ships in the night" contributed to this being your last chance?

Metaphors both reveal and mask different stories. Exploring the value of a metaphor can open up possibilities unfolding inner edges of understanding.

## WITNESSING AND POSITIONING

Implementation of a witnessing and positioning approach in couple therapy discloses deeper insights into each partner's narrative, creating space for alternative stories to emerge. Operationally, this approach facilitates a process whereby partners take turns speaking, listening, and observing. Learning to be witness to each other's experiences encourages the development of empathy and shared understanding, leading to stronger relational connection.

Alari and Stella's acrimony presented many challenges. Both partners felt unheard, unsafe, and disconnected. Communication became charged, and conversations that might have been opportunities for closeness turned into arguments and silence, leading to an erosion of trust and emotional safety, and a failure to see each other as they are. Witnessing has many benefits, including opening possibilities to develop and affirm positive identity stories for each partner about themselves and their relationship. When partners witness the other's narrative openly, the potential for new identity stories about self, the other, and the relationship grows exponentially.

Alari and Stella, however, were paralyzed by a blame/attack–defend sequence that left only one possible perspective from which to witness the other person: seeing them as the problem. The attack/blame–defend sequence produces a counterattack/blame–defend sequence—a reciprocal enterprise that leaves both parties feeling victimized and unable to escape the pattern's grip. Each views the other through a veil of negative emotions, which inhibits possibilities for change in the identity and relationship stories.

The following dialogue captures the couple's estrangement from each other. It took place shortly after Stella returned home after a long day's work. Exhausted, she headed straight to the bedroom:

> ALARI: [Talking as if Stella was not in the room] I can't believe that she came home and went straight to the bedroom.
>
> THERAPIST: Help me understand what happened.
>
> STELLA: (*looking straight at Alari*) I have told you that Thursdays are long days for me . . . I need to unwind after such a long day. Last week, you were buried in your work. You could not even acknowledge me when I came home.
>
> ALARI: I have feelings, and you do not care about my feelings.
>
> STELLA: No, you do not care about me. I have to support us. My earnings do.

It was valuable for me to witness the couple's animosity in action. I took the opportunity to share my observations about their communication patterns. I pointed out how often they interrupted each other, conveying that this might unintentionally reinforce the stories they have created and limit their ability to see each other in new or different ways. Indeed, this pattern of communicating could be contributing to their dynamic of being "ships in the night." I also noted that Stella talked directly to Alari while Alari spoke about Stella in the third person.

Couples often bring individualizing discourses to their interactions. Inviting them to step outside individualistic notions of communication helps them witness themselves from a new perspective. Alari and Stella were clearly locked in deficit-saturated stories that required active intervention to be freed from their entrenched mode of communication. I was poised to encourage Stella to witness Alari's story.

The following interaction took place after Alari chose to skip spending the holidays with Stella's family. Alari felt alienated from Stella's parents, who had berated him for not having a "real job." He associated her family's criticism with his belief that it was solely his responsibility to repair the relationship:

ALARI: I feel stressed even visiting with Stella and her parents. I do not know and do not feel the need to visit her family. After 9 years, Stella cannot do anything different. She can't do anything about it. It is like the amputation of the limb. If the relationship is important, the onus is on me. I need to do whatever it takes to keep the relationship alive. Stella is not able to do it. Either I get out of the relationship, or I have to be the person to find ways to make it possible to be healthy.

THERAPIST: You are not exiting the relationship, are you? You are submitting yourself to the work, or resigning to be in the relationship?

Alari paid meticulous attention to words. The word "resigning" struck a chord in Alari, who immediately disowned it. Instead, he asserted that he was fighting for a cause. He went on to outline his creative solutions to improve the relationship:

ALARI: I do not like that word. *Resigning* is defeat. I cannot engage in the type of fighting that ends up destroying oneself. It is clear to me that if you try to fight more, you will destroy yourself or the system itself. If you do not have power, you will destroy yourself. If you are genuinely weak, all you can do is to keep yourself useful or negotiate to get your space without being pushed to the corner. I am committed to be as creative, and I have to go about it in my own creative way.

THERAPIST: And what would that look like?

ALARI: I need to take care of the chores in the home. Stella is a taskmaster. I try to be sensitive to her needs. They are very simple. She does not want much from me. Not even romance or sex. I know what I need to do or not do. To not leave dishes in the sink. Cook once in a while. (*pauses, reflecting*) As for me, it is difficult to give me what I want. A few things I can do is not to put pressure on her. Not leave the apartment messy. Once in a while, clean the bathroom. Help her bring up the groceries. I need to be sensitive and be kind or loving toward her. Not simply do tasks but pay attention to her.

THERAPIST: And how might you see yourself doing that?

ALARI: Well . . . she is so self-contained. I am naturally a very expressive person. But (*pauses*) I need to try to increase my income to relieve pressure around her. Improve on my contributions of finances. As for making time, I will not make demands on her. This makes it okay. The problem is I came to this marriage with a lot of expectations.

THERAPIST: I hear you outline the tasks you want to accomplish. Tasks, affection and kindness, consideration for her and making time . . .

ALARI: Can I add one more? Do not expect any change of behavior from Stella. Do not give her feedback. She snaps. Do not expect her to apologize. This is the secret ingredient in the relationship. It is my responsibility to bear it and not take it seriously.

THERAPIST: You mean accept it, not even question it or dialogue with Stella about it?

This question made Alari reflect on an important storyline in his life: his self-avowed agnosticism. Although he held no formal religious or spiritual beliefs, his relationship with Stella was making him reflect on this in a different way.

ALARI: (*laughing*) I am not a religious person. I do not use spiritual terminology. I am allergic to it. I believe this relationship is making me be a better person. (*pauses*) It is making me into a different person. Turning into a spiritual person: having patience, expressing gratitude. All these things . . . Stella is forcing me to reckon with all of these things.

THERAPIST: It is giving you a sense of calm. I see you seem relaxed even as you speak about this. How are you feeling it for yourself?

ALARI: A sense of calm, not allowing my ego to get bigger.

THERAPIST: How is this helping your work?

ALARI: I am now adopting this stance. To stay calm. When Stella is nasty, I am going to be careful. I have to accept she may be rude, nasty, or insensitive . . . but I have agency and will be able to take it. So, expect no worse or better, I will still myself, expect the way of being, and roll with punches. I had hoped that as a person interested in conflict negotiation, she would be able to do this. But she does not challenge herself. She does not do any of this stuff with her friends, but she has the freedom to react like that with me. She acts with no self-awareness. She cannot see her own face in a moment like this. I accept this myself. I do not see her happy.

At this point, Stella almost chimed in but held her breath so that she could continue witnessing Alari. Later, she described this as one of the low points of the therapy session. Stella prides herself as having a great sense of self-awareness and self-observation. I commended Stella on sitting through this challenge and suggested she continue to notice what Alari's words conjured up inside of her:

THERAPIST: (*looking at Alari*) I hear the acceptance on your part. Do you get a sense Stella hears you . . . is able to accept?

ALARI: I do not. (*laughs*) Look here. In 9 years, I have seen her happy only when there is an extrinsic event. At our wedding you could see she was happy. When she goes to conferences, she is happy. When she dresses up for an event and wears a nice dress, I can see she is happy. Her happiness does not come from inside but from outside . . .

The subject of happiness frequently surfaced in our sessions as something both Alari and Stella deeply longed for; its absence cast a shadow over the viability of their relationship. While Alari often approached the topic in abstract, philosophical terms, in the earlier story, he was able to ground it in tangible, everyday acts of kindness. The exchange revealed undertones of blame.

Alari reflected that he often experiences happiness vicariously, through Stella's joy, noticing his personal struggle to recognize it for himself. He expressed a growing belief in cultivating happiness internally, especially through intellectual engagement. In contrast, he perceived Stella's happiness as being more externally stimulated. He realized that giving her massages is a shared source of joy—an act that brings them both connection and happiness—and recognized it as a simple, meaningful way to nurture their relationship.

Therapy became a vehicle for the couple to bridge empathic attunement between them. A big part of Alari's frustration with Stella focused on what he perceived as her inability to engage in deep thought about things he valued. For him, the ability to think is transformational and helps to build and sustain relational connection.

Alari described hopes for his relationship by sharing a Zoroastrian myth that told of a wandering group of refugees in a foreign land. Unable to communicate with them in the local language, the chief who received them filled a glass of milk to the brim, to indicate that there was no space for them in his territory. In response, the leader of the refugees added a spoon of sugar to the milk saying, "we will add sweetness to you."

Alari's story was his way of expressing commitment to improving the relationship by acknowledging his relational accountability:

ALARI: We need to make the other [person] better. We cannot keep demanding. That gesture of adding sugar is radical. I have tried to do just that with Stella. We need to make people better.

THERAPIST: What do you mean?

ALARI: We need to make them better but not by trying to change them. With Stella, I have tried for 9 years. I seek not to change her.

Alari was highly sensitive to how Stella responded to him, the language and tone she used. He experienced her replies as judgmental, and this stirred feelings of anger within him. The following dialogue occurred after Stella announced that she had to travel to a foreign country for business. Alari understood the couple could not afford to go on this trip together, a painful reminder of shattered hopes to travel together. However, his frustrations and disappointments erupted despite this knowledge:

ALARI: I wish I could come too.

STELLA: (*anger in her voice*) I do not know what you expect me to do. You know we cannot afford it. You do not have the means.

ALARI: (*clearly frustrated*) Here we go again. Must you say it like that? (*looking at therapist*)

THERAPIST: How would you have liked Stella to say it?

ALARI: With some kindness. . . . We both know that I do not have the finances but (*looking at therapist*) she does not have to throw it in my face all the time.

STELLA: But you and I know we can't afford it.

ALARI: I know our financial limitations. I need to increase my income. But you could just wish we could go together.

Alari's distress left Stella feeling conflicted about enjoying travel. Traveling brought Stella happiness and a sense of renewal—something she needed for herself. Yet being away from Alari filled her with worry. Happiness, for them, had always been complicated; they struggled with it for different reasons. Their time apart also surfaced deeper, unspoken feelings toward each other. The following dialogue illustrates both relational accountability and the bidirectional process of how couples' words and actions shape each partner's experience:

THERAPIST: Oh, yea, that reminds me of something we have talked about before . . . Stella's concerns about being able to travel without you. Do you see yourself letting her travel? Letting her enjoy what she truly loves? Pursue her interests?

ALARI: I have no problems with her travel. She worries I am going to go into a depression. But I can feel alone, and I can still want her to travel. I am not stopping her.

THERAPIST: You want her to enjoy herself. Yes . . . there was a time she worried about you being alone.

ALARI: Again, this is what distinguishes good thinking and bad thinking. . . . Because I might feel alone does not mean I want to prevent her from traveling. I am not going to pretend that I will not feel sad but I cannot stop her.

This exchange offers a poignant example of relational accountability. It illustrates how assumptions and actions shape a couple's responses to each other. Partners are inescapably responsible for these shaping effects, intended or not. Alari's ability to capture the polarity of his feelings, feeling sad but at the same time, wanting to support his partner's happiness, brought clarity and comfort to Stella. An expression of relief came over Stella's face. She explained how worry about Alari had prompted her to sacrifice her pleasure in travel. Her choices were made because she cared but came across as distancing. Alari went on to express his own caring for Stella:

THERAPIST: So, you care about her. You are saying to her that she should enjoy her travel, pursue her joys. (*turning to Stella*) What are you hearing?

STELLA: (*big sigh*)

ALARI: Yes, she is my wife. I am committed to her. I want to become more of the sugar in her life.

This transformative relational exchange exemplifies what White (2000) calls "the absent but implicit." These are interactions leading to unique outcomes that become the foundation to preferred stories. Witnessing brought new clarity to Alari and Stella's story, beginning a new chapter in their relationship. A sparkling moment of connection unexpectedly emerged when Alari committed to adding more sweetness to Stella's life. It cut through his disparagement, signaling how much he wanted to voice his love and commitment for his wife. Nurturing small acts of empathy also opened doors of understanding between the couple. In turn, the couple was able to appreciate the shaping effects of their actions on each other.

Stella and Alari's couple relationship invites feelings of compassion for them. Alari tends to live in his head, which tends to push intimacy away. As much as he yearns for closeness and for Stella to want his presence, his intellectualizing defends against it. Stella wants to grow the relationship and be accountable. She says she wants a partner she can feel connected to. Listening to the couple interact with each other one could not miss noting the age and cultural differences as key markers of the relationship. While Alari is vocal, Stella's voice is muted. Therapy aims to engage these narratives in ways that permits the couple to witness each other in empathic attunement.

### VIGNETTE: DARYL AND KARLY

The case of Daryl and Karly illustrates how couples can move between Fraenkel's (2023) categories of non-last chance and last chance using witnessing to help them navigate challenging life circumstances as an interracial couple. Daryl, a White 75-year-old man, was born and raised in an upper-middle-class household. His wife Karly, a Black 70-year-old woman, was raised by middle-class African American parents whose lives were profoundly shaped by the Civil Rights Movement. Daryl is a retired high-powered attorney, and Karly, a retired college professor. They have no children. They had envisioned their retirement as a period enriched by cultural engagement and shared activities. However, persistent arguments, worries about aging, and uncertainties about their future undermined these aspirations, leaving their hopes unrealized.

Many of Daryl and Karly's conflicts were rooted in race and cultural differences. Together for 40 years and married for 30, both had considered divorce a few times. Over the years, they had been to several couple therapists and vacillated between commitment to rebuilding their relationship and ending it. At the time they entered therapy with me, they were experiencing high conflict, low connection, and violation of each other's values—common characteristics of last-chance couples.

Racial tensions were at the forefront for the couple this time around. In the weeks prior to starting therapy, Daryl's father had died—a death that sparked intense arguments about their future choices for long-term care and burial plots. While Karly wanted to be cremated, Daryl wanted to be buried in a cemetery. Karly was deeply hurt by Daryl's refusal to acknowledge how divisive race and religion were in their relationship.

Tensions escalated when they researched retirement communities. Most of older-adult housing units in their community were populated by White residents. Karly knew she would not feel that she belonged in any of them as a person of color. Lack of options fueled the couple's disappointment, adding to frustration and fear about being able to enjoy aging together. Daryl's resistance to addressing the issues they faced made Karly feel isolated and alone.

Another issue that surfaced for the couple at this time surrounded intimacy. Both Daryl and Karly had been married before; both carried the weight of painful past relationships. The wounds from those earlier unions lingered, shaping the questions they now asked of one another. In seeking to understand each other's past relationships, they were also trying to make sense of the losses and betrayals that had come before. Like many couples, talking about sex and sexual intimacy was taboo. Karly often raised the issue, while Daryl avoided discussing it.

## Empathy and Shaping Effects of Stories

It became clear that Daryl and Karly had been significantly hurt by their previous relationships, leaving them reluctant to be fully open to each other. They struggled with understanding each other's perspective, unable to reach a position of empathy. Karly initiated discussions like the one below:

KARLY: Coming here, we got into another fussy thing we often do. Daryl will not tell me that he is attracted to me. Is he? (*looking at him*) Are you?

DARYL: (*silent*)

THERAPIST: I am curious what you think about Karly's question.

DARLY: (*silent*)

KARLY: (*looking at therapist*) I do not know how much he must react toward me like his previous wives. (*looking at Daryl*) Do I matter? What is different between me and your previous wives?

Discussions about previous relationships triggered old wounds and ruptures. Karly voiced her hurt; Daryl's silence spoke volumes. Our work together targeted building mutuality and empathy. Both partners needed reassurance of love and commitment to their relationship.

I encouraged each partner to tell their story while the other listened and then reverse the process (Freedman, 2014). Like with Alari and Stella, a witnessing structure would give Karly and Daryl permission to speak about what truly bothered them with a goal of moving the relationship forward. The goal is to encourage that each speak their truth with integrity; that they speak it with the goal of moving the relationship forward; and that they speak it in such a way that their partner is most likely to hear it. The exchange unfolded like this:

THERAPIST: I'd like to invite you both to listen to each other. I know both of you have very important things to say to each other. I'd like each of you to speak your truth without compromising its integrity. I'd also like that you speak it in a way that seeks to move the relationship forward. Finally, I'd like you to speak your truth in a way that your partner is most likely to hear it. I caution that if any speaking is punctuated by denigrating remarks or behaviors, your partner is not likely to hear.

KARLY: (*without hesitation*) I will start. I do not think Daryl sees me. We do not talk to each other. We do not laugh in our home. Everything is gloomy. We have become strangers to each other.

Karly's narrative illuminates how interactions are shaped by words and behaviors. She spoke of feeling unseen and unheard by Daryl, lamenting the absence of simple, yet meaningful, moments like conversation and shared laughter. It was evident from the start that their relationship was caught in an inescapable interactive cycle, where every word, action, thought, and feeling contributed to a negatively reinforcing pattern. Daryl's and Karly's narratives sustained a limiting view of the other. The exchange below highlights these issues:

KARLY: I like to talk to Daryl about many things.

THERAPIST: What kind of things?

KARLY: About the holidays, race, sex, many things. He does not.

DARYL: I feel you have your own views about these things, and we end up fighting. I cannot win.

KARLY: But we can have a conversation about race, about how your family has not quite accepted me. It is not about winning.

DARYL: Well, there is nothing I can do about that.

KARLY: But you could be on my side when they make insensitive comments. You do not see me. You will not talk about sex, about whether you find me attractive, or talk about race. How come you do not stand by my side when your family ignores me?

DARYL: Each time we talk about race or sex we end up fighting.

Therapy addresses relational accountability through storying (Carlson & Haire, 2014). Daryl's and Karly's stories, like all stories, do not exist in isolation. Story construction evolves, shaped by social, interpersonal, relational, and cultural contexts and by lived experience. Each time a story is told it is changed by the listener, whether that is an individual, a group, or within community with others.

I invited Daryl and Karly to reflect on the types of stories they were telling each other and also the stories their families of origin were telling them. I asked them to examine possible impoverishing stories they were telling themselves and to be curious about ways to reauthor them. Not wanting to compromise her truth, Karly asked Daryl to reflect on how Black women are stereotyped as hypersexual and whether that had any bearing on how he perceived her. For Karly, talk about race and sex were intertwined:

KARLY: I cannot understand why you can't say if you find me attractive or not.

DARYL: Well . . . (*silence*)

THERAPIST: What are your feelings when Karly asks you that question?

KARLY: (*immediately chimes in*) I wonder if you think of me in that hypersexualized manner that often White men place on Black women.

DARYL: I am afraid I am going to say the wrong thing.

THERAPIST: What feelings do you have for your partner? I will start with Karly.

KARLY: I married Daryl. I felt safe with him after I was assaulted. I love him. But I cannot hear any words like that being said to me.

DARYL: I do, but maybe we should not be together. I just do not like being compared to all White men.

THERAPIST: [highlighting Karly's positive feelings for Daryl] I wonder what it is like for you to hear Karly say those words.

DARYL: I am just afraid I am going to say the wrong thing. I cannot speak to my family about other things. They have their own mind.

KARYL: What does that have to do with your finding me attractive or hypersexualizing me?

DARYL: I find you attractive and I am not hypersexualizing you. (*silence*)

Witnessing new stories asks couples to entertain moments of caring and empathy, especially around their hurt and pain. In our work together, Karly and Daryl sought to find relational understanding. They moved away from problematizing their relationship to seeking mutuality and empathy in their communication. With couples, communication that relies exclusively on a one-direction notion of the individual self tends to fail. One directional communication creates a monologic discourse of the speaker keeping the other out. Communication that happens through a relational understanding engages a shared appreciation for the other (Carlson & Haire, 2014).

Daryl and Karly have applied what they learned about empathic attunement to their changing life circumstances as an older couple. For example, Daryl was becoming increasingly overwhelmed by driving so Karly offered to drive. Instead of causing conflict, Daryl welcomed her offer with great relief. Tensions in locating a retirement community have eased, and they are better able to discuss other aging and end-of-life issues. Mutual empathy has also paved the way for them to confront difficult conversations, such as declining physical abilities and the loss of so many family members and friends.

Racial issues, however, remained a difficult story to pursue. Karly experienced considerable silence from Daryl around their racial differences and thus took it upon herself to raise the issue of her being Black whenever it felt appropriate. Although she had grown up in a proud Black family, in Daryl's company she felt shame about her skin color. She discussed how over the years she had learned to not receive, internalize, or welcome projections that defined her on the basis of race, but it was a struggle:

KARLY: Then, I just started thinking how Daryl and I got married in the first place. A Black woman married to a White man.

THERAPIST: Some important stories to revisit.

DARYL: Last time we were talking about stories. We have a lot of stories together. I guess we need new stories. But old stories connect us to each other.

Karly recalled a book written about a White woman who adopted two Black girls. She appreciated the family's openness in talking about race and lamented Daryl's discomfort with it:

KARLY: For me it is a sign of closeness to talk about these things. For Daryl, anything upsetting is not okay to talk about. I think it would be good to find ways to talk about these things. Talk about race and sex so that it is not something forbidden. It is painful that we cannot have these conversations.

THERAPIST: Glad you brought that up. Now that we are back in the office, what is it like for you, Daryl? [For context: following the COVID-19 pandemic, sessions were held remotely, during which Daryl did not feel comfortable talking about certain subjects due to privacy concerns.]

DARYL: I do not know. I guess I am not the expert, and Karly is, and sometimes I do not know what to say.

KARLY: (*pushing back*) Can you tell me how I am an expert?

DARYL: When I say something, I feel I am saying the wrong thing.

THERAPIST: Well, what is it like to be married to a Black woman?

DARYL: It is hard. I think we have done a good job. Things come up. But it is hard. My family is not used to Black people. My family has said some stupid things.

THERAPIST: When you say Karly is the expert, are you relegating responsibility to Karly to bring up these issues?

DARYL: I know she will bring them up. I certainly think it is important. We live in a screwed-up society. Things always come up. Even when I have thoughts about something I see on TV or the news, I do not know how to bring it up. Karly knows more than I do.

THERAPIST: Are you afraid of bringing up these conversations with Karly?

DARYL: I am afraid we are going to get into a fight. It seems to lead to more pain and conflict.

THERAPIST: But Karly wants to talk about it.

DARYL: Yes, some of the times I am being defensive. I do not think I am as dumb. Or she thinks I am a dumb racist.

KARLY: Of course, I am going to bring up some things even in these last 5 minutes. Of course. Because I was assaulted by that guy and I made up something. I felt very safe with Daryl when I met him. I appreciated being safe with him, but I really never knew whether Daryl was attracted to me. I do not know if Daryl is really interested in me.

DARYL: (*visibly with anger*) Is that really related to race?

KARLY: We did things together. We did not have a sexual attraction. Race would be something we would like to talk about.

DARYL: It does not have to do with race.

THERAPIST: Yes, she mentioned race and sex. Karly mentioned proximity, attraction. She is not sure if you were attracted to her, or if she was a convenience of sorts. How has it been for you to be in a relationship with your partner?

As an older interracial couple that had both been in previous relationships, Daryl and Karly could not be further apart regarding their experiences. It is common however, "for couples to come into therapy feeling at odds with each other in terms of their experiences and struggles in the relationship" (Carlson & Haire, 2014, p. 5). Because of the power of individualistic interpretations, it was important to explore the couple's shared relational experiences if they were to progress in the therapeutic work.

For Karly and Daryl, the witnessing structure approach worked well. In the exchange above, they shared moments of honesty and empathic attunement revealing previously silenced stories about race, sex, assault, and power dynamics. They intentionally listened to each other and openly expressed their struggles, hopes, and dreams.

Carlson and Haire (2014) explain that relationally focused questions

> help couples begin to understand how their shared relationship struggles have had real and personal effects on the story of self of their partners, and therefore, have the effect of inviting couples into a more appreciative position in relation to one another. (p. 6)

Questions provide guidance for couples to enter into each other's stories from positions of accountability, respect, and witnessing. Questions additionally aim to help partners develop capacity for attunement. Below are some questions a therapist might ask to facilitate the process of witnessing:

- What has it been like for you both to experience the struggles of race (sexual attraction) in your relationship over the years?

- What has it been like for you to live with the knowledge that your hopes and dreams have not been met?
- How do you like yourself in this relationship?
- What impact has this had on your partner and their experience as a partner and as a person?
- How has your experience of your partner made you become someone different than you once were?
- How valuable has this difference been to you?
- How have you appreciated your partner and their experience of themselves in this relationship around this issue?
- What is it like for you to know that your partner has struggled with these issues and to know how these struggles have influenced how your partner feels as a person and as a partner?
- What would it mean to take your partner's side or understand your partner from the inside out?
- How has what you now know about your partner influenced your hopes and wishes to be a friend to your partner?
- What values, beliefs, hopes and dreams drive your preferences? Which values, beliefs, and hopes of your relationship with your partner do you embrace?
- What hopes do you have for how your partner feels about themselves?
- What kind of feelings would you hope that your partner could feel coming from you about how you feel about them as a person?

Being attentive to issues of power, inequity, and abuse in couple relationships cannot be overstated. For Daryl and Karly, discussing power differentials opened the door to meaningfully address how being an interracial couple played out in their relationship. As an assault victim, however, Karly was able to acknowledge that Daryl had provided her with the safety she needed. Eventually, the couple developed a mutual presence and commitment to understand and appreciate the other's story, which exchanged defensiveness for being one's honorable self.

Karly and Daryl oscillated between empowering and disempowering storylines though they increasingly were able to find ways to comfort each other without devolving into blame/attack–defense patterns. They expressed moments of genuine empathic attunement exemplified in this exchange that took place while preparing for a visit to Karly's cousin whose husband had recently died. The couple felt good about planning the visit together despite feelings of sadness and apprehension. Karly's cousin had five children. The couple's previous visits had triggered remorse about not having children of their own. Despite these difficult emotions, both Daryl and Karly felt positive about their collective contributions to make this trip happen:

KARLY: Over the weekend we learned that my cousin had lost her husband.

DARLY: Yes, we both knew him well and we shared good moments together.

THERAPIST: I am sorry for your loss. What was it like for you?

KARLY: Well, I notice how much Daryl steps in in moments like this. He planned the entire trip. I feel he cares and although we fight, we come together in caring ways.

THERAPIST: That feels special to notice that about Daryl. *(turning to Daryl)* What is it like to see your efforts noticed by Karly?

DARYL: It feels good. Karly means the world to me. Although we do not have children, we have each other.

Practitioners are frequently challenged by couple therapy as the process and progress can be halting, regressive, and at times, infuriating. Fraenkel (2023) however, cautions against the tendency to rush toward solutions. Instead, he emphasizes that clinicians stay attuned to the pace of clients' stories. Couples often need to hold on to their problem-saturated narratives until they feel genuinely heard, psychologically safe, and understood. Attempting to dismantle these stories too soon can risk invalidating experiences and hindering progress.

Alari and Stella brought many challenges to the therapeutic encounter. Their relationship was shaped by complex layers of culture, family backgrounds, and personal identity. Alari, having immigrated to the United States, felt isolated from his family of origin, and disempowered by his inability to support himself financially. Stella, on the other hand, was closely connected to her family but found it difficult to express her emotions openly. Both partners needed to bear witness to each other to attain empathic attunement for each other's stories.

Viewed through a lens of witnessing, empathy, and relational accountability, Daryl and Karly's struggles can be understood not just as interpersonal conflict, but a meeting point of deeply rooted social identities, family histories and lived experiences. Their differing perspectives on many issues represent stories of belonging, pain, and meaning that shape how each partner moves through the world and through the relationship.

Working together with empathy means holding space for vulnerability. It encompasses witnessing the emotional cost of exclusion, the ache of disconnection from one's identity, and the fear of being misunderstood or judged. Relational accountability on the other hand, calls for each partner to reflect on how their words, silences, and assumptions impact the other—not with blame but with care.

## Conclusion

Couples get caught up in cycles of vulnerability causing them to use mechanisms such as defensiveness and blaming to cope with their emotions and to manage their relationships (Scheinkman, 2017). For Alari, his need to intellectualize created a relational distance when what he really wanted was intimacy and to be cared about. For Stella, independence gave her time away from worry and was a necessary survival strategy to protect herself from Alari's incessant criticism. Daryl's vulnerability showed up as emotional distance, driven by fear, uncertainty, and a persistent undercurrent of anxiety and unworthiness. Feeling unheard left Karly feeling vulnerable, sad, lonely, and stuck in an unsatisfying relationship. Her survival strategies were expressed by anger and confrontation.

Couple therapy meets people where they are in relationship. The role of the therapist is to pay close attention to how their stories, both individual and relational, shape the context, words, and actions that may reinforce problem-saturated narratives. As couples commit to witnessing their partner's stories, they develop empathic attunement that binds them to each other. Therapeutic strategies for helping couples no matter where they are in their relational lives include separating them from their problems, expanding openings and possibilities, and developing relational understanding and accountability through witnessing practices.

The next chapter explores and expands the theme of witnessing in the face of illness narratives. How providers and systems engage caring and curing unfolds important storylines.

CHAPTER 8

# Illness Narratives

## FROM CURING TO CARING

Illness narratives are highly diverse, requiring therapists to be equally adaptable, focusing on the possibility of cure, but more importantly, emphasizing the necessity of care. Weingarten's (2001) ocean metaphor says it best:

> The progressive illness narrative [movement toward incremental health improvement] orients people to cure. Yet if there is one thing I feel I have learned from an adult life lived inside an unreliable body, it is that care, not cure, will keep us floating in the ocean. It is my hope that understanding the different kinds of constraints facing people with illness, with regard to the stories they can tell, will make it more likely that care will circulate among us. I hope that this will create, metaphorically, a variety of rafts and docks and buoys and life preservers for us to cling to—together—in the illness-waters that we will all face at some time in our lives. (p. 124)

There is abundant literature on the experience of illness that describes its confounding nature (Adams, 2015; Jaouad, 2021; Lorde & Smith, 2020; Mukherjee, 2015; Penn, 2001; Simblett, 2013; Sontag, 2003; Weingarten,

2000,2010, 2022; Weingarten & Worthen, 2017). Writing extensively from experience, Weingarten (2001, 2010, 2013, 2022; Weingarten & Worthen, 2017) has detailed illness's diversity of features, and its contradictions. Adams discusses the ways in which chronic illness shifts personal schemas, changing one's previously held beliefs, worldviews, and the ways in which meaning is made. Penn called for new metaphors and alternative voices to counter the predominantly negative imagery that shape the meaning and experience of illness, including within relationships.

Simblett (2013) contends that dominant cultural narratives construct how illness is understood, and how they influence the ways people position themselves when faced with medical and psychiatric conditions. He cites the *Diagnostic and Statistical Manual of Mental Disorders* (*DSM*), a classification system used by clinicians as a tool to diagnose psychiatric conditions (American Psychiatric Association, 2013), as an example of how medical culture establishes categories that are absolute, leaving no room for variability or individual difference. Instead of "dancing" with the *DSM*, Simblett suggests moving away from constricted narratives to "loosen *DSM*'s tight embrace on defining the truth of the person's reality and identity" (p. 121). This includes placing more value on insider knowledge to gather individual truths from those experiencing illness.

Health is a precarious position that can change at any moment in time. In her book *Illness as Metaphor*, Susan Sontag (2003) suggests that people hold dual citizenship, one in the kingdom of the well and the other in the kingdom of the sick. This description highlights the fine line that divides people's daily existence, separating good health from bad. For therapists working with illness and disability narratives it is essential to recognize insider knowledges and pursue alternative storylines that reveal multifaceted thick descriptions of people's lives. Factors that affect good health and poor health tell very different stories from a wide range of citizenships.

## Illness Narratives

Illness narratives defy single-story descriptions (Weingarten, 2001). They reside in multivariate contexts, such as medical disorders, mental health conditions, disability, chronic health conditions, genetic disorders, and terminal disease, among others. Their outcomes may be equally disparate, from full recovery, lingering symptoms, permanent or temporary disability, and death. Some illnesses are rare, having few comparisons or likenesses to others, while there are many that share common features and similarities. Certain narratives depict a unique progressive or regressive journey, while others challenge modern medicine's ability to treat them. Some illnesses are experienced on an individual level, while most not only affect the patient but also their family members and communities. As Weingarten asserts, "Illness is huge. Illness or, more accurately, our relationship to it, threatens the way we know ourselves and how others know us also" (p. 112).

Some illnesses are well recognized, eliciting people's empathy. A cancer diagnosis, for instance, is understood by the vast majority and not questioned or judged. There are illnesses however, for which there are no specific categorizations or reliable treatments, yet people suffer from their physical and emotional effects. When the medical community fails to understand or acknowledge certain illnesses, it can lead to reductionistic explanations, blaming their origins on mental health or psychological problems or vague causes, such as stress.

People who suffer with these illnesses often experience themselves as deeply flawed. Without explanation or context for their experience, they are mired in uncertainty and loss of control. They search for explanations, yet illness narratives too often have more questions than answers, leaving people caught in an ever-evolving sense of unknowing.

Unanswered illness questions also unmask major flaws in society's ability and desire to care for its people. Larger systems such as health care institutions, providers, and payers all play integral roles in shaping illness narratives. Health inequities are pervasive in the U.S. healthcare system. Systemic racism, poverty, trauma, and other social drivers characterize a society that consistently chooses winners and losers. Indeed, the 2020 pandemic shone a light on the politicization of health and laid bare global inequities in access to care.

The rotator cuff story highlights the physical, emotional, and systemic challenges of healing—revealing how medical experiences, especially for marginalized bodies, are shaped as much by trust, power, and visibility as by pain and procedure.

## The Shoulder, the System, and Me: A Rotator Cuff Story

When I was diagnosed with a torn rotator cuff, I expected physical pain. I didn't expect to be thrust into a world of medical jargon, procedural detachment, and emotional uncertainty. I thought it would be a straightforward process: Identify the problem, fix it, heal. But this story quickly became about more than my shoulder—it became about trust, identity, and what it means to navigate pain within a clinical system. The medical jargon didn't soothe my anxiety; it intensified it. I was looking for reassurance—what I found was confusion.

The magnetic resonance imaging (MRI) results gave me technical descriptions, tendon tears, fluid buildup, degeneration—but still no clarity. I expected the physician to explain my condition—what I was going through and why. I suppose I also expected compassion. But to my dismay, the doctor simply recited the test findings. There was no warmth, no pause for emotion, no invitation to ask questions. I sat there wondering how to make sense of this sterile narrative. What did any of this mean for *me*? What was expected of *me*? And more urgently: who was advocating for my well-being?

When the doctor said surgery was the best option, I hesitated. Were there other paths? Could physical therapy work? I recalled comments made by a former client, a physical therapist, who observed how Black and Brown bodies were judged and treated differently in clinical settings, especially around expressions of pain. How much of what was being recommended for me was standard care, and how much reflected implicit bias?

I found myself in a precarious position. I was doubting a medical system that I had to depend upon. One moment, I was certain that surgery was the right choice. The next, I was overwhelmed by suspicion. There was something mechanized about the whole process, like I was being moved along a conveyor belt with different choices at every stand.

My uncertainties deepened when discussing reimbursement systems with my doctor. He spoke candidly about navigating insurance authorizations and preparing for "all possible scenarios" in the operating room. "It's a tough capitalistic world," he said, and for a moment, he sounded human, almost empathic. And yet, his words didn't allay my fears. Who gets left behind in a system like this? Was I already slipping through the cracks? As a Black man would they underestimate my pain? For someone with expertise in narratives, I was without words to calm my anxieties.

The surgery was successful, but the recovery process was a different kind of trial. I was completely unprepared. No one told me how grueling it would be. When the anesthesia wore off, the pain was piercing—shocking in its intensity. Painkillers barely dulled it. I couldn't sleep. I couldn't move my arm or perform tasks of daily living without assistance. I spilled food, dropped utensils, and struggled to open bottles. It was humbling, frustrating, and emotionally draining. I thought about people who go through recovery alone—and those who live permanently with limited mobility. Mostly, I felt angry that no one had warned me how bad it could get. I began to question whether anyone truly listens to patients when they describe their pain—especially patients like me.

In quiet, pain-filled moments, I came to understand how fragile independence really is. I also began to see how illness forces us to confront not just our bodies but our place in the world—how we're seen, how we're treated, and how deeply flawed and insensitive the systems around us can be when we most need their support.

As I recovered, I moved through grief, frustration, and eventually—slowly—toward acceptance. I learned new ways of doing old things. I cried. I prayed. I sulked. I hoped. Recovery, it turns out, isn't linear. It's filled with questions, long silences, and with moments when faith is the only thing left to hold.

As you have surmised, this isn't just a story about my shoulder injury.

It is one of many that mirror other people's illness narratives. It speaks to how care is experienced at vulnerable times and how the medical system responds (or doesn't) to the person behind the diagnosis. What does it mean to be cared *for*, and to be seen—not just as a body in need of repair but as a whole person. In many respects, I'm still recovering, maybe not in body but in existential pursuit of finding meaning for illness and care. I'm still asking questions and hoping to find answers. I am also grateful. I now carry deep within me an appreciation for how complex healing truly is and I am reminded that the person, not the illness, always comes first.

Client stories tell of ways they have been let down by systems, especially those meant to help them when they were feeling most vulnerable. Oloo's story encompasses the ways he suffered as witness to lack of essential resources during the pandemic.

### THE STORY OF OLOO

Oloo's life came to a screeching halt shortly after the 2020 pandemic struck. Oloo, age 50, had come to the United States as an immigrant from Kenya, and was struggling to make ends meet working as a care nursing assistant (CNA). He financially supported his family in the United States and also his extended family back in Africa.

During the early days of the pandemic, Oloo watched in horror as so many of his Black and Brown patients succumbed to the virus. He saw his face in the eyes of these people. Nonetheless he had to work, exposing himself to great risk with no health insurance coverage. He worried for his life as he closely monitored for COVID symptoms.

In therapy, Oloo lamented his loss of professional status in United States. Back in his home country, he was a certified registered nurse. He struggled with life's contradictions, caring for his patients, including White people, while at the same time, not being able to take care of his own family. He could not reconcile the disparities he witnessed—the differential treatments offered to certain patients over others.

Oloo experienced the pangs of moral distress daily. He witnessed how some patients were chosen to live while others were left to die. These were hard questions and choices. What roles did race, class, and age play in these life-affecting decisions? Was his role about curing or about caring, and how did either of these play out during the horrors of a global pandemic? How was he to make meaning of his experiences?

## Curing or Caring: Patient Voice

Patient/client voice is often left out of traditional medical discourse. Although the phrase "patient-centered care" has been popularized in the business of health, in health care practice client-driven narratives, metaphors, and "insider knowledges" are rarely represented in diagnosis and treatment (Simblett, 2013, p. 123). Sedgwick (2013) characterizes contemporary medical discourse as primarily influenced by a "modern technocratic attitude toward health care," a binary conceptualization, or "restitution plot" that erects boundaries between "normal health" or "wellness" and "illness" or "sickness" as opposites (p. 309). This linear definition of illness ignores the postmodern or constructionist stance of multiple truths and excludes client voice entirely (Leimumäki, 2012; Sedgwick, 2013). Within this paradigm, pain and suffering are seen "as a temporary condition to be overcome" (Sedgwick, 2013, p. 310) rather than a condition to be managed. Leimumäki further points out that by eliminating multiple and overlapping illness experiences, the restitution narrative essentially dismisses the idea that those living with chronic illness, though not cured, and perhaps still experiencing levels of pain and suffering, can still experience a fruitful life (Leimumäki, 2012).

Oloo wrestled with many troubling thoughts. He observed his patients struggling to survive, but nothing stemmed their suffering, their emaciated bodies told the story. It seemed to him that being isolated from families and loved ones exacerbated his patients' distress.

Oloo watched people die with no one to hold them or to listen to their dying words. He lamented his patients' helplessness as well as his own. Although he understood the desperation felt by the medical community, he did not understand why finding a cure for the virus had to come at the expense of caring.

Tensions between care and cure permeate medicine, leaving the patient's experience of illness unacknowledged and misunderstood. Medical metaphors, acronyms, and jargon are prevalent in medicine, used as a mechanism to distance the person from the illness (Dai & Peng, 2024). Without insider knowledge, the medical script of illness can "alienate the sufferer from their illness and hence, ultimately, from themselves" (Sedgwick, 2013, p. 319). Seriously ill patients by necessity put their trust in health professionals hoping to recover and badly needing their compassion and care. However, as Sedgwick cautions, relinquishing power over to providers renders patients vulnerable. Most try to be compliant but in doing so "the ailing individual takes on the role of one who is well-regulated and thus (perhaps) easier to treat, but powerless" (p. 309). Loss of control during illness can lead to an additional form of suffering, an existential crisis during which the "sufferer's illness no longer belongs to them" (p. 309). This dual experience of suffering and powerlessness was evident in no uncertain terms during the 2020 COVID-19 pandemic.

The pervasiveness of the restitution narrative in contemporary health care practice has both social and deeply personal implications for how people experience illness. Leimumäki (2012) proposed that narratives are by their very nature, social because they are always told to someone, even an imagined audience. In effect, the way that we narrativize experience is always contextual. Even when creating it just for ourselves, the story's narrative elements, sequencing, and coherence are embedded in a social context.

Examining the social construction of an illness story offers valuable clues to meaning making, and in particular, how a person attempts to reframe the dominant restitution plot to one more resonant with a "quest narrative." A quest narrative makes meaning of illness through the experience of bearing witness to suffering and illness. Rather than being unspoken, hidden, or focused only on cure, the quest narrative is situated in identity work shaped by the patient's experiential knowledge, expertise, and voice (Leimumäki, 2012). It resists labels and assumptions, recognizing that unlike the restitution plot, each person's illness journey is unique.

Communities too, seek to construct quest narratives as they create their collective stories around illness. Pain and suffering is not minimized but it is contextualized within a broader life, not catastrophized into "chaos narratives" or stories focused only on incurability and tragedy (Leimumäki, 2012; Sedgwick, 2013). Quest narratives shift the storyline away from the contemporary technocratic model to a holistic stance that prioritizes caring whether or not curing is possible.

Oloo's distress was increasingly palpable as he told stories of sitting at the bedsides of so many dying patients. Because of pandemic restrictions, Oloo and I met over Zoom shortly after his overnight shifts. He was typically prompt to our sessions but, on this one occasion, he was late to the call. I was about to turn off my laptop when I heard the familiar click:

THERAPIST: Oh, there you are!

OLOO: I do not know if I can continue to do this. There is so much death all around me. I do not even know what I have been doing. A man was dying before my eyes. I ask myself what it means to suffer.

THERAPIST: That's a very important question. How do you understand it for yourself?

OLOO: As I sat with this man, I thought about the people in his life, especially his family that could not be there with him in his dying moments. I thought of what I was offering him and if it really mattered. What stories was he telling himself about illness?

THERAPIST: Clearly, he has had such a big impression on you.

OLOO: I had been with him a week before when he came into the hospital, and he had asked me to talk to his family. I felt in those moments that the best way I could be there for him was to talk to his family. So, I spent the whole night talking to

> his wife who kept asking me to describe every little motion he made. Being with him that way felt more present and caring to him than anything else.

Oloo told me of the long silences he experienced in the presence of his patients. He neither comprehended nor had the language to express how these felt. What were his patients going through? What were they thinking? Were they able to make meaning of their illnesses? And how was isolation and loneliness affecting them? Oloo was deeply troubled by not having answers to these questions. He also struggled with not knowing how the virus would further unfold. It was still early in its spread and information about COVID seemed to fluctuate daily.

## How to Engage Stories of Illness: The "Dance" Metaphor

Simblett's (2013) "dance" metaphor is frequently used to explain how to engage with stories of illness. Dance invokes movement, expression, and creativity. In narrative practice, dance as a metaphor replaces static classifications with openness, allowing for difficult conversations and opportunities "to use the dance to refuse the possibility of being assigned a set place within a discourse and in the process cocreate new discourses, new dance-floors for the dance to continue upon" (Simblett, 2013, p. 118). He advised clinicians to avoid the temptation to define people by their illness and encourages clients to do the same. Reinforcing an identity that goes beyond illness significantly helps people thicken their narrative to include richer stories, including those about times when they are feeling well.

Daryl and Karly (see Chapter 7), both in their 70s, exemplify ways in which people assimilate their physical limitations into broader, richer identities. They described themselves as being "in decline," particularly due to hearing loss. Yet, they were not defined or limited by their encroaching auditory deficits. Instead, they sought new dance floors to enrich their lives, finding joy in outdoor activities among other undertakings that were not dependent on their hearing. Adapting to deficit, disability, and illness does not deny their existence but neither does it thwart one's ability to have a quality of life.

People like Daryl and Karly remind us that no life is a single story, and similarly, illness is more than one narrative. They demonstrate resilience in the spaces between good health and poor health. According to Sedgwick (2013) the body has "many healths . . . akin to places one visits . . . in this way likened to alien landscapes hidden beneath the familiar surface of one's everyday health" (p. 307). The idea of "many healths" is counter to the traditional medical discourse, one that views illness as static, mechanistic, and void of potential for insight, meaning making, and growth.

This single-story perspective is even more evident in discourse surrounding mental illness. Although some progress has been made to demystify psychiatric conditions, improve treatments, and reduce harmful stereotypes, mental illness continues to be significantly misunderstood, undertreated, and stigmatized. The *DSM* (American Psychiatric Association, 2022) is constantly being revised to address new knowledge. However, classification cannot accurately represent how people living with mental illness differ from one another even within the same diagnosis. To perceive diagnoses as fixed and true is to put people at risk for internalizing the stigmas and characteristics proffered by unyielding categorizations. Everyone's experience of mental illness is unique, affecting different areas of life and at varying degrees and times. Simblett (2013) might say that we must be nimble dancers when using the *DSM*. Flexibility, curiosity, and openness are essential to assess the impacts of mental illness on individuals and communities. Indeed, the dance metaphor can be applied to many different discourses: politics, race, religion, gender, any category that society paints in binary, linear, or black and white images. Gray areas are vast and must be explored.

## Finding Moments of Connection

Moments of connection are cornerstones of narrative practice and are especially salient when working with clients experiencing illness. The quality of connections with health professionals is identified by patients and family caregivers as critical to positive adaptation when a diagnosis of chronic illness or permanent disability is received (Konrad, 2007). However, despite being poised to support those who have received difficult news or are living with ongoing health struggles, health professionals are unprepared or unwilling to enter into connection, resorting instead to the mechanistic and distancing language of the medical script (Konrad, 2007).

The stories of Nana and Anisha illustrate the value of meaningful therapeutic connection for people living with illness. Through relationship, narrative approaches invite clients to find ways to make meaning of highly complex life situations.

### THE STORY OF NANA

Nana's story incorporates the core principles of narrative practice. Upon reflection, I have come to deeply appreciate how much I learned from Nana, and the ways in which her life experience was intricately woven throughout her story, offering valuable insights into how one's personal history and culture shape the construction and telling of illness narratives.

Nana, 70, had been diagnosed with high blood pressure, diabetes, and macular degeneration. As an independent woman who used to have control over her life, having multiple chronic health conditions left her with a deep sense of loss due to an unreliable body.

Experiences of loss, including those of family, children, and community, were prominent in Nana's self-understanding. Like most people, Nana's losses were intimately experienced as an individual and also as part of a community. A mother of eight children, six had died from various illnesses. Her husband too, had passed, compounding her grief. Nana's identity was strongly connected to being a caregiver. Taking care of others was always at the expense of taking care of herself. Given her circumstances, it was now Nana's time for self-care.

Together we explored what motherhood meant to Nana and the strength it took to raise her eight children. After the deaths of her children, she became the primary caregiver for her grandchildren, a role she had clearly not anticipated but embraced with pride. Nana held the family together through many of life's challenges and now, here she stood faced with struggles of her own. Nonetheless, she refused to see herself as vulnerable. She insisted on inhabiting Sontag's (2003) kingdom of the well.

Redefining wellness was a central theme in my work with Nana. Equally important was finding moments of connection:

THERAPIST: Help me to know what I should know about you. What makes you, you?

NANA: (*long pause*) . . . well, my name is Nana. The name has a long history.

THERAPIST: Tell me about your name.

NANA: (*another long pause*) . . . The name has gone through many iterations. My children called me Mama . . . and when they had children of their own, they taught their children to call me JajaMama, which literally means Grandmother.

THERAPIST: And how did it become Nana?

NANA: (*smiles*) . . . Well, my grandchildren switched it to JaNana and it eventually became Nana. This name seemed easier for them to say. And I like it.

THERAPIST: That is a beautiful story of your name. And . . . also nice that you like it.

NANA: Actually, it is more than that.

THERAPIST: More than what?

NANA: My name reminds me more of who I am or what the doctors tell me about my body.

Nana took a long pause. When she spoke again it was with a softer, less certain tone. She described feeling disconnected to a body she no longer understood. Nana was desperate for answers as it seemed, despite myriad diagnoses she had received, there still was so much about her health that remained unknown. She spoke of seeing multiple specialists, each offering only fragments of understanding. "It's as if I handed my body over to the medical system," she said. Rarely, however, did anyone ask Nana about her own experience. She felt isolated, trapped in a body that didn't make sense. She longed for connection, but being with others, even those she loved, drained her of what little energy she had.

Nana's health anxiety became all encompassing, exacerbated by medical experts who could not find effective remedies for her symptoms. She became resentful toward providers that began to interpret her symptoms as signs of mental illness, as one doctor put it: "Illness is all in your head." She voiced significant frustration with a medical world that ignored her physical suffering.

Nana's experience is not uncommon. Health professionals are known to dismiss or minimize physical symptoms for which there is no apparent explanation. In the literature, this is called "symptom invalidation" and is more apt to occur with women; people of color; and lesbian, gay, bisexual, transgender, and queer/questioning (LGBTQ+) individuals whose physical illnesses are attributed to stress or psychological sources (Bontempo, 2025; Wolfe & Hintz, 2024).

Like others in her position, Nana began to wonder if she was being seen by her health providers as an object rather than a full human being. Appointments focused on measurement: whether it was blood levels, surveys, pain rating scales, or standardized questionnaires. Numbers, she said, could never capture the full reality of her experience. Pain and suffering were not fixed, they ebbed and flowed, defying quantification. What disturbed Nana most, however, was what little attention was being paid to her as a person. She felt invisible, marginalized, and desperately ill.

Nana did not fit the plots and subplots of traditional medicine's conceptualization of illness. Moreover, social drivers other than the illness itself affected her health. These included racism, food insecurity, houselessness, and other forms of oppression that rarely get factored into doctors' appraisals and intervention plans—social factors known to be influential in shaping health across populations, circumstances, class, and environments (Braverman & Gottlieb, 2014). Medical knowledge alone is not sufficient to produce positive health outcomes. Life circumstances must also be considered as part of assessment. And Nana knew that well. She wished that those responsible for her care checked in with her about what she called the totality of her life.

## Caring as Bedside Manner

When we began our work together, I made a conscious effort to see Nana in the context of the "totality of her life," beyond her diagnoses. I think of this as the *bedside manner* of my practice—a commitment to engaging in dialogue that fully welcomes clients in their being. It is a way of connecting that honors how a person wishes to be seen, actively resisting forms of Othering and reductionism:

THERAPIST: You said your name reminds you more of who you are or what the doctors tell you about your body. Tell me more about who you are.

NANA: Well . . . I am, first and foremost, a mother. As a mother, I connect to all my children and grandchildren, dead or living. I draw my strength from having raised eight children. Not everyone turned out as I would have wished but I did my job. And I am proud of it. I have given them what my mother gave me, a gift of a lifetime. I care about them. But I do not think the systems I interact with care as much about me.

Nana's account of Othering she experienced points to a health care profession more deeply rooted in the pursuit of curing rather than in the practice of caring. Her narrative exposes how objectification disconfirms the personhood of a patient. A clinician's genuine expression of caring fosters connection. Clients are recognized and affirmed as unique individuals, not objects to be analyzed, interpreted, and categorized. Such attentiveness opens pathways to deeper insight and allows for a more holistic view of the individual, one that acknowledges the full complexity of their being.

In a later session, Nana offered a culturally grounded interpretation of illness, describing it as a state of imbalance. She referred to it as "not being in harmony with nature and God." This perspective prioritizes cultural humility by situating illness not solely within the confines of the physical body but within broader spiritual, emotional, and relational contexts. To have focused exclusively on the body, without recognizing the interplay between body, mind, and spirit would have been to overlook fundamental aspects of Nana's identity and worldview.

As our work continued, Nana gained agency. She became confident to ask questions, especially when she felt her providers were too quick to blame stress or mental health for her illnesses, invalidating her experience as a person. Because her symptoms fluctuated it was often difficult to clearly explain how she was feeling, which caused a disconnect in communication with her health care team. Although her symptoms fluctuated, they helped her to know herself and appreciate herself better.

Learning how Nana made meaning of suffering was an important and inspiring aspect of our work. She often spoke of "suffering, but never of suffering alone." She embraced suffering not merely as personal hardship but as a communal and spiritual experience. At times illness left Nana depleted, causing her to experience uncharacteristic loneliness and disconnection from her family and community. Attending closely to Nana's belief about "never suffering alone" reconnected her to the ways she could draw upon family, cultural memory, and faith as sources of resilience.

Through her suffering, Nana developed a deeper appreciation for a higher power, which she referred to as God. Nana also invoked her ancestral African homeland—its earth, valleys, mountains, water, and other natural resources—all of which she described as "wellsprings of connection." Nana's invocation of Africa's natural elements suggested that for her, healing was rooted in a sense of belonging to a larger lineage and ecological world. Together, we examined these symbols—the earth, valleys, mountains, and water—as metaphors for stability, endurance, and life-sustaining connection, and explored ways to integrate them into our therapeutic conversations to strengthen her sense of identity and purpose.

Through her illness, Nana embraced uncertainty as an inherent part of life. Narrative practice positions Nana's acceptance of uncertainty as a rich aspect of meaning making, personal agency, and strength, which runs contrary to traditional Western cultural priorities of control and certainty, cure over caring. Accepting life's unpredictable nature, especially during times of illness, crisis, or change, has a mediating effect, decreasing fear of the unknown and reducing stress and anxiety (Gilles, 2017). Together Nana and I reflected on these "wellsprings of connection," deepening our therapeutic alliance and supporting her ongoing narratives of resilience, faith, and cultural rootedness.

## THE CASE OF ANISHA

Unlike Nana, whose health issues emerged gradually as she aged, Anisha's were unexpected, affecting both her identity and the stability of her family life. Anisha, a 43-year-old Black woman, was feeling frightened and confused following a diagnosis of Stage 3 breast cancer identified by a routine mammogram. When we first met, she had just learned that the surgical team wanted to operate within the week, news that "hit like a ton of bricks." Feeling understandably confused and scared about her new diagnosis, she was gathering information and weighing options. Anisha also conveyed not wanting to be a "guinea pig" with the treatments offered to her. Thus, she read widely and asked detailed questions about her diagnosis.

Anisha was also worried about the impact her diagnosis would have on her two sons, ages 7 and 9, and her parents, who "have a lot of health problems." She was the primary earner for the family and caregiver for both her children and parents. Anisha was divorced and did not receive support from her ex-partner. She knew about the high costs of health care, recalling an outstanding emergency department bill she was still paying off for her son who had fallen off a bike the year before. She was apprehensive about potentially losing insurance coverage should she be unable to work. Anisha's faith community was always there for her in times of need, but this unanticipated illness rocked her faith in God.

## Trust, History, and Healing: Reflections on Narrative Practice With Anisha

My work with Anisha revealed a deeply complex array of issues that extended far beyond the crisis of breast cancer. Although Anisha sought treatment at one of the premier medical institutions in the United States, our conversations quickly illuminated a series of layered questions—questions rooted not only in her personal experience but in the wider historical and cultural context of care.

Anisha had observed that the cleaning persons and janitors were all persons of color. The treatment team were all White. Anisha stated that no one represented her race and color on the treatment team. On several occasions Anisha stated: "I do not trust the system." Her suspicions about the system raised more concerns and questions. These included the following questions: How did this institution fit into Anisha's own understanding of health and healing? What did it mean, for her as a Black woman, to place trust in a system that has a long history of marginalizing, excluding, and even exploiting people of color? Furthermore, how do we, as practitioners, hold space for the narratives of medical mistrust—stories shaped by the legacy of unethical experimentation on Black bodies, particularly Black women—and still offer hope, guidance, and presence?

These were not merely rhetorical questions but practical and ethical ones. They shaped every aspect of our work together. Our discussions invoked even more questions: How does one address historical inequalities without allowing the narrative to eclipse the person in front of us? Does this narrative of distrust provide an opening for deeper engagement, or does it risk creating distance? Within the constraints of medical timelines and institutional demands, how much time is enough to truly explore the depth of a person's story? Is there a temptation to focus only on the "presenting problem," bypassing the unspoken or unfinished stories that linger beneath?

More questions emerged. How do we attune ourselves to healing narratives—not just stories of trauma or illness but those that sustain and uplift? How do we amplify the strengths that have helped a person endure? In Anisha's case, how could I best listen for the values and sources of meaning that shape her experience: her faith, her devotion to her children, her care for her aging parents, and her volunteer work?

In situations like Anisha's, therapeutic conversations become less about solving a problem and more about witnessing complexity. They involve listening for what is precious—for instance, Anisha's beliefs, ethics, guiding principles, and hopes. They direct attention to what she intends for her life: her specific purposes, ambitions, objectives, and deeply held pursuits. Such witnessing is messy, there are no neat answers, no closure. Instead, they open space to wonder, to pause, and to witness more fully the story of a woman navigating not just illness, but an entire moral, ethical, and cultural landscape of care.

So, how do we attune ourselves to healing narratives—not just stories of trauma or illness but those that sustain and uplift? How do we amplify the strengths that have helped a person endure while not minimizing their pain and suffering? In my work with Anisha, I had multiple challenges. I needed to listen closely to the values and sources of meaning that shaped her experience. I had to acknowledge and validate her faith, her devotion to her children and community, and her care for her aging parents. And I could avoid bypassing the fears she legitimately harbored toward medical systems that had exploited people of color, women, and the most vulnerable. We reframed mistrust as a needed protective response to systemic harm.

## UNDERSTANDING STORY: EXTERNALIZING TO REAUTHORING CONVERSATIONS

Narrative practice facilitates the development of alternative storylines that incorporate people's lived experiences, imagination, and meaning making. Reauthoring conversations offer "a point of entry to the alternative storylines of people's lives . . ." (White, 2007, p. 61), and it was my goal to find those entry points in conversation with Anisha. It did not take long to discover that Anisha was in the process of grieving her health as well as her sense of identity. She was uncharacteristically experiencing emotional dysregulation, anger, loneliness, distrust, sadness, and suspicion, and was trying to understand the emotional roller coaster she was on.

Learning more about Anisha's background brought me to a better understanding of the different worlds she inhabited. In college, Anisha studied journalism and developed a passion for investigative stories. During one session, she described several interviews she had conducted that brought forth feelings of agency and joy. This information prompted me to suggest that Anisha write a letter to her present self, which we could investigate together, identifying recurring themes and patterns that could guide her identity work. Anisha cautiously seized the opportunity. She was somewhat afraid of what might surface but I assured her that the therapeutic space was a psychologically safe and supportive environment for such exploration.

Themes that emerged in her writing included self-protection through self-deprecation, loneliness, sadness, fear of abandonment, impermanence, distrust, fear of medical procedures, and conflict within her family relationships. Anger and fear were also recurring themes, anger toward her ex-partner and emerging doubts about God. Anisha additionally uncovered a profound fear of the unknown. A final major theme was her deep-seated resentment and negativity toward herself. Our work centered on helping Anisha strive to understand how these themes played out during the illness crisis and throughout her life. Journaling and letter writing have since become valuable tools for Anisha to express her fears, hopes, wishes, and expectations.

## SEPARATING FROM THE PROBLEM

Diagnoses have power. They greatly influence how we perceive ourselves and also how others see us. In narrative practice, the quest is to help clients experiencing illness separate themselves from the problem, a daunting task given how illness encompasses one's body, mind, and spirit. Externalizing conversations offer clients and clinicians opportunities to co-construct the meaning of illness as just one story among others toward a preferred sense of identity (Duvall & Beres, 2011).

A concrete separation of problem and person allows for a multifaceted self-representation, the illness only being one facet, and facilitates a thickening of the narrative.

With Anisha, part of our work together was to understand and draw out exceptions to her experiences. This foundational element of narrative practice, the development of exceptions, was crucial to create greater meaning throughout her illness narrative. Empathic questioning assisted me in drawing out exceptions, opening doors for Anisha to examine her relationship to the problems named by the medical community. We worked diligently to coauthor narratives in her voice, attuned to her values, priorities, and virtues. Later, at Anisha's request, we invited family members to witness her story. Anisha shared her diagnosis with her two young sons and her aging parents. Her fears and concerns about how they would receive the news dissipated as she felt a depth of care and love from her family members. Freedman (2014) notes the specific positioning of family members as witnesses to another's story, allowing each member to listen openly and consider other perspectives in the ultimate process of thickening or re-storying the narrative.

## Conclusion

Clients, patients, and clinicians are all witnesses to illness stories. We cannot, not witness. As is often the case, theoretical concepts gain clarity when we experience them in the context of our own lives. In reflecting on my own experience, I recognize that I have lived through the different witness positions articulated by Weingarten (2000). I vacillated between feeling empowered and aware, disempowered and being clueless, unaware, and helpless.

This chapter described varied experiences of illness. My experience underscores the significance of relational support; having a partner present during illness highlights the impact of companionship on coping and meaning making. Such presence can be understood as both a gift and a reminder of the disparities between those who face illness with support and those who do it alone. As Weingarten (2000) notes, "matters of life and death are too hard, too onerous, too painful to 'do' alone" (p. 399). Anisha regretfully felt alone throughout her ordeal. Oloo was the sole witness to his patient's tragic death. Nana and Anisha, each in their own way, had ancestral connections to their illness yet both experienced times of disconnection and aloneness.

To be ill is not merely about managing disease. Illness forces one to re-story one's life—to construct a new narrative that is involuntary, deeply unsettling, and is often misunderstood. It is a narrative marked by gaps, openings, noises, and silences—a story characterized by limitations, uncertainty, and many unknowns. It is a story that vacillates, continually shifting in meaning. It is also a story that seeks caring, especially when curing is not an option.

Illness narratives chart unique journeys for every person. Narrative practice provides opportunities for those who live with illnesses and those who care for them to give voice to their experiences, search for new meaning, hope, and purpose, and build connections within the context of curing, caring, compassion, and empathy. The next chapter explores spirituality in relationship to stories of purpose and connection.

CHAPTER 9

# Spirituality and Social Justice

## SEARCHING FOR PURPOSE, CONNECTEDNESS, AND MEANING

For many cultures, spirituality, storytelling, and healing are interrelated. Many people understand healing as a form of spiritual transformation within the context of community. The connection between spirituality and storytelling is also deeply personal, creating space for one to journey inward and explore their inner voice. Spirituality and stories can build upon and help cultivate community between individuals who engage in relationship to one another—promoting respect for personhood, uniqueness, history, and the complexities of being an individual within community (Mueller, 2010). For Latinx and Africana communities in particular, stories are a means of disseminating shared experiences that offer spiritual comfort and guidance (Comas-Díaz, 2006). For older adults across a variety of cultures, storytelling serves to establish and renew community bonds (Snyder, 2005). And for children, stories offer moral messages, education, and comfort.

However, when it comes to healing, Western societies tend to prioritize the knowledge of experts. For example, the status of physicians is elevated because they are seen as knowing more about health than the people who are experiencing illness. Health, health care, and wellness are viewed from individualistic rather than communal vantage points and patient privacy is highly guarded. Healing, intervention, and evaluation take place in sterile environments across clinical settings where spirituality is not emphasized. Although patients are asked about their spiritual preferences on intake and offered pastoral guidance when in a hospital, spirituality is not integral to Western healing philosophies. This is a problem as I'll discuss below. For many people, spirituality is a source of strength, growth, and self- understanding. This chapter will discuss how narrative practitioners can help nurture people's spiritual stories to enhance healing.

Like physical health, trends in Western behavioral health prioritize measurable outcomes and evidence-based practices, preferring one-size-fits-all interventions rather than individualizing clinical care to fit the uniqueness of clients, including their relationship with spirituality. There is considerable debate about the pros and cons of integrating spirituality into clinical therapies. Some studies find that being attuned to clients' spiritual belief systems enhances therapeutic efficacy and improves overall functioning (Captari et al., 2018). Others cite ethical boundary issues and cultural missteps as reasons to avoid using spirituality or religion to address client issues in psychotherapy (Plante, 2007).

Damianakis (2001) contends that neglecting spirituality as an aspect of healing dilutes ways of knowing, such as intuition, reflexive knowledge, spiritual meaning, and creativity. Similarly, Pouchly (2012) contends that because spirituality is so much a part of a person's identity, it is neglectful, and potentially harmful, to not address it with clients and patients:

> Clients with spiritual beliefs should have their views heard and explored. Belief systems form a part of the individuals' identity. By not encompassing this culturally sensitive component to therapy choice is removed as are key issues and contexts for expression. (p. 81)

However, Damianakis (2001) cautions that spirituality must be understood as separate from religion to avoid getting caught up in dogma. She writes: "Spirituality can be operationalized as the search for purpose and meaning in one's life, whereas 'religion' entails a systematic body of beliefs and practices related to such a spiritual search" (p. 23). As human beings, our search for a good life is also our spiritual need to experience a meaningful role in our inner and outer worlds.

In many parts of the world, and especially within indigenous societies, spirituality is regarded as an extension of religion (Mugisha et al., 2013). Humanity and spirituality are inextricably linked, understood as a human quest for purpose, relationship, and meaning, as well as a way to cultivate connectedness among communities, groups, the non-human environment, and higher powers (Damianakis, 2001; Kamya, 2013; Moore et al., 2015; Sandage et al., 2020).

My therapeutic work with African immigrants and refugees in the United States heightened my own appreciation for stories and storytelling with spiritual properties that serve as healing agents. From this perspective, healing is a holistic endeavor that balances spiritual realms and the physical world (Chioneso et al., 2020). Furthermore, spirituality is a form of "self-transcendence," a step above self-actualization on Maslow's (1968) hierarchy of human needs. It includes ". . . a deeper sense of connection to others and the cosmos" (Damianakis 2001, p. 26). Spirituality has also been described as a human yearning for connection beyond oneself, the universe, a higher power, or the search for the sacred (Bell-Tolliver & Wilkerson, 2011; Oxhandler & Pargament, 2014; Pargament & Mahoney, 2021).

Cultural healing practices tell stories through performance rituals, such as drumming, dancing, signing, and oral histories. Community knowledge is highly valued and takes precedence over that of individuals. To paraphrase Teilhard de Chardin (1955), we are not human beings having a spiritual experience but we are spiritual beings having a human experience.

As I will explore further, reframing crises through a spiritual lens helps individuals better adapt to stressful circumstances, such as illness, trauma, and loss. From a neuroscience perspective, spirituality and religion come together to form a "cognitive framework that can reduce suffering and increase one's purpose and meaning in life" (Kagimu et al., 2013, p. 1212). I've argued that the body, mind, and spirit all tell important stories; therefore, clinicians seeking to provide holistic, culturally responsive care must take them into account in a collective manner (Kamya, 2013, p. 16).

Engaging spirituality in clinical care promotes a movement from monologic to dialogic discourse creating compassionate interaction (Kamya, 2013). As I've written, such conversations open space for "a new language through which pain and love are shared" (p. 29). In narrative practice, conversations that invite spiritual discourse nurture alternative stories that are client driven and permit collaborative "remembering" and "reauthoring" to bloom (Baldwin & Esley, 2015; Damianakis, 2001; Kamya, 2013). When we use narrative practice, "spiritual conversations like prayers and mindful or centering practices provide alternatives to stifling conversations or conversations that oppose the subjectivity of the other" (Kamya, 2013, pp. 29–30). Together, the client and practitioner witness the telling of old stories and the birth of new and meaningful ones to create healing.

## Spirituality, Ethics, and Social Justice

In my view, spirituality and social justice go hand in hand—spiritual beliefs can help people oppose social, political, and environmental injustices that besiege private and public lives. Human beings from all backgrounds, immigration statuses, and identities collectively belong to a broader ecological family. For Perry and Rolland (2009), the therapeutic benefits of a justice-seeking spirituality are powerful, especially for individuals, populations, and communities that experience marginalization. As Powell argues, "if spirituality is to engage suffering and its causes, it must also be concerned with how institutions and structures function in society" (Powell, 2012, p. 199). Spirituality needs to be anchored in tenets of social justice and the principles of caring: the same principles that undergird caring narrative practices. Accordingly, practitioners must work toward repairing hurts incurred by social injustice (Perry & Rolland, 2009).

For many societies, justice and spirituality are deeply rooted in the natural world. Natural harmony is strongly associated with social responsibility. As Perry and Rolland (2009) write:

> Spirituality by its very nature not only inclines but requires one to engage the world with a sense of responsibility for the well-being of creation, and with a commitment to repair what is amiss and to act in defense of creation. Spirituality and justice seeking are thus inextricably tied; like a Möbius strip, they are not distinct realms, but flow seamlessly one to another. (p. 384)

Adherence to ethical behaviors and standards is the third leg that supports a just practice. Every helping profession is guided by a code of ethics. As an example, the preamble of the National Association of Social Workers (NASW; 2021) code of ethics is clear when it states that

> the primary mission of the social work profession is to enhance human well-being and help meet the basic human needs of all people with particular attention to the needs and empowerment of people who are vulnerable, oppressed, and living in poverty. (p. 1)

The core values embraced by helping professions include service, social justice, dignity and worth of a person, the importance of human relationships, human rights, empowerment, strengths perspective, social transformation, compassion, hope and witness, and the ethics of care. These values evoke a deep spiritual core of the human condition.

The reformist spirit movement in mental health is committed to combating inequities, advocating for justice, and raising awareness of how social drivers—such as poverty, gender inequality, and racism—impact illness and health. As early as the 19th century, activists such as Dorothea Dix fought to reform asylums and improve care for people with mental illness. Around the same time, Jane Addams and Ellen Gates Starr cofounded and led Hull House, where "workers employed the arts to engage those same communities in pro-social activities that sought to build community amongst the diverse residents they lived amongst in low-income neighborhoods" (Kelly et al., 2024, p. 192). Aldarondo

(2007) views mental health practice and the drive for social justice as inextricably connected. He writes: "good mental health professionals are neither strangers to the pervasive presence of inequality and injustice in our society nor are they naïve about its effects in the inner life of the people" (p. 4). Care, justice, equality, and dignity form the heart and soul of narrative practice, qualities it shares with spirituality.

Practitioners address injustice in all its permutations, including but not limited to race, gender, age, disability, sexual orientation, and economic class. Oppression impacts the lives and well-being of children, families, and communities; immigrants and asylees; those in poor health or struggling with substance use; and people affected by mental illness. To commit to social justice is an invitation to care about everyone, a call with spiritual import. It is full recognition of the human condition that binds all people regardless of the differences between them.

People's stories speak to their own deep concerns for justice. They address the dignity and worth of persons, the importance of human relationships, human rights, self-determination, and integrity. They compel practitioners to listen with what Reik (1983) calls "the third ear," this refers listening to what is *not* said, rather than only to what is said. Codes of ethics provide guidelines for practitioners as they attend to people's stories. They do not, however, offer specific direction for decision making, especially when practitioners face complex situations, conflicts, or dilemmas. Narrative practice and the iterative process of telling and witnessing supplement ethical decision making in ways to ensure human dignity is preserved, and the client's voice is respected and heard.

The next sections briefly describe some core values espoused by narrative practitioners. Within the framework of human rights, these values include the dignity and worth of the person, and the importance of human relationships as contributing factors to people's stories of purpose, connection, and meaning.

## DIGNITY AND WORTH OF THE PERSON

Stories express clients' quests for dignity and worth. Narrative practitioners bear witness to these from a place of honoring the dignity, worth, and value of all people; this is inclusive of social class, race, color, creed, gender, sexual orientation, and age, and the ways these intersect with one another. We understand the problematic narratives as only one aspect of a person's identity. In this way, practitioners can acknowledge and uphold the many ways in which a person is separate from, and much more than, the disruptive problems that bring them to therapy. Our role is not minimize the suffering clients are experiencing, but ensure that a person's worth is never diminished in the process of problem solving.

### THE IMPORTANCE OF HUMAN RELATIONSHIPS

Practitioners help people build and/or restore relationships. Spirituality, too, aids in repairing relational ruptures and establishes communities where connections can grow. People develop and thrive through meaningful relationships. Relational-cultural theory (RCT) contends that healthy relational connection fosters growth, self-worth, and a zest for life, whereas relational disconnection, both individual and societal, culminates in marginalization, isolation, and overall emotional distress (Baker Miller & Pierce Stiver, 1997).

From a narrative perspective, relational connection is seen as essential to human survival. The development of healthy human relationships fully engages identity, including social, cultural, developmental, psychological, spiritual, occupational, and economic elements of a person's being. Altogether, they represent the many stories that make up a human life.

### HUMAN RIGHTS

Foundational to human rights is the belief that all people deserve to be treated fairly and share universal freedoms. Social justice advocates for human rights, including equity, equality, and access to common resources (Caputo, 2001; George, 1999; Reichert, 2003; Sharp, 2021; Stainton, 2002). Justice additionally refers to the nondiscriminatory allocation of burdens and opportunities in society (Miller, 1999; Sharp, 2021).

Spirituality is a just-seeking practice, based in pursuit of a just world and inclusive of all who seek its comfort and guidance, regardless of distinctions between self and other and between self and the world (Sharp, 2021). The United Nations Universal Declaration of Human Rights (UDHR), adopted in 1948, spells out the rights due to all people as well as the international community's responsibility to ensure that these rights are protected (United Nations, 1948). The UDHR further links human rights with human dignity without exception. Social, economic, religious, political, and family rights are among UDHR's fundamental protections.

The UDHR sets universal standards, guiding professionals to consider human rights in the assessment of clients' well-being. It should be noted that although the United States was a signatory to the UDHR, one of the treaties of the International Bill of Rights, to date it has not yet been fully ratified by Congress.

UDHR standards along with codes of ethics compel practitioners to engage in social activism on behalf of those they serve and in service to the greater good. As stewards of universal rights, practitioners are poised to protect individual rights as well as the rights that preserve communities. Stories often bring forth the role that spirituality plays in activism through facilitating personal, relational, and collective spiritual wellness in the context of human rights.

## EMPOWERMENT

Rappaport (1987) defines empowerment as "a process, a mechanism by which people, organizations, and communities gain mastery over their affairs, and involve themselves in the democratic processes of their communities and institutions" (p. 122). Spirituality is a facet of identity that acts as an empowering agent that helps people harness their inner and social resources, especially at times of adversity. In a study of spirituality and empowerment with women of color, Sengupta et al. (2025) found that for these women,

> spirituality was more than a philosophical orientation but comprised a core facet of their identity, empowering them to cope with adversity and uplift others through a leadership style defined by compassion, trust, strong interpersonal relationships and purpose. (p. 1)

Participatory engagement is a collaborative approach that empowers people of all backgrounds and experiences to be agents in decision-making processes that affect their communities and their personal well-being. Inclusive participation considers insider and local knowledge to be essential to successful outcomes and contributory to self-empowerment and community control. Participatory engagement values people's critical skills, seeing them as indispensable informants to the institutions that affect their lives.

Paulo Freire (1970) produced a critically reflective model of participatory engagement for social transformation. The model outlined a step-by-step process using the terms "see," "reflect," "analyze," and "act" that helped people identify the limits that had been imposed on them, and act toward change. At the same time, Freire conceived the concept of critical consciousness to describe one's ability to analyze and critique existing social and political conditions. Such critique set the stage for action that challenged oppressive and disempowering forces that inhibited the people's control over their circumstances. A model like this echoes the human yearning for purpose, connection, and meaning.

Freire's (1970) model promoted critical consciousness through a dialectical process where people stated their differing standpoints with the goal of activating change. Given the oppressive times in Latin America, Freire's ideas were perceived as radical as they dared "to perceive social, political, and economic contradictions and to take action against the oppressive elements of reality" (p. 35). Sobrino (1988) called such action a spirituality of liberation.

Freire's theories and those of liberation activists are rooted in the "preferential options for the poor" (Dault, 2015, p. 46). Preferential option invites action on behalf of those who are marginalized and on the fringes of society. It is also rooted in biblical traditions and scriptures that elevate the oppressed masses and recognize lessons learned from their plight in the quest for purpose and connection.

## STRENGTHS PERSPECTIVE

Spirituality and the strengths perspective share values and concepts that emphasize individual and community resilience and hope (Lee, 2019;

Saleebey, 1996). Spirituality acknowledges and values the richness and strengths of all people and cultures: It is about discovering the human-ness that lies in the restoration of people's transcendent and collective relationships.

Strengths-based spirituality directs attention to human capacity, purpose, talent, possibility, resourcefulness, and vision. It encourages individuals and communities to write new stories that separate the problems they are experiencing from the strengths they have to remediate them. In this way people and communities enable hope in the face of hopelessness and become agents of change, no longer objects being acted upon but subjects actualizing their potential (Chazin et al., 2000; Freire, 1973; Rappaport, 1987).

Narrative practice values indigenous and local knowledges that reveal a people's spirituality and strengths (White & Epston, 1990). It engages in affirming and curious practices, what Freire (1973) called a "problem-posing" approach in which learning becomes a mutual process of discovery, what others have referred to this as a movement from one voice to many voices (Kamya & Trimble, 2002; Morson & Emerson, 1990). Prehn (2025) proposes that to validate indigenous voices we must move past dominant deficit narratives and adopt a strengths-based approach rooted in indigenous worldviews and spirituality. Openness to others' knowledges and beliefs expands people's narratives and validates the strengths and spirit that reside within each individual and community.

## HOPE AND WITNESSING

Witnesses listen to people's evolving stories as they are told and retold over time. As narratives unfold, their plots are continuously constructed, deconstructed, and reimagined in ways that reflect growing awareness and reemergence of hope. Witnesses facilitate the thickening of stories by engaging clients in dialogue that elicits richer descriptions (White & Epston, 1990). New meanings become possible.

To achieve these ends, practitioners hold hope when clients are unable to carry it. Therapists calibrate when to infuse hope, thoughtfully balancing it with validating clients' pain. In essence, they work with clients to find meaning, purpose, and connection.

### SPIRITUALITY AS AN ETHIC OF CARE

To be a narrative practitioner is to participate in an ethic of care, described as a "relational stance" (Madsen, 2007), an "emotional posture" (Griffith & Griffith, 1992), or a "way of being in relationship with our fellow human beings, including how we think about them, talk with, act with, and respond to them" (Anderson, 1997, p. 94). In therapy, we invite trust from those we work with, recognizing the honor and responsibility such trust entails. We respond using thoughtful and caring approaches that recognize our shared humanity, and in some instances, we act to challenge injustices that clients have experienced. In many respects, the "notion of care is at the heart of ethical practice" (Reimer, 2017, p. 16).

Clients tell stories with spiritual import. These stories highlight purpose, connection, and a search for meaning. An ethic of care positions practitioners as unwavering allies, both culturally curious and humble, committed to collaboration and partnership. It prioritizes respectfulness and behaving humanely regardless of a person's social circumstances, problem, or readiness for change. An ethic of care is not only about "doing no harm" but also about enhancing well-being and improving quality of life in the quest for meaning, purpose, and connection.

In the next section, I describe my work listening to and supporting the spiritual narratives of immigrants and refugees. An important aspect of this practice was being anchored in my own spiritual narratives, or as described in Chapter 3, my co-centering stance (Beaudoin & Monk, 2024). This is no easy task. One might ask: How does one act upon such spiritual self-awareness? Once found, what is the best way to engage with clients' spirituality and what is its role in helping them construct meaning? And finally, where does practitioner–client synergy lie?

## The Life of Immigrants and Refugees

Although many immigrants come to the United States for economic and educational reasons, many have unwillingly been forced to flee their homelands under traumatic conditions. Many left lucrative jobs or steady employment in their home countries, only to find themselves unemployed or underemployed in their new host country. Family roles and power structures are significantly altered by relocation. Parents may work long hours, leaving little time and energy to care for their children, with few or no opportunities to pass on cultural traditions and values to their children. In addition, immigrants frequently have difficulties securing housing due to discrimination and lack of affordable housing.

Immigration laws and economic difficulties impede family members from joining relatives in the United States. Without the supportive presence of extended family, many are left feeling isolated and marginalized in a country they had hoped would embrace them. I should mention that while writing this book (during 2025), mass deportations by the federal government have caused shock waves of fear and uncertainty. Anti-immigrant sentiment and federal policies have exacerbated the plight of all immigrants regardless of their status. For too many, fears of deportation loom.

The immigration process causes significant cultural and psychosocial impacts in the lives of immigrants. "Relocation means leaving one world behind and entering into a new and unfamiliar culture" (Cohen Konrad, 2019, p. 369). Emotions associated with relocation are understandably mixed—immigrants must adapt attitudinally and behaviorally to entirely new environments. Fear, depression, and insecurity coexist with excitement and hope. Losses associated with language are especially salient. Language not only encompasses words but also their meanings that too often get lost in translation.

For those living in the United States acculturation to American ways leaves immigrant parents with profound feelings of regret as they watch their children reject ethnic cultural traditions and native language in favor of a world they do not understand. "Children typically acculturate more quickly to the language and behavioral norms of their new homeland. In some families, youth act as translators for their parents and other family members . . . " (Cohen Konrad, 2019, p. 372), creating tensions and intergenerational conflicts due to changes in family roles and positions of authority.

Losing contact with loved ones can instigate ruptures within families and cultures of origin. Family members become strangers to one another, leading to major relational strains and disappointments. Prolonged separation diminishes possibilities to share and sustain family history. One young man from Uganda told me about his desire to pass on to his children the cultural, spiritual, and religious beliefs of his homeland, including traditional rites of passage, but the structures necessary to support them did not exist in the United States. "My children will never be able to worship in the same way that my parents taught me," he lamented.

Escape from war-torn countries unfortunately does not guarantee immigrants' safety in the United States. Social inexperience often leaves them vulnerable to crime and in some cases to exploitation by the host culture. The 24-hour U.S. news cycle is another source of great distress. A 50-year-old man from the Democratic Republic of Congo, told of how he became plagued by nightmares of the killing fields triggered by constant replays of war and violence in the daily news. When he sought community and comfort at church, he was met with intense divisiveness reminiscent of the conflicts that he had fled. Like many immigrants, such experiences are not only disappointing but are felt as betrayal. He built an altar in his home and burned incense with his family, a ritual that helped him connect with ancestors and get through hard times. I have listened to my clients expand their stories as they connect to smells and scents.

Exploring spirituality and its connections to therapeutic healing is a two-way process. When we invite clients to explore their connections to spirituality, we must be willing to do likewise if we are to genuinely witness their stories. This is true regardless of one's religious affiliation, or belief system, or even a person's disregard for spirituality altogether. Reflexivity is essential to conduct effective and ethical practice. Fook and Gardner (2007) remind us that practitioners work best when they appreciate how their own biases, values, experience, and backgrounds, including how they relate to spirituality, affect practice efficacy. Attending to clients' narratives—whether grounded in spirituality, traditional religion, or alternative ritual practices—is integral to the *process* of healing.

## My Religious and Spiritual Beliefs

As a religious and spiritual being, I draw from my African beliefs. These African beliefs are rooted in natural and spiritual worlds and are experienced as both "instrumental and metaphysical" (Rivett & Street, 2001). As such, they serve as functional guides to day-to-day life and as a basis for pondering existential questions and the unknown. People pray to a supreme God, divinities, and community ancestors. They also invoke the natural world populated by spiritual beings that reside in the mountains, rivers, lakes, trees, rocks, and other natural environs. In some instances, they call upon the living dead, considered kind and helpful gods/spirits, who are perceived as protectors (Mbiti, 1990). These gods and spirits are held in reverence and are thought to preserve harmony between the human and spiritual worlds.

Altogether, spiritual entities comprise a system through which many Africans who practice or accept traditional religions make sense of their lives. Spirituality guides family structure, child-rearing practices, naming, and the life cycle. Among the Baganda of Uganda, the living dead are believed to dwell around homesteads, protecting the inhabitants from danger or evil spirits. Knowing that spiritual protection surrounds them provides individuals and families with comfort, connectedness, control, and a sense of belonging.

At various historical junctures, religious and spiritual practices have been threatened with elimination. European colonialism brought monotheistic religions, such as Christianity, to the African continent claiming that it was their aim to bring civilization and progress to uncivilized nations (Nunn, 2010). The perception of religious superiority rooted in colonial imperialism instigated significant tensions between African spiritual beliefs and monotheistic religious practices. The endurance of African spiritual beliefs today is a testimony to the resilience and determination of African people.

Bearing witness to spiritual stories obligates me to reflect upon and acknowledge how my spiritual values and beliefs intersect with my clinical practice and personal worldviews (Fook & Gardner, 2007). The act of sharing but not imposing my spiritual being is essential to my ethic of care. I believe it adds authenticity and efficacy to my therapeutic work and aids in building trust. I have been honored by my clients' willingness to name oppression rooted in historic enslavement and submission, especially when in the process of reauthoring their stories. It is important to note that I do not hold an anti-Christianity stance. Rather, I am opposed to religious and cultural practices imposed on indigenous people and cultures.

My own faith is rooted in African religious traditions that embrace the mystical powers of the universe. Understanding the legacies of colonialism and Christianity in Africa influence how I practice my religion and heighten my empathy for the many generations that struggled to maintain their spiritual integrity. I translate my belief in spiritual beings into a commitment to worship that sustains my sense of connection, purpose, and meaning. Worship through prayer centers me. It strengthens my relationship to self and deepens my connection to community. In some respects, I am aware of the mystical powers that surround me; in other ways I am not. One belief I hold firmly is the presence of the divine within my life, a presence that sustains harmony and order amid uncertainty. The crack in the window has come to symbolize the persistence of hope—evidence that light finds its way through what is broken.

## REVISITING MOT'S STORY

You may recall Mot's story from Chapter 2. A Sudanese immigrant, he was 17 at the time we worked together and had newly arrived in the United States. In retrospect, I've come to appreciate Mot's story in two distinctive ways: as one that is emblematic of the lives of many immigrants and refugees, and as a story that resonates with my own spiritual core.

Mot was one of a group of children who came to be known as the "lost boys" (a term they disliked, since they didn't think of themselves as lost). He belonged to the Sudanese Dinka tribe. At a very early age, due to imminent threat, he roamed the devastated

> war fields in Southern Sudan, crossing many rivers in fear of attack from warring groups and predatory animals. Too often he went without food. Mot finally crossed Northern Uganda into Kenya and settled into a refugee camp at Kakuma, Kenya, before finally being resettled in the United States through the United Nations Refugee Resettlement Program.
>
> In the United States, Mot was placed with a foster family. He was referred for therapy because of increasing behavioral problems at school, labeled by his teachers as "aggressive, angry, threatening, and uninterested," among other labels. For his part, Mot found his new peers to be disrespectful and suspicious of him. He described how one White girl had sprayed him with water while telling him to take a shower. These stories told of racism and palpable anti-immigrant sentiments. Mot began perceiving his dark skin to be "bad and offensive to others." This was new to his identity, something he hadn't experienced in his homeland. He blamed himself for this predicament.

When I met him, the young man was deeply troubled by larger questions. He asked himself, "Why did this happen to me?" "What happened to my brothers and sisters? "Why do brothers kill each other?" "Why did the gods do this to us?" "How can I forgive them as we have been taught by Deng [a spirit God in the indigenous spiritual tradition of the Dinka tribal group]?" He also wondered when he would finally belong.

Mot's questions are equally spiritual, psychological, and existential in nature. They speak to an unsettled relationship with God and a desperate search for purpose and life's meaning. His questions echo those of other refugee children who have witnessed atrocities and been wounded by violence, yet cannot find answers to such senselessness. Their trust in others was shaken, their sense of safety shattered. Their identities, too, had been disrupted as they struggled to discover who they were while living in a foreign land.

The migration process brings many forms of loss—of kin, community, identity, and a sense of belonging (Falicov, 2002). Separated from familiar people, places, and possessions, refugees and immigrants undergo long and difficult transitions. In their new environments, they must reshape who they are while adapting to unfamiliar customs and languages. They often encounter barriers in the host society that can leave them feeling lonely and disconnected. Encounters with racism and anti-immigration sentiment deepen their sense of exclusion. With such upheaval, many immigrants struggle with physical, emotional, and spiritual tolls of displacement.

Earlier in the chapter I referenced Rivett and Street's (2001) concept of "instrumental and metaphysical" spirituality. I have found this paradigm helpful in addressing spirituality with immigrants and refugees in therapy. The authors distinguish two methods of integrating spirituality into therapeutic work. Using an "instrumental" approach, the therapist focuses exclusively on a client's experience. They explore the influence of religion or spirituality—such as prayer, worship, and spiritual practices—on the client's life as a source of strength or distress.

The "metaphysical" approach invites interaction between client and therapist whereby the therapist participates as a fully embodied spiritual being with the client. This may mean being explicit with clients about the therapist's own journey and relationship with the spiritual world. This may include one's own intuitive knowledge that comes from realms beyond the material world.

Both the instrumental and the metaphysical tell important stories. Attention to spiritual resources aids in the development of alternative stories. For Mot, prayer and metaphor were influential in his healing, as they were in my own. Mot was able to draw from familiar spiritual beliefs and practices to name his experiences. Metaphor functioned as a metaphysical medium to access the spiritual presence. Integration of prayer and metaphor into therapeutic narratives is something I've come to greatly appreciate, as illustrated in my sessions with Mot.

## Prayer as a Form of Communion and Healing

Mot deeply values prayers and rituals, using them to express faith and to guide his life as a religious person. Raised a Christian, he found ways to integrate African traditional prayer into his family's beliefs and practices. This occurred through repetitive prayer, recitation, and chanting, which helped him become centered when overwhelmed by painful wartime memories. Repeating certain words and phrases, akin to mantras, provided comfort. He told me that prayer brings about personal transformation, leading to new ways of self-understanding and openness to new possibilities.

Mot also experienced the protective power of prayer. In his view, it shielded him from evil and misfortune while simultaneously strengthening his determination to overcome life's difficulties. At other times, prayer allowed Mot to acknowledge vulnerability and surrender to something larger than himself. Surrendering full control opened opportunities for us to explore his inner life, the psychological and existential implications of his experiences, and to consider growth, healing, and change. The exchange below illustrates his own relationship to prayer:

MOT: Sometimes, I pray alone. Sometimes, I pray with my family, alive or dead.

THERAPIST: Tell me about it.

MOT: I carry them with me. They are always with me. They remind me where I came from. They remind me of my own escape.

Hence, prayer for Mot was metaphysical as well as spiritual. When praying, he could feel close to those he left behind and to those he lost. In many ways, prayer served to spiritually hold the complex stories of his life. In terms of practice, he prayed both out loud and in silence. In vocal prayer, he openly prayed for loved ones, using naming and remembrance to honor them and weave their stories into his own. In silent prayer, he imagined himself sitting in the presence, stillness, and reverence of the divine, trying to make sense of surviving the ordeal.

Survivor guilt is one among many psychological injuries that accompany the immigrant and refugee experience, often leading to disconnection and crises of faith. Mot spoke of "those people who lied to me," describing how some people exploited his vulnerability in the guise of offering shelter. The betrayal left him with a deep sense of mistrust and the painful conviction that genuine care might be an illusion. In that state of disillusionment, even his faith wavered, and he began to question whether God could still be trusted.

When I sat with Mot, I humbly acknowledged that I did not know what to say and did not have the answers. It turned out that me admitting to not knowing forged connection with Mot rather than disappointed him. His mistrust of others, and perhaps of God, was justified. I was there to listen and validate his existential wonder and angst. Together, we used narrative practice to deconstruct deficit-saturated stories, exploring the strengths he and the other "lost boys" used to survive the nearly unsurvivable.

The value of prayer for health, well-being, and healing for people facing adversity has been well documented across religions and cultures (Dossey, 1993; Koenig et al., 2001; Walsh, 2008). Dossey suggests that prayers originating from any faith have a positive impact, reducing depression, anxiety, and strengthening one's belief in possibility. I have found this to be the case with the refugees and immigrants I have known. Many who have met with distrust and tragedy do not question God. Rather their unequivocal faith in a caring and loving God helps them manage life's difficulties and maintain hopefulness despite extraordinary adversity.

Mot vacillated between doubt and exceptional faith. He recounted:

> Sometimes, we crossed the same river two or three times to escape being noticed by the enemy. We kept running. We did not know who we were running away from. We could not trust anyone. It was very scary. Some of the children belonged to the enemy and they reported on us. We were too scared to sleep at night. We wondered what would happen to us. We hated them and I suppose they hated us. We hoped God who created all of us would save us from danger. And God did!

Working with Mot, I used Beaudoin's (2005) narrative therapy reauthoring map. Beaudoin proposes "a theoretical map that details a list of explicit clinical micro-practices bringing forth experiences of agency

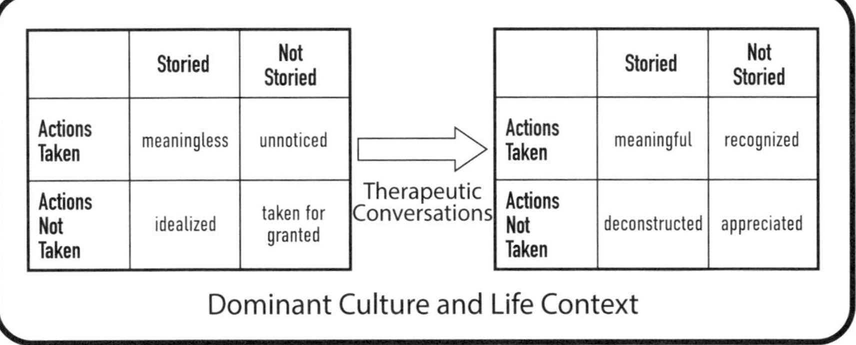


**Figure 9.1** Therapeutic Conversations Foster Reauthoring of Choice and Agency Within the Client's Story of the Trauma

*Reprinted with permission of Guilford Publications from "Agency and choice in the face of trauma: A narrative therapy map," Beaudoin, M. N., Journal of Systemic Therapies, 24(4), (2005); permission conveyed through Copyright Clearance Center, Inc.*

and choice" (p. 33). The map explores obstacles that disrupt meaning making and offers recommendations to mitigate them in clinical practice. She identifies four ways to explore clients' agency, choice, and meaning making:

1. *Actions taken and storied* as meaningless or unhelpful are rendered meaningful.
2. *Actions taken and not storied* are recognized.
3. *Actions not taken and storied* as ideal are deconstructed.
4. *Actions not taken and not storied* are noticed and appreciated.

Beaudoin (2005) notes that these positions are more "likely to make visible their actual ability to first, generate options; second, choose options that are congruent with their values; and third, engage in these actions in ways that are more successful than initially storied" (p. 34). Using a reauthoring map, my conversation with Mot went like this:

THERAPIST: I am very impressed you had to cross the same river two or three times to escape being noticed by the enemy. Where did you find the energy to do that?

MOT: We just had to do it. There was no other way out.

THERAPIST: How did you do that?
MOT: (*shrugs shoulders*)

I noted that Mot minimized the tremendous effort that went into his escape. Not everyone can garner the energy to act under such circumstances. I hoped he could recognize the unique insights and abilities he brought to bear in those dire moments and the major obstacles he had to overcome to escape. It was important to elevate the choices he made in those moments:

THERAPIST: What was the hardest thing about this moment?
MOT: I felt trapped. We did not know who we were running away from. We could not trust anyone. It was very scary.
THERAPIST: Did feeling trapped and scared make it harder even to think? What is it that allowed you to overcome those feelings in that dire moment?
MOT: I trusted in God who would save me from all my fears and burdens.

Mot's faith was thus an internal resource, something that helped him survive. However, I felt it important that he also acknowledge the inner resources and personal attributes that he himself had brought to this harrowing situation. I engaged him about these abilities:

THERAPIST: I am curious, how did you cross the river? What did you have to do?
MOT: I had to swim across the river.
THERAPIST: Had you learned to swim before?
MOT: Yes, I knew how to swim but my swimming had never been put to the test. I feared less for drowning. I was more afraid I was going to be eaten alive by crocodiles in that river. I prayed all the way.

Mot's prayer as well as his imagination brought him clarity and calm:

THERAPIST: What happened for you in those moments?

MOT: I prayed. I have never prayed as hard. At times, I imagine I was swallowed up by a crocodile. I was lying in its belly. I just continued praying. I felt calm. I knew I had to do it.

Mot's belief in prayer helped him rise above the dangers before him. It propelled his courage and determination to survive. Heiler (cited in Shorter, 1975) proposed that prayer is an awakening into one's consciousness that both transcends and reinterprets human experience. Similarly, Shorter describes recurring themes in African prayer, one of which is divine governance: a belief in God's master plan that both challenges and protects. Mot's words echo this both/and paradox. He worried about a possible crocodile attack while simultaneously maintaining a tenacious hope that God would provide and protect. For Mot, prayer offered a spiritual narrative to embrace that paradox.

As our work continued, Mot began to speak of the sense of interconnectedness he felt through prayer. This spiritual practice helped to diminish his loneliness, isolation, and mistrust. He became more relational and involved in his community, gaining meaning and purpose from interactions that are part of building a new life. Prayer served as rite of passage and transitional object marking and celebrating moments of renewal.

## Metaphors as Narratives of Healing

Many cultural groups and indigenous traditions use metaphors as a means of communication. Among immigrant and refugee groups, metaphoric images are used to explain reality and mystery. Babits (2001) describes metaphor as holding "the inner edge of possibility" (p. 22). Metaphors suggest new and varied ways of understanding experience while also leaving a lot open to interpretation. Most importantly, metaphors help to engage new narratives in people's lives, thus expanding possibilities. They provide new windows of understanding.

Meaning making is crucial to cultivating resilience and achieving recovery, particularly in the wake of trauma and loss (Walsh, 2007). Meaning making using metaphor helps people acquire a sense of coherence in the service of adaption after tragedy (Walsh, 2008). Gaining new perspectives on senseless atrocities, unbearable suffering, and overwhelming struggles is critical to translating such experiences into comprehensible, manageable, and meaningful challenges while never minimizing them.

Metaphors transcend polarized "either/or" dichotomies. They offer ways to build capacity and find both/and solutions to complex personal, familial, social, and transformational experiences (Falicov, 2002). For example, forging a bicultural identity with roots in two worlds—the homeland of origin and the new nation destined to become home—fosters adaptation and well-being for many immigrants and refugees.

Metaphors contribute to novel and expansive narratives that take into consideration the many worlds we inhabit. In my work with Mot, as with many others, metaphors offered a window of understanding into the plight of life and the journey ahead. For Mot, river metaphors embody how he held firm even when things seemed impossible. Frequently, he used the metaphor "a river flowing with joy" to describe his hopes and wishes. Alternatively, he spoke of the "angry rivers" that nearly cost him his life:

> MOT: Most of these rivers were furiously angry at us. They swept everything that came our way. They carried off my cousin. We never saw him again. I would like to swim in a new river that flows with joy . . .

Together we explored the river metaphor, seeking to expand its imagery. I asked: "What does the river give to you?" "What has it taken away?" "How and when is it soothing?" While Mot recognized the turbulence of the river, he also noticed its ability to calm. Through metaphor, he could acknowledge goodness alongside tragedy, helping him manage moments of frustration and appreciate the balance between life's joys and challenges.

The young man eventually expanded the river metaphor to address the exigencies of life in the United States. He described adaptation to American culture as a "long river with winding twists and turns. Sometimes, I like them, sometimes, I hate them." When things did not go well at school, or in his foster family, or community, Mot talked about the "river letting him down." Meanwhile, "drinking from the river fountain" was how he expressed his pursuit of agency and courage. His life was a "river that still flows in many different directions."

You might be wondering, how can the river metaphor open one's vision for healing? Water is a life-giving and life-saving force. Mot described how he walked miles in his home village to fetch water. He remembered how the river provided a habitat for fish that his tribal group ate. The waters of the Nile River irrigated his family's crops and farms. Ultimately, Mot used the river metaphor to connect to sustenance, growth, possibility, and hope.

At one point I asked Mot if he could recall inspiring family words of wisdom or encouragement. He recalled a proverb: *An elephant never fails to carry its tusks*, which refers to never letting go of the task at hand. I have since used this metaphor many times to connect to other clients' narratives of survival and resilience. It is an invitation to "drink from the river fountain" when strength and fortitude are needed.

The rich imagery my clients have brought to the therapy space resonate with my core beliefs and the ways in which I express them. Such empathic synergy has helped me build trust and authentic bidirectional understanding with clients. I have come to the realization that it is not only the sharing of metaphor that brings such therapeutic connection but also the very experiences that underlie them.

In Chapter 1 I shared the story of the violent assault on my father and how he escaped through a window and wasn't seen again for years. I was a 10-year-old boy whose life abruptly changed when brought face-to-face with political violence. Over the years, what was once a literal crack became a metaphor for hope. "A crack in the window" was the expression that held the potential for reconnection and healing. My own use of metaphor to describe violence, loss, and transition enhances my ability to appreciate what so many immigrants and refugees in the United States have witnessed and survived.

Narrative practice offers a wide range of avenues to explore and expand the metaphors in people's lives to aid the healing process. Metaphors enrich storytelling by offering people ways to speak about trauma, tragedy, survival, and resilience without having to repeatedly relive details of the horrific experiences people have suffered. They also allow for multivarious communication. For example: a river flowing, a crack in the window, or the tenacity of elephants never losing their tusks are concepts that transcend specific communication. Instead, they speak to our shared humanity, spirituality, and hopes for a better future.

## Intersection of Therapist's Story With Client Stories

As therapists, our own stories matter. It's natural that clients' stories activate our own spiritual beliefs, metaphors, and practices. These conversations are inescapably metaphysical, exploring many existential questions that cannot be answered (Rivett & Stret, 2001). They are also intrinsically subjective, reminding us that therapeutic work is never neutral. We are present in the stories people tell us. How we weave our own stories into the work we do with clients matters as well. The "crack in the window" metaphor became an important marker in my life and signaled my family's rite of passage, forcing us to reevaluate our lives within the context of our plight. It opened us to a place we had never been, bringing with it many losses and new possibilities.

My work with African immigrants and refugees has been one of *faithful companioning* and *faithful hoping*. Together we seek to locate the "inner edge of possibility" (Babits, 2001) that grounds our work. Therapy is a sacred space where clients can bravely acknowledge and regard their own discomforting deficit-based stories as necessary for growth and change. They are also safe spaces where pain, sorrow, and anger are met with compassion and care. The therapist's faithful companioning and hope are conduits for clients to journey into new territories. This has brought immense meaning to my work.

## Conclusion

Spirituality, storytelling, and healing are deeply interrelated. Attending to the meaning of spirituality in clients' lives affirms their dignity and worth, acknowledges their search for purpose, and reinforces their capacity for choice and agency. It also highlights the centrality of relational connection in the therapeutic process. In my experience, spirituality can activate and sustain strength-based narratives. Bearing witness to clients' spiritual stories honors their efforts to reestablish meaning and coherence in life through therapy.

Spirituality is as deeply personal as it is metaphysical. If practitioners ask clients to delve into their spirituality, we need to do likewise. Narrative practice acknowledges that therapists are not objective. Awareness of one's subjectivity requires continuous reflection on how our own backgrounds, experiences, and spiritual perceptions influence our work. We owe this to our clients as they courageously allow us to enter their worlds. As they expose their most vulnerable selves, we cocreate sacred spaces where they can pursue their healing journeys.

CHAPTER 10

# Engaging the Story of Social Identities

This chapter considers narrative practice in the context of social identities. Clients of all social identities seek therapy. Their stories reveal personal struggles with family, romantic partners, and colleagues as well as challenges related to sexual orientation, sexual expression, and gender identity. For many, broader social issues populate their narratives, including impacts of discrimination, social exclusion, and other systemic injustices. In the words of Audre Lorde (2015), "There is no such a thing as a single-issue struggle because we do not live single-issue lives" (p. 138).

Social identities are personal and interactional and thus exist in relationship to others. People possess multiple identities: their individual self; their relational self, which may include being a spouse, partner, parent, friend, or relative; and a professional self, among other aspects of personhood that people inhabit. Whether marginalized, privileged, intersectional, or shades in between, identities constantly evolve, responsive to stories that are told or assumed about them. They are deconstructed and reconstructed, influenced by narratives, both good and bad. And because we are social beings, they are affected by systemic and structural messages, including those that foster discriminatory, misinformed, and oppressive stories. Mulvale (2021) contends that assumption and misinformation about any person or population fosters inequality, domination, and oppression, including "patriarchal assumptions about and treatment of women; heterosexist oppression of queer and non-binary people" (p. 38). All identity stories affect all other identity stories. This is true across the life span and in interpersonal, cultural, and systemic domains where social identities form and exist.

### THE CASE OF TAMARA

Tamara's story illustrates the complexity of identity and its multivariate impacts. Tamara was both reflective and critically curious about the many ways she had been affected by her identities. When we first met she was 29 and identified as a queer woman using she/they pronouns. She described her relational life as embedded in two related stories. One was her parents' divorce. The other was her own engagement. Her parents met in their early 20s, got married in their mid-20s, and raised three children before divorcing after 32 years of marriage. Tamara remembers a mostly happy childhood. She felt loved by both her mother and her father. However, her parents' marriage was at the same time a story about contention, high conflict, palpable stress, and family tension that worsened over the years.

## Community and Cultural Expectations

Tamara would agree that her parents' marriage conformed with the cultural norms and community values of the times. They identified as a monogamous, married heterosexual partnership. They followed traditional social expectations, having children and becoming a family. They practiced traditional gender roles: Her mother took on household responsibilities and her father worked and earned household income. Looking back, Tamara would describe her parents' roles as unequal in both distribution and power.

In our sessions Tamara often reflected on her parents' marriage and divorce. It had challenged the dominant story that a marriage is a lifelong partnership, and that staying together and "making it work" is almost always the preferred choice. While her mother had found some social support, she also encountered stigma and social criticism for being the party to end the relationship. Her father faced less social pressure, in part because the divorce was not his choice and also because of the gendered perception that women were responsible for keeping families together, prioritizing others over themselves. These entrenched cultural narratives were reinforced and exerted power over the stories Tamara internalized about her parents, their divorce, and the tenuousness of intimacy and trust in relationship.

Now engaged to be married, Tamara found that her same-sex relationship and engagement faced different but parallel critical judgment. Like her parents' divorce, Tamara's marriage defied social norms and cultural expectations. She met her fiancée in her early 20s, and they formed a monogamous relationship. Now in their late 20s, Tamara and her partner were engaged to be married. The story of her relationship was challenged by cultural standards that were opposed to gay marriage and to the overall gay/lesbian "lifestyle."

In many ways, Tamara was unprepared for the responses she got to her relationship. She grew up in a household that was predominantly silent and uninformed about LGBTQ+ identities, culture, and history but generally accepting. She had gay uncles who were accepted by the family, but their sexual orientation was never mentioned. Her family's overriding beliefs and expectations of marriage were strongly aligned with cultural and gendered ideals of marriage and Tamara's marriage did not fit into this mold.

### Holding the Edge of Possibility Through Metaphors

As we've discussed throughout the book, metaphors are essential narrative tools for expressing difficult-to-describe thoughts, experiences, and feelings. They are rich with imagery, both illustrative and hyperbolic, able to exaggerate a characteristic or action, or express a complex idea. In therapeutic conversations, metaphors offer therapists opportunities to enter clients' inner and sometimes previously silenced worlds. Clients will use metaphors to describe their lives. Like Mot, Tamara found metaphor useful to reflect upon her social identities. Similar to Mot's river metaphor, Tamara saw her life as a "map with many roads and paths":

> A metaphor that encapsulates this for me is that a map was laid out before me with many roads and paths, some outlined more boldly than others. All of them pointed toward a destination of success that looked like cisgender, heterosexual partnership, and marriage, alongside career satisfaction and success.

Asked what all this means, Tamara launched into an insightful and critical dialogue about her social identities, heaping one metaphor upon another:

> THERAPIST: Tell me more about this metaphor.
>
> TAMARA: If you looked closely, you could see that other people might chart their own path through a forest or across an ocean. Perhaps there was a gay uncle or two dwelling in the unmarked territories of liberal acceptance.
>
> THERAPIST: What was it like for you?
>
> TAMARA: There were no marked paths that could take me in a different direction. The ultimate destination of cisgender, heterosexual partnership and marriage was synonymous with happiness, and it occluded possibilities of both unhappiness in heterosexual marriage, as well as happiness in other types of relationships and other paths of life.

I listened attentively as Tamara spoke about how her words and images helped explain the challenges she now faced. They also illustrated the intersectionality of her social identities and their heterogenous elements. Her use of metaphor as well as her willingness to share their meaning with me was indicative of her commitment to explore problem-saturated narratives in the trusting space we had formed together.

Stories are fueled, supported, and often encumbered by larger stories.

I asked Tamara what fueled the direction of her story, exploring them in safe increments:

THERAPIST: What do you think supported these ideas?

TAMARA: It was this discourse and the systemic oppression of cisheteronormativity that delayed me in knowing and accepting both my sexual orientation and my gender identity. When I told my parents that I was attracted to women, as a young adult in college, their reactions revealed broader cultural discourses that stem from systemic oppression of queer identities.

THERAPIST: What did they say?

TAMARA: My mother told me that it is natural to "experiment," a sentiment with which she probably intended to convey support. Yet her words told me that she either thought or hoped that this attraction was only experimental, a temporary phase to be outgrown.

THERAPIST: How do you understand this? How did she hear you out?

TAMARA: At the time, I had come out as bisexual, and one of her first questions for me was whether this meant I could still end up with a man. This question and her relief when I reluctantly said "yes" told me that she valued heterosexual pairings over queer ones, and that she did not care to celebrate my identity but rather wanted to hold out hope that the narrative she had envisioned for my life might still have a chance of coming true.

THERAPIST: How did you counter her story and begin writing your story?

With this question, Tamara paused, looking pensive. She seemed tentative, appeared tearful, and yet I could tell that there was something she desperately wanted to reveal:

TAMARA: Over time, through immersing myself in queer community, I found the strength and bravery to reauthor my story.

THERAPIST: Hmm . . . to reauthor your story?

TAMARA: Yes . . . what I initially saw as failure to be heterosexual and to have the "normal" and "correct" type of desire and relationships, I slowly came to understand instead as a journey of bravery, curiosity, discovery, self-acceptance, and connection with community.

THERAPIST: A journey . . . ?

TAMARA: I was able to thicken the description of who I was both as an individual and in relationship to others.

Tamara went on to describe her newfound voice that rejected discriminatory challenges in favor of self-love and embodiment of her social identity:

TAMARA: This enabled me to find a deeper level of self-love and love for a new community.

THERAPIST: Love for a new community?

TAMARA: It was because of community and hearing other people's narratives of queerness, both in media and from friends and community members, that I was able to continue learning about myself and gather the courage to eventually come out as a lesbian and a nonbinary person.

Growing up Tamara was told that there were only two genders, male and female, and that marriage required the presence of both. She was not exposed to stories about or from LGBTQ+ people. Neither was she aware of the pervasiveness of transphobia and cisnormativity in dominant culture. Gay, lesbian, and transgender people were portrayed to her as the butt of jokes or as serial killers in horror films and detective stories. Stories about them were invariably tinged with shock, disgust, and disenfranchisement. Transgressions against LGBTQ+ individuals were not included in the history books she read.

Tamara's emerging identity story radically broke through stereotypes and cultural denial. She recognized how deeply her identity and self-worth were negatively influenced by bias, hatred, and socially constructed mythologies about gay, lesbian, transgender, and nonbinary people and their communities. They were also born of silence and the invisibility of stories that spoke of nonheterosexual life and love. Tamara's breakthrough resulted in re-storying her feelings of failure and coming to reframe her life as a queer woman "as a journey of bravery, curiosity, discovery, self-acceptance, and connection with community."

Now more than ever, mental health practitioners must recognize the significance of social identities and the pervasive yet often invisible role of systemic oppression in shaping understandings of gender and power. These forces are deeply entangled with Western cisheteropatriarchy, influencing both individual experiences and broader societal structures. LaSala and Goldblatt Hyatt (2019) note:

> the trans-gender community exists within a larger context of prejudice, gender bias, racism, classism, and unequal access to health care. Because clinical social work practice often focuses on the intersection of individual and societal issues, clinicians must be especially informed regarding the principles of autonomy, nonmaleficence, beneficence, and justice . . . (p. 504)

Mental health practitioners are increasingly providing clinical care for transgender clients, charged with doing assessments that open access to medical treatments for gender-affirming care. Reamer (2014) cautions that clinical practitioners must be critically reflective, aware of beliefs, biases, and conflicts of faith that could impede their objectivity in working with this population. As such, those offering services to LGBTQ+ individuals can find themselves having to manage their own issues as well as being caught in the conundrum that Tamara describes—navigating the very systems they seek to challenge.

One might ask: "What purpose does a binary gender system serve?" It undoubtedly upholds capitalism and patriarchy. Binary gender supports capitalism by legitimizing and maintaining hierarchy and the unequal distribution of power. It reinforces rigid social roles, preventing women, gay, lesbian, and transgender individuals from disrupting patriarchal structures while also constraining society's collective imagination of identity both in terms of being and becoming.

Transgender people, and those who fall outside of cultural gender norms, have existed throughout time and across global cultures (Independent Television Service, 2023). However, in today's world rigid adherence to binary gender identities seems to be on the rise as is discrimination against gender-nonconforming people. Dismantling systemic transphobia, cisheteropatriarchy, and rigid gender expectations would undoubtably be liberating and in effect, would do no foreseeable harm. However, dominant cultural stories imply a potential threat to dismantling systemic transphobia, cisheteropatriarchy, and anti-gay/lesbian sentiments, seeing them as destabilizing, overturning zealously held belief systems, and upsetting "the way things have always been."

People have the right to follow cultural scripts—indeed, they offer security to those who seek to follow expected behaviors. But they should never be imposed at the expense of others whose social identities and choices fall outside those expectations. When that happens, it becomes a toxic form of oppression. Tamara's journey aimed to stand up against oppressive cultural scripts, and to compose new ones that aligned with her identity and values.

## Multiple Stories Coexisting

We have spoken many times of how single stories rarely sufficiently explain the human condition, especially when describing complex social issues. It is most often the case that multiple stories, which may all be true to one degree or another, coexist, overlap, or intertwine. Narrative practices foster the creation of thicker stories that embrace complexity, struggle, and resilience.

A complex and sometimes contentious social issue that illustrates multiple true, yet conflicting stories is marriage equality in the United States. In 2015 the U.S. Supreme Court decision in *Obergefell v. Hodges* (National Constitution Center, 2015) ruled that all states must recognize and allow same-sex marriage. This landmark ruling was a major social justice victory for the LGBTQ+ rights movement. Same-sex marriage, an institution aligned with existing social norms, was recognized by the courts as a legitimate and legal union but not necessarily accepted by those who opposed it for religious or cultural reasons. Same-sex couples were allotted the same rights to be married as heterosexual couples.

Parallel to marriage equality for same-sex marriage is the story of unjust influence, inequality, and lack of choice for people with disabilities. Many people with disabilities face an unjust choice between marriage, an institution that brings ritual, happiness, legal protections, and financial benefits, and the life-saving assistance they receive through Social Security Disability Insurance (SSDI). Due to the marriage penalty embedded in SSDI policy, people with disabilities may lose their benefits if they marry (Luterman, 2023). Until these ableist policies are repealed, Americans with disabilities, regardless of gender or sexual identity, do not experience marriage equality. The marriage equality narrative becomes even more complexified when LGBTQ+ and disability identities coexist.

The argument that LGBTQ+ Americans have won the battle for marriage equality is appealing but misleading. It overlooks ongoing challenges to marriage equality for LGBTQ+ individuals living with disabilities as well as for people with disabilities of all identities. It fails to account for persistent and systemic homophobia and transphobia as well as for implicit biases toward people with disabilities rooted in perceptions that they are of less value to society than those who are fully "able" (Huang et al., 2023). These discriminatory attitudes and behaviors tell complicated and multifaceted stories about marriage equality that must be reconciled if true equality is to be achieved.

Systemic forms of oppression, such as racism, sexism, and classism, among others, coexist in the broader stories of human rights. They live in housing projects and corrections facilities, where LGBTQ+ people and those with disabilities are rejected, exploited, and their safety is often at stake. The story of marriage equality is a partial story. Like many other social and cultural narratives, it erases rich and powerful histories of people, movements, and continued struggles for equality and liberation. In our practices we are morally obligated to recognize and honor the coexistence that underlie our clients' narratives. If we are educators, we are similarly compelled to teach the history of underrepresented populations and inspire new generations to imagine fresh narratives and possibilities for their own futures.

Tamara's story of discovery is not unique. And while she faced marginalization as a queer woman, she also recognized that her overall experience was shaped by race and class privilege. She was both marginalized and protected: marginalized due to systemic oppression of LGBTQ+ people, privileged because of her social identities as a White, middle class, educated, able woman, and a U.S. citizen by birth. Tamara also had many sources of support in her life, including meaningful and reliable relationships and a community that helped her build and strengthen her resilience.

Tamara came to understand her life as a tapestry of many stories, micro-identities, perspectives, and biases. Rather than setting these aside, she has found a greater sense of authenticity from accepting them all as part of her rich and complicated identity. She no longer rejects aspects of herself but rather acknowledges that we all navigate the world through unique and variable personal histories that shape our behaviors, attitudes, and experiences. Such understanding allows Tamara to be meaningfully present in her relationships.

### POLYAMORY: ONE WOMAN'S STRUGGLE TO FIND ACCEPTANCE

Like Tamara, Lianne's story tells of a journey to embrace social identity. Her life unfolded from an unforeseen rupture—an experience born of rejection and deep emotional disruption.

Nothing could have prepared Lianne for the abrupt termination of her 2-year marriage. She learned of her husband's intention to file for divorce from a text message she received when driving home. She barely averted getting into an accident as she tried to make sense of this sudden turn of events. Lianne recognized that she and her husband had been drifting apart. They argued about having little time together and their diminishing sexual intimacy. Lianne was bitter about their growing disconnection.

Her husband, too, cited many resentments. In the end, and to Lianne's dismay, the couple divorced.

Lianne actively sought new connections after the divorce. She tried dating but nothing seemed to work out. Lianne began questioning to whom she was attracted: men, women, or both. She was unsure what she was seeking in intimate relationships. This quandary led to a deep depression that eventually brought Lianne to therapy.

Lianne had researched polyamory, the practice of having multiple intimate consenting partners at any given time and found it to be intriguing. She began engaging in polyamorous relationships, which to her delight she found satisfying. While Lianne was pleased with her discovery, she struggled with how to explain her newfound relationships to her family that were still coming to terms with the divorce. What would she tell them?

Lianne's family did not take the news of her polyamorous relationships well. They could not understand or respect her choice, and their disapproval led to a disruption in communication, something that exacerbated Lianne's already vulnerable emotional state.

To address the family disconnection, we decided to invite Lianne's parents to one of her therapy sessions to "hash it all out." To her astonishment, they accepted the invitation. At the session, both Lianne and her parents were cordial toward each other. Her parents expressed their concerns about polyamory, especially how they were going to announce the news to family members and friends. Lianne desperately asked for their acceptance. She told them she was finally feeling "a sense of calm." Her parents reassured her of their love.

A week later, I checked in with Lianne. As it happened, the outcome of the session was not what Lianne had hoped for:

THERAPIST: How have things been going since our last meeting?

LIANNE: I don't know. Just, I just can't get over my parents, you know? I really thought that things were going to go better after the session. And now my parents don't even want to talk about it at all. It's like it never even happened.

THERAPIST: So, since we met, you haven't talked about polyamory at all?

LIANNE: No. No. Now, things just feel weird. Like, I feel like they're not talking to me at all, like they're embarrassed of me or—I don't know. I feel like they came into the session thinking that I was going to change when I really wanted them to accept me. Either I am the problem, or they see everything around me as a problem.

Lianne's wish for her family's acceptance did not come to fruition. Instead, she was feeling like she was the problem. Lianne and I had previously worked on deconstructing her problem-saturated stories with the goal of expanding her self-perceptions and acceptance. This included accepting herself as polyamorous and rejecting internal body shaming that resulted from externally generated messages about her large body size. In therapy, pathologizing gazes related to fatphobia and polyamory were debunked. In the following dialogue we sought to identify times when Lianne had successfully explained aspects of herself to others:

THERAPIST: It seems like they really see polyamory as a problem.

LIANNE: I feel like that's how most people see it. And I thought that especially my parents could see it for what I see it as and try to understand me.

THERAPIST: Are there times in the past where you feel like you have had to explain something to them or sort of get them to understand a part of you?

LIANNE: Yeah, I guess so. And I guess they're not the most understanding people. But like when I was with Gary, and Gail, and now Jim . . . I guess—I don't know. They still don't understand what happened there and they just, they never really wanted to comfort me. They just, they were just judging it.

THERAPIST: What do you think it is about Gail and that

relationship and now your relationship with Jim that is difficult for your parents to understand?

LIANNE: I think they just have their own version of what's normal, society's version of normal, and they can't stand to think that their daughter is anything but that. And I don't know, I guess, I mean, I'm still me. I'm still their daughter, and maybe it makes them uncomfortable to reflect on their own relationship that way. I don't know. I mean, I don't see why they can't just try and see it my way and see what's good about it.

THERAPIST: Yeah. You mentioned the good things. What are the things that you've enjoyed about being you, and what has that sort of brought for your relationship, and brought for you personally in terms of the good parts?

LIANNE: It's given me a chance to explore who I really am. I mean, I felt really lost after Gary left and I didn't know who I was, and I really didn't like myself. And I mean, I still don't like myself, but I feel like I'm trying to grow. And I don't know, this is giving me a chance to be with different people and find out more about myself. (*pauses, sighs*) And Jim is just amazing, and I feel like he really sees me for who I am in a way that Gary didn't, and my parents don't. And he's just—he is who he says he is and he's true to himself and to me. And I just don't feel pressured or like I'm put into a box or anything like that. And it's—I feel like I can just express myself being poly.

THERAPIST: Sounds like you feel like now you can be your true self, that you're becoming more of your true self.

LIANNE: Yeah.

THERAPIST: Yeah. And your parents' reaction to that was hurtful and sort of a rejection in some ways.

LIANNE: Yeah. That's why it hurts, because I feel like this could be a good thing for me. And I don't—I don't know why they wouldn't want the best for me. It just feels, it feels really selfish of them.

THERAPIST: Yeah. So, you feel that they're being selfish in telling you that they don't want you to explore this part of yourself or to be poly?

LIANNE: Yeah. And I just feel like they're making it all about them. And that's how I felt during our session. Like the way that they were talking about it, they were just talking about themselves when it's really—I mean, this is about me.

THERAPIST: In the sort of history and story of your family, has that been the case where you feel that your parents sort of take on aspects of you into themselves and feel that what's going on with you is a reflection of them?

LIANNE: Yeah, I guess so.

THERAPIST: Okay.

LIANNE: And that's why I think it's about them protecting their image to their friends and our family. My mom was talking about seeing it on Facebook. I mean, she's just—she's so self-conscious about it. And now I feel like things are weird with the family and I'm scared to go to family events. And I don't want to be the odd one out. I don't want to be seen as weird just because I'm being myself.

THERAPIST: They feel uncomfortable, or you feel uncomfortable?

LIANNE: I guess it's both, because I can feel that they're uncomfortable and that makes me feel uncomfortable. Because now I feel like I'm supposed to be hiding something about myself to make them feel okay, which doesn't really feel fair.

THERAPIST: What about in your other relationships, friendships, or at work, do you feel like you must hide that part of yourself as well or—I know with all things like with your bisexuality coming out, it's like a lifelong process, right? Is this something that you feel like you're able to be out with in other places outside of your relationship with Jim or your other partners?

LIANNE: Somewhat. I think I'm really trying to figure it out. I want to have more confidence, and that's—it's really something that I struggle with. And you know I struggle with my body and the way that I feel and the way that people see me, and this is just another layer of that.

Lianne's work to reframe her coexisting identities, as both polyamorous and a larger-bodied woman, was an uphill battle against cultural judgment and disapproval. In our conversations she wrestled to move past negative and blaming labels reclaiming "fat" as a self-descriptor rather than an insult. Being open, however, was a risk that Lianne was understandably reluctant to take. Her experiences had built a legacy of mistrust. Therapy sought to help Lianne locate times she felt understood:

LIANNE: (*takes a big sigh . . . and continues*) And I feel like my first step was being open with my parents, and they just really squashed it. And now I feel kind of scared to tell other people. I don't know. I mean, I don't know if they're telling their friends and our family and I just—I haven't really told too many people. Their opinion of me was, I guess, the most important, because I think I seek their approval first. And now I just feel like—I feel like people judge everybody who's poly because they don't get it. They can't imagine themselves doing it.

THERAPIST: Yeah. So.

LIANNE: In society there's sort of this idea that people are supposed to have slender ideal bodies . . . that people are meant to be monogamous and that not being monogamous is like infidelity, right? I think that's sort of what most people think of when they think of multiple partners, that that's infidelity. (*pauses . . .* ) Yeah, exactly. And I mean, that's just—that's not what it is for me or I know for Jim. And it just feels like it's impossible to explain my side. And I don't know, Jim was the one who really opened me up to this idea. And I was really; I am open to it. I was open to it then and it doesn't mean there aren't difficult aspects of it and I'm still learning and trying, and I just—I need a support system.

THERAPIST: Yeah. Who is there for you?

LIANNE: Jim is supportive. He's great, but I can't have just him. And with him and him sleeping with Julie and—who am I supposed to talk about that with? I can't talk to him about that because that was the whole problem. And now my parents are just going to judge me and judge Jim, and I don't want that.

THERAPIST: You mentioned Julie. I don't think I've heard her name before.

LIANNE: Julie. Jim slept with Julie and that's, I mean, that's fine. I don't have a problem with that. I know that he has other partners, but he didn't tell me, and I found out months later. Just makes me feel insecure, because . . .

THERAPIST: It's an insecurity that he didn't tell you or how is it different from the other partners he's had? Do you feel insecure about him and his wife or anything like that?

LIANNE: Yeah, it's that he didn't tell me. And I guess I still feel a little anxious about him and his wife, but I get it. We're still working things out, and he's still working things out. But I thought the whole agreement that we had was that he was going to communicate with me. It's all about our communication. I just didn't like feeling like I didn't have any control in that situation.

THERAPIST: Yeah. I mean, it sounds like both with your parents and with Jim that there's sort of been this lack of recognition for your feelings. That you're feeling not heard and not understood. Has Jim, has he understood sort of your reaction to what happened with Julie?

LIANNE: Yeah. Yeah, I think so. I mean, he's a really understanding person, which is why I like him so much. It's just that I'm kind of afraid of it happening again. And I don't think he was trying to hurt me, you know. I don't know. I feel like I can't really—I trust him, but after what happened with Gary, I feel like I have to have my guard up all the time.

THERAPIST: Sounds like both with your parents and with Jim to some extent, different situations, but having to sort of have your guard up around all the people who are close in your life. If they do something that's going to hurt you, it's really hard to come back from that.

LIANNE: Yeah.

THERAPIST: Yeah. I know we have to wrap up, but thinking about next week, I'm wondering if this is something that you feel like you would be comfortable bringing up to Jim, maybe talking about how this has sort of affected your trust in him and maybe where that comes from for you.

LIANNE: Yeah. Yeah, I can do that.

Lianne's willingness to be open with Jim marked a step toward self-acceptance. As with so many who have weathered disapproval and harsh judgment, Lianne had to embrace her own identities before she could ask others to do the same. She was committed to polyamory, and over time, Lianne found the words to communicate her feelings with increased confidence. She went on to expand her audience, becoming an advocate for people who live in the intersection of these marginalized identities, a role that has contributed to writing new narratives of self-acceptance.

## What Is in a Name?

In Chapter 1 I described the significance of names and naming and how they provide opportunities to explore meaning in people's stories. Names carry weight. A name is the first gift given to a child. A child might be named to honor ancestors and relatives, a significant life event, a place of birth, a nickname, or even a sacred location. Names communicate intentions, hopes, dreams, and connections to the past, present, future, and the spiritual. They carry stories, values, and meaning. Just as companies invest significant time and resources in selecting names that align with their brand, a person's name serves as an indelible symbol.

However, whether it is one that parents have agonizingly selected or one that is assigned by family or historic tradition, a name is given to the child, not chosen. As children grow, given names may fail to align with their emerging identities. For many transgender people, choosing a name is a powerful first step in affirming their gender identity. According to Pamfile et al. (2024):

> Considering that naming practices are based on the gender presumed at birth, it appears that, very frequently, for people who identify as transgender, both in binary and non-binary ways, the given names fail to express accurately their gender identity, both to themselves and to others. The renaming act, part of the social and administrative gender-affirming pathway, provides them with the possibility to perform their gender . . . (p. 1)

For transgender people, the accepted use of chosen names and pronouns by people in their lives enhances self-esteem and solidifies feelings of inclusion, especially for youth (Pamfile et al., 2024). It is not surprising then, that when people refuse to address transgender individuals by their chosen names, what is called deadnaming, they feel invalidated and disrespected. Names hold powerful significance; they tell stories about identity and self-definition. Therapists play a crucial role in affirming those stories as illustrated by Oliver and Lara.

### CALL ME BY MY NAME

Oliver's mother Lara was intent on not using his chosen name. Now 16 and a transgender male, he was already struggling with relentless bullying at school. His mother's insistence on calling him by his birth name, Olivia, exacerbated his distress. He felt misunderstood at home and among his peers. Disagreements over his name became a constant battle. It was Oliver's request that he and Lara attend a therapy session with me, a session that proved helpful in understanding their relationship.

From the moment we began, Oliver demonstrated a strong sense of agency, standing firm in his advocacy for identity. It wasn't long, however, before he and his mother slipped into a familiar argument. My role was to create space for both of their experiences and perspectives to be heard:

THERAPIST: Cool. Great. Yeah, let's start out with Oliver. Can you tell us a little bit about what we're doing here?

OLIVER: Well, I mentioned to you the last time we met that I finally asked my mom to start calling me Oliver and using he/him pronouns, and she didn't really take it well. And she hasn't talked to me all week, so I'm sort of surprised she came. But yeah, if we could just actually try to have a conversation about what's going on, that would be really helpful.

LARA [MOM]: Well, I stopped talking to you because all we were doing was yelling at each other, and you weren't listening to me. You weren't listening to me. Just once—can you please, just once, listen to me? Put yourself in my shoes. (*turning and looking at therapist*) This is my Olivia. (*then, looking at Oliver . . .* ) This is—Olivia, you're always going to be my baby girl. Olivia is always going to be my baby girl. This is a huge ask . . .

OLIVER: (*clearly, speaking angrily*) Do you—like, do you know how transphobic that sounds, though? Like, I . . .

LARA: I'm asking you to please just put yourself in my shoes.

THERAPIST: Lara, I'm hearing that you're having a lot of feelings about this—this ask, that Oliver has brought to you. I am going to ask that you do your best to call Oliver by his name. I think that is something that he has asked of you, and I think that we can work toward trying that out here, okay?

LARA: Okay. (*looking at Oliver*)

OLIVER: Okay . . . thank you. (*ignoring smile*)

THERAPIST: Yeah. You're talking about imagining being in your shoes. I can't imagine being in your shoes. I think this has been a lot of small steps for Oliver—that he's been working on for a while. And maybe it seems like kind of a big step for you, because you maybe haven't seen those steps. So, it's—maybe there's a little bit of difference in what this feels like for each of you.

OLIVER: (*looking at his mom*) I mean, I—actually, I feel like, one, I feel like I've been extremely considerate of you this entire time. And I also just feel like, yeah, I've been doing these things. I cut my hair, and you thought it looked great. And then, like, we went shopping and I asked you if I could buy things from the men's section, and you said it was fine. Like, you bought me this button-down (*pointing at his shirt*) . . . and I thought that meant that you supported me. I—

LARA: I do support you. I've always supported you.

OLIVER: Yeah. I don't understand why it's such a big deal to try to call me something different. Like, Oliver is not that different of a name. And he—you would just have to think of me—you would just have to think of me a little differently. It's not—I just don't feel like it's that big of an ask. And I feel like I've been waiting for so long to tell you this, not because I'm trying to keep something from you but because I wanted to make sure this is, like, real, you know?

LARA: I don't get it. Three years ago, you came out. You came out as queer—as lesbian. You said, Mom—and then you brought your girlfriend, Jen. And you know how—

OLIVER: And you love Jen.

LARA: Yes. Yes. I really do like Jen. But it was difficult for me. But you know what? I accepted it, right? Because you know how much I love you. I love you so much.

OLIVER: Yeah, and I—

LARA: You know that. And I try my best. As a single mom, I try my best. I'm always there for you.

OLIVER: I know. And that's why I expected something different. And that's why I was so hurt when you come back with the "I can't see you as anything else." Because I sent you articles on social media, and I had a friend at school come out, and you were just so supportive. And I thought that, with me, it would be the same, and it wouldn't be such a big deal.

LARA: It is a big deal. Because you are telling me you want to transition. Not only that—okay, the whole change thing. But then you tell me, mom, I want to do hormone therapy eventually. I mean—and—what? And you've been fine with me calling you Olivia all this time, for the past 3 years. We—it's my child. You are always going to be my baby child—always.

OLIVER: I just—

LARA: Always. Please.

THERAPIST: I'm hearing that who Oliver is to you is your baby. And I'm trying to think, is there a way that we can make it so that Oliver can still be everything that he is to you—your child?

In saying this, I hoped to set the stage where both Oliver and his mother would find appreciation in the unfolding of their relationship. It also gave Oliver an opportunity to educate his mother about transitioning, highlighting what he needs in his relationships. His mother could learn something from the way Oliver's friends were treating him. Wong and Drake (2021) emphasize that affirmation, communication, and advocacy foster well-being, while misgendering, rejection, and suppression cause harm. Oliver went on to clarify his position:

OLIVER: Like, just to clarify, I said that I was thinking about hormone therapy. I never said that I wanted to go on HRT [hormone replacement therapy], and I never said that—there are so many things to think about transitioning. Right now, I just want to socially transition. Like, my friends support me. They call me Oliver. That feels really good. They use he/him pronouns. Like, I'm thinking I want to use he/him pronouns in school. And I don't think I can tell my teachers before I tell my mother. I'm sure there's paperwork involved, and like, I want your support there. And I'm not going to be a different person. Transitioning—I feel like I already have transitioned. My hair used to be down to here. And then I cut it, and you said it looked great. And I'm wearing men's clothing, and you're supporting that. I feel like, in some ways, I've already done the transitioning. And you care about me in that way, it's just like this one thing—this one thing—the name, that's—

THERAPIST: Oliver, what is it about the social transitioning that you've done with your friends—they call you Oliver, and they use he/him pronouns—what about that feels good for you? Can you tell us a little bit about that?

OLIVER: It's, like, the best thing in the world. It's like, I feel like me for once. Like, when somebody says Oliver, I'm like, oh, yeah, that's who I am. That's where I'm at. It's not like somebody would deadname me, and I'd be like, yeah, I guess that's me. And hearing somebody call me he, it feels right. It's just like, that's who I am. And especially in public spaces, when I'm dressed like this, I get called Oliver at a coffee shop when I give them my name, and it's just—and . . . all of my friends are using he/him, so other people believe that I'm a guy. I'm not even on HRT, and people treat me like a guy. And that feels—it feels right. It feels good. . . . Yeah.

LARA: I just don't get it. I don't get it. I just—I think about the past 16 years. I think about my daughter and all the times—all of the special moments we've had together, how much you were so—you'd watch me put on my makeup. We'd be—you loved shopping with me. I thought you loved it when I would help you pick out an outfit or a dress. So was that—I'm just—I'm so confused.

OLIVER: I mean—

LARA: And it hurts, because—and you know the last thing I want to do is hurt you. I don't want to hurt you. You know how much I love you.

OLIVER: I know, I know.

LARA: You know that.

OLIVER: I know. I know.

LARA: This is really difficult for me.

OLIVER: I know. I mean, I—

LARA: Because I love Olivia.

THERAPIST: Oliver.

OLIVER: I hear that. I know "I don't want to hurt you." And from when I was a kid, I didn't—I was uncomfortable sometimes, and I saw how happy those things made you, especially the dresses—God, some of them, I was just so—I felt so humiliated in. But you said it looked good on me, and you said it fit me, and you—like how proud you are of me whenever I go out and I look pretty or delicate. It's like, I . . .

LARA: And you're still pretty. You're still beautiful. You are. But I hear you. And I am concerned. Because I know the depression has been a big factor, as well, and I'm concerned for—

OLIVER: I've been so much happier living in this way. And I've felt so happy. And the fact that you actually—like, you supported . . . you supported this (*gesturing over his body*) and that felt good. But all those other times—I mean, some of the times—like, I think it's nice watching you put on makeup, and I just don't feel comfortable in dresses. That was something that I used to do for you—for you and you'd say—

LARA: (*interjecting*) I'm sorry it was so hard for you. I had no idea. I'm sorry. I had no idea.

OLIVER: I don't know. I just didn't—I didn't say anything because I didn't want to make a fuss, or shame the family, or whatever.

LARA: You know what? There's already a lot of shame in our family when it comes to me. I come from a broken marriage, as you know. I'm divorced. And I've been a single mom. It's a big shame factor—a very big disappointment. But that's on me. It's not your fault. I'm here because I love you.

THERAPIST: That's really big. That's really important.

OLIVER: Thank you.

THERAPIST: And I think that that's what is connecting all of us here. We all care about Oliver. And—

LARA: I'm sorry to interrupt. But I just wish—I—please, please, just put yourself in my shoes, okay? Please try to understand, I'm not your enemy here.

THERAPIST: Lara, what are you hoping to get out of Oliver putting himself in your shoes?

LARA: I'm hoping that he's just going to take his time, just slow down. Just slow down.

OLIVER: I don't—I don't understand how you see me going fast. As I said, I feel like I've been—

LARA: Well, fast—oh, mom, call me Oliver now. My whole—your whole life that—

OLIVER: (*sarcastic laughter*) I don't know how that slows down. Like, where does that slow down? Do I say, oh, yeah, just call me Oliver some of the time? No, it's like, that's what a name is. That's how you change your name. And it's hard when you go out, and your friends are calling you one thing and your teachers are calling you another thing, and then like you come home—like, I just want to come home and feel like you see me—like I'm seeing—

LARA: I do see you. I see you every day. I see you all the time. I see you.

OLIVER: But you don't see me as Oliver.

LARA: I don't know. I'm going to need some time with this.

THERAPIST: That's okay.

OLIVER: This is just, like—

Oliver and Lara struggled as they both sought to make sense of their evolving stories. Lara struggled with the loss of the child she knew, causing her to hold on to a single story and risking alienation in their relationship. Her experience is not uncommon. Parents often experience grief in response to gender identity issues. As Wahlig (2015) notes "... the person they once knew is gone" (p. 305) though they are still present in their lives. As Boss (2000) explains, ambiguous loss is the sorrow tied to profound changes in a loved one short of death—something that captures Lara's experience.

For his part, Oliver actively sought to rewrite his story. To do so, he desperately needed his mother's support and understanding, especially as he faced ridicule and marginalization at school and among his peers and teachers. Indeed, both Lara and Oliver needed support to untangle their overlapping, multilevel stories.

## Therapy and Culture

Oliver's and Lara's stories are representative of how broader cultural conflicts across differing social, political, and ideological beliefs with families can generate relational disconnection. Researchers have found that social and political divisiveness in families increases the odds for depression and anxiety among family members (Laszloffy & Platt, 2024). For Oliver, asserting his gender identity was a way to advocate for his mental health and well-being, mitigating the risk of depression and suicide experienced by sexual- and gender-minority youth (Guz et al., 2021; Price-Feeney et al., 2020; Russell et al., 2018). The use of correct names and pronouns is found to be one way to significantly reduce these risks (Russell et al., 2018) as is the provision of gender-affirming care (Tordoff et al., 2022). In many respects, Oliver's frustration and the health risks associated with being a transgender person underscore the vital need for his mother to recognize and affirm his identity.

Narrative practitioners play vital roles in helping to reshape stories that cause disconnection and disenfranchisement. Their skills and strategies offer a safe and trustworthy structure that acknowledges and affirms identity, fosters understanding, and creates space for healing. Narrative conversations capture and curate stories that activate new possibilities. With Tamara, for instance, reauthoring helped her successfully reconceptualize life through metaphor, gaining self-acceptance in a cisheteronormative world, finding love and experiencing worth as a queer, soon-to-be-married woman. During our time together, we identified many examples of preferred-self acceptance, something Tamara called little moments of self-celebration.

Lianne, too, found self-acceptance as she embraced her polyamory story, freeing herself from oppressive judgment and self-directed shame around her choices. For Lianne, polyamory was not the problem, nor was her size. The problem was communication and learning how to speak her truth and worry less about others' opinions. Over time, practicing self-care and establishing trust took precedence in Lianne's life.

My work with Oliver and Lara focused on helping them reconcile conflicting needs and desires surrounding Oliver's gender identity. Embracing new knowledge was a struggle for both, but in very different ways. Lara needed support to befriend the story of her son and to manage her ambiguous grief at "losing" her child. Expanding the story within the context of our work together helped Lara support Oliver while reconciling her losses. It was also a space for her to voice her isolation and vent her fears. In this way, a coalition of resources was being built to aid Lara in expanding her own story. Lara loved Oliver, and in the end, their relational connection would heal their disconnection:

THERAPIST: We'll take some time. We'll work on this . . . a lot of conversations for us to have. I would love to take some time just talking with you, Lara, about how we can support Oliver, what that looks like, answer any questions you might have, and begin to befriend Oliver's experiences. There are some resources that I can connect you with. This is a big step for you, right? And it's a big step for Oliver, too. We've been talking about this for a bit. And—

LARA: Oliver . . . (*catching herself calling him Oliver*) . . . Oliver has you. Oliver has . . . See, I'm calling you Oliver already.

OLIVER: Yeah, I noticed that. It really means a lot.

LARA: But I have no one. I have no one. I have no one to listen to me. I have no one to vent my fears to.

Lara clearly felt alone. However, her desire to be listened to and heard opened doors to co-centering work and progress for everyone. Lara and Oliver began to actively listen to each other. When they spoke, they leaned into each other, their body language speaking as loud as their words. I supported them to elevate their individual and collective work:

THERAPIST: It sounds like you're feeling a lot of this on your own. And that's—it's a lot for any parent to think about what this means for their child, and what this means for their family. And Oliver is very much aware of what he's asking of you. And from what he said, it sounds like he trusts that this is something that you can do.

OLIVER: Yeah. I've given it a lot of thought. I feel like—I really do try to think about you. I hope you know that.

LARA: I hope you know how much I love you. I hope you'll never forget how much I love you, and that I've always been there for you, and how difficult this is for me.

OLIVER: I mean, that's why I trusted that I'd be able to even come out to you, is because I—I know that you love me. And I have faith that you'll be able to change, I hope. And we can meet in the middle, or something, you know?

THERAPIST: Yeah. And I think we're going to work hard to make this work. And a lot of making it work is going to be supporting Oliver in what he needs. Because that is really what we know as the best way to support youth. And, Lara, this is a lot for you to be dealing with on your own. So, I would love to connect with you about ways to get you a network of support, whether that's parents—other parents of trans youth—or referring you to a colleague of mine.

LARA: That would be great.

THERAPIST: Yeah.

LARA: I could use all of the help.

THERAPIST: Yeah. And I think it's great that you're open to that.

These conversations precipitated a discussion of radical acceptance, a concept that promotes full acknowledgment and nonjudgmental recognition of things as they are rather than what we wish they would be (Brach, 2004). Oliver knew what he wanted but did not know whether Lara could meet his expectations. At the beginning of sessions, his body language appeared constricted but as his mother befriended his experiences, his expression and disposition were transformed. He smiled. Lara, however, remained visibly upset and confused. At the same time, she diligently moved forward making the changes she needed to keep their relationship intact. During our sessions we also sought to recognize significant others, an audience of supporters, who might notice their progress.

With Lara's story unfolding, her bond with Oliver deepened. She still needed gentle reminders to use his name, and sometimes made mistakes, yet she also began giving herself permission to embrace a wider range of emotions: joy, pride, anticipation, and excitement. As Beaudoin and Monk (2024) note, "the preferred story increasingly becomes laden with many complex layers of affective experiences crisscrossing many aspects of preferred identity and relational experiences" (p. 92).

Our work together was a triumph of sorts for Oliver. Though uncertain about the extent to which his mother was truly "befriending" his transition and its complexities, he felt calmer knowing that they had embarked on a journey together. Neither of them was alone. Lara was his support; he no longer had to navigate contradictory storylines on his own. Lara had slowly let go of overriding fear, stepping into the unfamiliar as she sought to understand her son. It was not easy, but she was determined to try.

It was important that our therapeutic conversations provided spaces with clear boundaries and understandings that reinforced Oliver's experiences. Therapy with Lara balanced gentleness and firmness; I empathized with her while simultaneously centering on Oliver's needs. For example, Oliver was the name to be used in all therapy interactions. I respectfully redirected Lara when she misgendered Oliver or used his deadname. Therapy became the co-centering space to foster relational attunement, described as a person's ability to sense the inner world of another (Siegel, 2010). As the therapist, being attuned to the inner worlds of Oliver and Lara modeled ways they could be attuned to each other.

While the therapy space belonged to Oliver, it was enhanced by acknowledging and exploring divergent perspectives that mother and son shared. Oliver's identity transition may have felt like a sudden and significant change to Lara, but it was long in the making. For therapy to be successful, both mother and son had to acknowledge their distinctive pathways and bear witness to their unique feelings and experiences.

Unfortunately, a common aspect of Lara's and Oliver's separate experiences was transgender discrimination. Witnessing had brought them back in relationship and once united, they sought support from the transgender community. For example, they chose to attend a "Healing Justice" event designed to acknowledge the historical harms and assaults experienced by transgender individuals and communities. Healing Justice as an organization advocates for public accountability as an act of love and justice, and a contribution to bidirectional healing. Oliver and Lara had reconnected in love; they were now collectively pursuing justice.

## Conclusion

LGBTQ+ and particularly transgender issues spur contentious social, familial, and political discourse. In this chapter, stories have illustrated issues that arise when individuals defy identity norms and boundaries. Names are one of many areas in need of critical consideration and radical acceptance for transgender people. Names hold deep significance. They shape and reflect our experiences, affirm our identities, and embody fundamental respect and human dignity. They connect us to our social worlds and broader cultural narratives, weaving together the fabric of our relationships. Through naming, we continually construct and reinterpret the meaning of our lives.

Resurgence of societal backlash against transgender rights in the first quarter of the 20th century has made the struggle for recognition and dignity even more urgent. Policies restricting gender-affirming care, banning discussions of LGBTQ+ identities, denying transgender existence, and criminalizing it in public spaces amplify the harm faced, particularly by youth. A return to more accepting times is certainly possible, but for this moment in history transgender rights and denial of their human dignity is at stake.

Narrative practices offer clinicians strategies to explore, honor, and affirm social identities in the lives of those they work with. These practices address the social and political struggles people face. When discrimination, oppression, and injustice enter the narrative, they are named, resisted, and addressed. This chapter addressed but a portion of the complex issues surrounding social identities. Narrative practices provide spaces to explore those stories.

In the concluding chapter, I return to the image of the crack in the window—a moment that significantly reauthored the narrative of our family's experience. This image operates as a generative metaphor for understanding how stories take shape in people's lives and within therapeutic conversations. In narrative practice, endings are not finalities but invitations: openings for new storylines to emerge. The central invitation of this book is to remain engaged with the multiplicity of stories people bring, and to cocreate space for alternative narratives to be richly explored and more fully lived.

EPILOGUE

# The Crack in the Window

## RE-STORYING

The stories I've recounted offer a slice of people's experiences generated through our therapeutic work together. I have been humbled by what these stories have taught me. They are unceasing reminders that we are never finished, never perfectly sealed. We are evolving, opening, breaking, mending, and through it all, re-storying our lives in ways that bring hope, healing, and empowerment.

Sharing insider stories and their deep personal meanings is, I believe, the most powerful way of gaining insight into the diversity of human experience. Exchanging stories is about forging relational connection that thickens understanding of ourselves and each other. Early on I committed to telling my own story throughout the book. Rather than merely recount the tales of others and offer my interpretations, I chose to include my story to connect with you, the reader.

The *crack in the window* is the guiding metaphor for my life and my work, one that holds multiple overlapping memories, meanings, and defining moments. In the aftermath of my father's brutal kidnapping, the crack in the window somehow reassured me that he would someday return to our family, and indeed he did. At first glance, a crack conjures damage: a break, a flaw, and danger. But no story stands alone. Over time the crack expanded in meaning as something that lets in light, air, and possibility, a threshold where something new could begin.

In narrative practice the work of therapy is about re-storying. As I learned from my own life, and from the people who graciously have shared their lives with me, we are much more than single stories. Our identities and worlds encompass multiple, ever-changing and unfolding stories that co-exist, interact, and very often conflict with one another. Stories are about adaptation, growth, and discovery. They recognize the past but are not meant to revise it. Like Mot's river metaphors, stories soften memory as well as offer guidance, renewal, and entrance to a new future.

Re-storying is the quiet, steady act of reclaiming agency and reimagining our place in the world. Trauma and suffering cannot be erased—the past is the past. Its impacts should never be minimized. Survival can wear out the soul and it is difficult to choose hope having faced terrible hardships. The beauty of re-storying is its ability to create new narratives that motivate us to think about ourselves in alternative ways, helping us to extract our inherent strengths and move forward. Working together, we engage in a process of breaking the silence, naming what has happened, regaining resilience, and then choosing what actions are needed to change direction.

Re-storying the meaning of the *crack in the window* moved me from stultifying despair to believing in possibility. It helped me recognize that stories have no end. There is always more to come. And because stories continue to evolve, we can hold on to hope, not as blind optimism but as conviction rooted in courage. During those long, tumultuous years of my father's absence, the crack in the window was simultaneously a reminder of his disappearance and his inevitable return. My hope did not negate the sharp edges of the window's crack—it was an undeniably painful time. But I chose to focus as well on the light that shone through looking for openings to the possibilities of the yet unknown.

Therapists hold the duality of pain and hopefulness alongside their clients. We bear witness to peoples' struggles, disappointments, trauma, and pain as well as to the birth of their hope. Once revealed, trauma stories speak volumes about clients' determination to survive under extraordinary circumstances. Re-storying trauma is cumulative, made up of small acts of resistance that pave the way to self-liberation. Tasha's story is an example of how one woman built upon her determination "to beat the odds," defy shame and trauma, and know that she mattered.

Individual stories exist within concentric circles of context, circumstance, and community. They are interactional, relational, cultural, and political. Couples' work, for example, is fraught with intersectional complexity. Not being able to talk about race and religion threatened Karly and Daryl's long-term marriage; gender and jealousies caused Alari and Stella's relationship to be riddled with seemingly unresolvable tensions. Therapists must hold in balance the narratives of both partners to help them successfully expand their stories toward a consensual resolution. At the same time, they must attend to relational accountability, witnessing, and empathic attunement, a highly complex therapeutic juggling act.

Cultural stories, especially those told by immigrants and refugees, are well represented throughout this text. They tell of historical and contemporary injustices, inequity, moral distress, dislocation, and disconnection. As a Black African immigrant, my story lives within these stories. But my story is only one of many diverse narratives. Listening to cultural stories has complexified my understanding of the immigrant experience in its variations, inclusive of the violence, racism, hostility, and discrimination so many have endured. Other cultural stories expose heterosexism and discrimination based solely on identity. Oliver's and Lara's parallel struggles as son and mother expose the ways in which social expectations shape personal stories.

However, hope and beauty are also well represented in cultural stories. Metaphors and vibrant imagery peppered clients' narratives permitting me to gain access to their inner worlds, existential thoughts, and personal dreams. Metaphors broke through Nana's and Anisha's illness narratives, helping them to see their lives as more than the problems illness brings. Nana's illnesses left her feeling "out of harmony with God," which helped me appreciate the role that spirituality needed to play in our work together. Inspired by Simblett's (2013) "dance" metaphor and Sontag's (2003) "kingdom of the well," I make every effort to grasp on to clients' metaphors to see where they will take us.

Throughout the book, I have outlined narrative practice theories and strategies that are commonly used in therapy. I hope they are helpful to you in your practices. I have equally tried to convey how acknowledgment of uncertainty, "not knowing," and humility are useful narrative interventions that invite therapeutic discovery. Not knowing the process or outcome of an illness can plunge therapeutic work into unchartered territory. The most potent stance in such cases is to embrace an ethic of caring. Caring, when curing is not a possibility, and even when it is, seeds purpose, bolsters connection, and aids in making meaning when life circumstances are unfair.

Not knowing is also a powerful therapeutic tool when clients ask unanswerable questions. They question God or wonder why they survived catastrophe when others did not. Mot felt betrayed by God when he survived the killing fields while his cousins, among other "lost boys," died. He asked me whether God could be trusted. I worried that without an answer Mot would lose faith in me, too. But that was not the case. Instead, my admission of not knowing made our relationship stronger, more authentic, as it did with others whose circumstances could not be simplified or readily explained.

As you have probably surmised from Chapter 9, I am passionate about the role of spirituality in therapeutic storytelling. Like other aspects of identity, spirituality influences whether and how people believe that recovery, healing, and redemption are possible. Therapists need to be curious about how a client's faith, or lack of faith, is woven into their storylines. To me, knowing and respecting a client's spirituality is an ethic of care. Nana and Mot, among others, reinforced my belief in the healing properties of spirituality. Their narratives illustrated the human yearning to find purpose and meaning in life.

As a practitioner, I have benefited from knowing my own spiritual beliefs and boundaries. My spiritual beliefs have provided me with a centering out of which I have listened to the spiritual yearnings of my clients. It has been important to engage in therapeutic conversations mindfully from my position as a spiritual being. In working with clients, the use of spirituality involves helping clients draw on their familiar spiritual beliefs and practices. I have learned to separate my own beliefs to create healthy boundaries in the therapeutic spaces. I have been careful not to impose my beliefs or practices on my clients. Instead, I have engaged in a collaborative exploration and understanding of instrumental use of clients' religious and spiritual resources, to listen to clients' language and metaphors, and to seek clients' informed consent. A co-centering posture allows opportunities to enter clients' spiritual experiences.

The search for purpose, connection, and meaning is part of people's stories. These stories, in essence their spirituality, are related to fairness and a search for justice.

## Endings as Seeking Home

I pondered innumerable words and phrases that would best capture my thoughts and feelings about how to close out this book. Endings hold all the elements of stories; it is easy not to know which pathway will lead to the right conclusion. Such words as "pauses," "terminations," "transitions," "closures," and "crossroads" came to mind, none of them quite fitting the enormity of what completing this book felt like to me. I also reflected upon personal and cultural rituals that accompany endings. Graduations, coronations, and of course, death, have recognizable rituals. But the ending of a project such as this has no diploma or crown. And in many respects, it has no ending. People's stories will go on and I will continue to witness them.

To be honest, endings fill me with trepidation, an understandable response, similar to so many of my clients, given the many traumatic disruptions and losses I've experienced. Endings fill me with countless emotions, whether they are anticipated, by design, or happen by default. They activate feelings reminiscent of the day our home was attacked and my father disappeared, and stir feelings that accompanied me on my journey of exile. My emotions equally run high when I contemplate the deaths and losses of family and friends. Remembering helps quell the more difficult emotional aspects of endings and loss. They become part of a larger story of a life, the partial narratives coming together to form a greater whole. In truth, I prefer to think of endings as beginnings in disguise. Possibility lives in the shadows of closure.

The therapeutic journey too, has beginnings, middles, and ends. We sit beside clients at the start of something new that they too may face with trepidation. We listen as their stories unfold, finding our way to empathic attunement. For some clients, the journey to healing is arduous: The road to hope is rife with obstacles that must be overcome before peace and tranquility can be achieved. Immigrant stories, for example, speak to lengthy and lingering journeys to find belonging in a new country, one that is not always welcoming, while still yearning for their homelands and families left behind. Therapy for them offers a sheltering place where they can speak their truth without fear of retribution or rebuke.

Therapists ensure that the therapeutic space remains a safe conduit for telling stories regardless of what their content brings. We hold hope for those who cannot yet see possibility. We remain patient and reflective, aware of the importance of staying close to our own stories and the feelings they generate. And when the time comes, we accompany people to their endings, hoping that they have finally located some semblance of peace and possibility, but not necessarily closure. Life continues.

When I started writing this book, I was overwhelmed by the many directions it could take. It was like being on a journey to a new country without a road map. Not surprisingly, writing evoked memories of my own story: I thought about factors, places, and people that contributed to who I am today. I asked myself: How do my clients' stories broaden my own self-narrative? Without exception, I am grateful to those who have been willing to share their stories with me in our sessions in all their messiness, beauty, tragedy, and complexity. Like the crack in the window, people's stories offered varieties of meaning; they represented pain and suffering while also offering possibility for light to shine through. Stories have taught me much about myself, the world, and have deepened my appreciation for the value of storytelling in narrative practice.

As a final footnote, while writing this book, my mother died. We were deeply close; her presence shaped me in profound ways, some of which I am still discovering. Her loss cracked my heart wide open. And yet, even in grief, the work of re-storying continues. I didn't stop being a therapist, or a writer, or a son. I learned, more intimately than ever, how loss and love walk hand in hand. I learned that the cracks we carry are also where our deepest stories reside.

Endings bring gifts. My final gift to you are tools you can use for re-storying. These apply to your professional work as well as to your own journey of self-discovery:

1. *Know your story.* Be honest about naming what has shaped you; include an accounting of your wounds, your strengths, and your lineage.
2. *Befriend your story.* Accept your story with kindness and compassion. Be open to letting yourself be rewritten.
3. *Re-story your old story.* Don't be afraid to question old narratives that are no longer helpful. You are allowed to grow beyond them.
4. *Reimagine your story.* Ask *what happened* and *why*, and also, *what is still possible*?

In closing, my hope is simple: that this book gives you strategies and language to celebrate the possibilities of change and the courage to walk beside your clients as they tell their stories and create new, empowering ones. Be curious; keep asking questions and stay open to the messages that stories are telling. Be a faithful companion to those who invite you into their stories. Light the way, notice the presence of hope shining through, and always trust in the power of human resilience. And remember, as a person possessed with an open heart you will inevitably be changed by this work.

# References


Adams, H. L. (2015). Insights into processes of posttraumatic growth through narrative analysis of chronic illness stories. *Qualitative Psychology, 2*(2), 111–129. https://doi.org/10.1037/qup0000025

Adichie, C. N. (2009, July). *The danger of a single story* [Video]. TED conferences. https://www.ted.com/talks/chimamanda_ngozi_adichie_the_danger_of_a_single_story

Aldarondo, E. (Ed.). (2007). Rekindling the reformist spirit in the mental health professions. In *Advancing social justice through clinical practice* (pp. 3–18). Erlbaum.

American Psychiatric Association. (2022). *Diagnostic and statistical manual of mental disorders* (5th ed., text rev.). https://doi.org/10.1176/appi.books.9780890425787.

American Psychiatric Association. (2013). *Diagnostic and statistical manual of mental disorders* (5th ed.). https://doi.org/10.1176/appi.books.9780890425596

Andersen, T. (1996). *The reflecting team: Dialogues and dialogues about the dialogues.* Norton.

Anderson, H. (1997). *Conversation, language, and possibilities.* Basic Books.

Anderson, H. (2007). Hallmark of collaborative therapy: The philosophical stance as "a way of being." In H. Anderson & D. Gehart (Eds.), *Collaborative therapy: Relationships and conversations that make a difference* (pp. 63–79). Routledge.

Angelou, M. (2010). *I know why the caged bird sings.* Random House. (Original work published 1969)

Babits, M. (2001). Using therapeutic metaphor. *Clinical Social Work Journal, 29*(1), 21–33. https://doi.org/10.1023/a:1005254410387

Baker Miller, J., & Pierce Stiver, I. (1997). *The healing connection: How women form relationships in therapy and in life.* Beacon Press.

Bakhtin, M. (1981). *The dialogic imagination: Four essays* (C. Emerson & M. Holquist, Trans.). University of Texas Press.

Baldwin, C., & Esley, J. (2015). The self and spirituality: Overcoming narrative loss in aging. *Journal of Religion and Spirituality in Social Work, 34*(2), 205–222.

Banyanga, J., Björkqvist, K., & Österman, K. (2017). The trauma of women who were raped and children who were born as a result of rape during the Rwandan genocide: Cases from the Rwandan diaspora. *Pyrex Journal of African Studies and Development, 3*(4), 31–39.

Beaudoin, M.-N. (2005). Agency and choice in the face of trauma: A narrative therapy map. *Journal of Systemic Therapies, 24*(4), 32–50.

Beaudoin, M.-N., & Monk, G. (2024). *Narrative practices and emotions: 40+ ways to support the emergence of flourishing identities.* Norton.

Belenky, M. F., Clinchy, B. M., Goldberger, N. R. & Tarule, J. M. (1986). *Women's ways of knowing: The development of self, voice, and mind.* Basic Books.

Bell-Tolliver, L., & Wilkerson, P. (2011). The use of spirituality and kinship as contributors to successful therapy outcomes with African American families. *Journal of Religion and Spirituality in Social Work. 1*, 48–70. https://doi.org/10.1080/15426432.2011.542723

Bird, J. (2000). *The heart's narrative: Therapy and navigating life's contradictions.* Edge Press

Bontempo, A. C. (2025). Conceptualizing symptom invalidation as experienced by patients with endometriosis. *Qualitative Health Research, 35*(2), 248–263. https://doi.org/10.1177/10497323241253418

Boss, P. (1999). *Learning to live with unresolved grief.* Harvard University Press.

Brach, T. (2004). *Radical acceptance: Embracing your life with the heart of a Buddha.* Bantam Books.

Braverman, P., & Gottlieb, L. (2014). The social determinants of health: It's time to consider the causes of the causes. *Public Health Reports, 129*(Suppl. 2), 19–31. https://doi.org/10.1177/00333549141291S206

Bronstein, I., & Montgomery, P. (2011). Psychological distress in refugee children: A systemic review. *Clinical Child and Family Psychology Review, 14*, 44–56.

Browning, D. (2003). Pathos, paradox, and poetics: Grounded theory and the experience of bereavement. *Smith College Studies in Social Work, 73*(3), 325–336. https://doi.org/10.1080/00377310309517688

Bruner, E. (1986). Ethnography as narrative. In V. W. Turner, E. M. Bruner, & C. Geertz (Eds.), *The anthropology of experience* (pp. 139–155). University of Illinois Press.

Campillo, M. (2012). Keys to a subjugated story: My favorite narrative therapy questions. *International Journal of Narrative Therapy and Community Work, 1*, 35–39.

Captari, L. E., Hook, J. N., Hoyt, W., Davis, D. E., McElroy-Heltzel, S. E., & Worthington, E. L., Jr. (2018). Integrating clients' religion and spirituality within psychotherapy: A comprehensive meta-analysis. *Journal of Clinical Psychology, 74*(11), 1938–1951. https://doi.org/10.1002/jclp.22681

Caputo, R. K. (2001). Multiculturalism and social justice in the United States: An attempt to reconcile the irreconcilable with a pragmatic liberal framework. *Race, Gender, and Class, 8*(1), 161–182.

Carlson, T. S., & Haire, A. (2014). Toward a theory of relational accountability: An invitational approach to living narrative ethics in couple relationships. *International Journal of Narrative Therapy and Community Work, 3*, 1–16.

Chazin, R., Kaplan, S., & Terio, S. (2000). The strengths perspective in brief treatment with culturally diverse clients. *Crisis Intervention, 6*(1), 41–50.

Chioneso, N. A., Hunter, C. D., Gobin, R. L., McNeil Smith, S., Mendenhall, R., & Neville, H. A. (2020). Community healing and resistance through storytelling: A framework to address racial trauma in Africana communities. *Journal of Black Psychology, 46*(2–3), 95–121.

Cohen Konrad, S. (2019). *Child and family practice: A relational perspective.* Oxford University Press.

Comas-Díaz, L. (2006). Latino healing: The integration of ethnic psychology into psychotherapy. *Psychotherapy: Theory, Research, Practice, Training, 43*(4), 436–453. https://doi.org/10.1037/0033-3204.43.4.436

Cooperrinder, D. L. , & Whitney, D. (2005). *Appreciative inquiry: A positive revolution for change.* Berrett-Kohler Publishers.

Copes, H., & Ragland, J. (2016). Considering the implicit meanings in photographs in narrative criminology. *Crime, Media, Culture, 12*(2), 271. https://doi.org/10.1177/1741659015623599

Dai, R., & Peng, S. (2024). The implication of the illness metaphors of *In America*: Mitigating negative effects of metaphors through illness narratives in the postpandemic era of

COVID-19. *Humanities and Social Sciences Communications, 11*, 778. https://doi.org/10.1057/s41599-024-03308-7

Damianakis, T. (2001). Postmodernism, spirituality, and the creative writing process: Implications for social work practice. *Families in Society, 82*(1), 23–34.

Dault, K. (2015). What is the preferential option for the poor? *U.S. Catholic, 80*(1), 46.

de Varennes, F., & Kuzborska, E. (2016). Language, rights and opportunities: The role of language in the inclusion and exclusion of indigenous peoples. *International Journal on Minority and Group Rights, 23*(3), 281–305. https://doi.org/10.1163/15718115-02303004

Denov, M., & Piolanti, A. (2019). Mothers of children born of genocidal rape in Rwanda: Implications for mental health, well-being and psycho-social support interventions. *Health Care for Women International, 40*(7–9), 813–828. https://doi.org/10.1080/07399332.2019.1571593

Denov, M., Woolner, L., Bahati, J. P., Nsuki, P., & Shyaka, O. (2020). The intergenerational legacy of genocidal rape: The realities and perspectives of children born of the Rwandan genocide. *Journal of Interpersonal Violence, 35*(17–18), 3286–3307. https://doi.org/10.1177/0886260517708407

Doherty, W. (2002). Bad couples therapy: Getting past the myth of therapist neutrality. *Psychotherapy Networker*, 26–33.

Doherty, W. J., Harris, S. M., & Wilde, J. L. (2015) Discernment counseling for "mixed-agenda" couples. *Journal of Marital and Family Therapy, 42*, 246–255. https://doi. Org/10.111/jmft.12132

Donald, M. (2017). Key cognitive preconditions for the evolution of language. *Psychonomic Bulletin and Review, 24*(1), 204–208. https://doi.org/10.3758/s13423-016-1102-x

Dossey, D. (1993). *Healing words: The power of prayer and the practice of medicine.* Harper.

Duvall, J. & Beres, L. (2011). *Innovations in narrative therapy: Connecting practice, training, and research.* Norton.

Falicov, C. J. (2002). Ambiguous loss: Risk and resilience in Latino immigrant families. In M. M. Suárez-Orozco & M. Páez (Eds.), *Latinos: Remaking America*. University of California Press.

Farran, C. J., Herth, K. A., & Popovich, J. M. (1995). *Hope and hopelessness: Critical clinical constructs.* Sage.

Fishbane, M. D. (2019). Healing intergenerational wounds: An integrative relational-neurobiological approach. *Family Process, 10*(10), 1–23.

Fook, J., & Gardner, F. (2007). *Practicing critical reflection: A resource handbook.* McGraw-Hill Education.

Foucault, M. (2002). *The archaeology of knowledge.* Taylor and Francis.

Fraenkel, P. (2009). The therapeutic palette: A guide to choice points in integrative couple therapy. *Clinical Social Work Journal, 37*, 234–247. https://doi.org/10.1007/s10615-009-0207-3

Fraenkel, P. (2011). *Sync your relationship, save your marriage.* St. Martin's Press.

Fraenkel, P. (2019). Love in action: An integrative approach to last chance couple therapy. *Family Process, 58*, 569–594. https://doi.org/10.1111/famp.1244

Fraenkel, P. (2023). *Last chance couple therapy: Bringing relationships back from the brink.* Norton.

Freedman, J., & Combs, G. (1996). *Narrative therapy: The social construction of preferred realities.* Norton.

Freedman, J. (2014). Witnessing and positioning: Structuring narrative therapy with families and couples. *International Journal of Narrative Therapy and Community Work, 1*, 11–17

Freire, P. (1970). *Pedagogy of the oppressed*. Seabury Press.

Freire, P. (1973). *Education for critical consciousness*. Continuum.

Freire, P. (2004). *Pedagogy of indignation*. Routledge.

Freire, P. (2016). *Pedagogy of the heart* (Bloomsbury Revelations ed.). Bloomsbury.

Freire, P., Freire, A. M. A., & Barr, R. R. (2014). *Pedagogy of hope: Reliving pedagogy of the oppressed*. Bloomsbury.

George, J. (1999). Conceptual muddle, practical dilemma. *International Social Work, 42*(1), 15–26. https://doi.org/10.1177/002087289904200103

Gilles, A. (2017). Viewpoint: Embracing uncertainty. *British Journal of General Practice, 67*(658), 215. https://doi.org/10.3399/bjgp17X690629

Gottman, J. M. (2011). *The science of trust: Emotional attunement for couples*. Norton.

Griffith, J. L., & Griffith, M. E. (1992). Owning one's epistemological stance in therapy. *Dulwich Centre Newsletter, 1,* 5–11.

Guarnaccia, P. J. (2019). *Immigration, diversity and student journeys to higher education*. Peter Lang.

Guilfoyle, M. (2015). Listening in narrative therapy: Double listening and empathic positioning. *South African Journal of Psychology, 45*(1), 36–49. https://doi.org/10.1177/0081246314556711

Guz, S., Kattari, S. K., Atteberry-Ash, B., Klemmer, C. L., Call, J., & Kattari, L. (2021). Depression and suicide risk at the cross-section of sexual orientation and gender identity for youth. *Journal of Adolescent Health, 68*(2), 317–323. https://doi.org/10.1016/j.jadohealth.2020.06.008

Hardy, K. (Ed.). (2022). *The enduring, invisible, and ubiquitous centrality of Whiteness*. Norton.

Hodge, F. S., Pasqua, A., Marquez, C. A., & Geishirt-Cantrell, B. (2002). Utilizing traditional storytelling to promote wellness in American Indian communities. *Journal of Transcultural Nursing, 13*(1), 6–11. https://doi.org/10.1177/104365960201300102

Hoffman, L. (2007). The art of "witness": A new bright edge. In H. Anderson & D. Gehart (Eds.), *Collaborative therapy: Relationships and conversations that make a difference* (pp. 43–59). Routledge.

Hogwood, J., Mushashi, C., Jones, S., & Auerbach, C. (2018). "I learned who I am": Young people born from genocide rape in Rwanda and their experiences of disclosure. *Journal of Adolescent Research, 33*(5), 549–570. https://doi.org/10.1177/0743558417713302

hooks, b. (2003). *Teaching community: A pedagogy of hope*. Routledge.

Huang, Y., Kim, J., Levine, A., Park, J., & Kuo, H. J. (2023). Measuring implicit biases about disability: A scoping review. *Rehabilitation Counseling Bulletin, 68*(2), 121–135. https://doi.org/10.1177/00343552231199246

Huemer, J., & Vostanis, P. (2010). Child refugees and families. In D. Bhugra, T. Craig, & K. Bhui (Eds.), *Mental health of refugees and asylum seekers* (pp. 225–242). Oxford University Press.

Independent Television Service. (2023, November 13). *A map of gender-diverse cultures: PBS.* https://www.pbs.org/independentlens/content/two-spirits_map-html

Jansen, S., Niyonsenga, J., Ingabire, C. M., Jansen, A., Nzabonimpa, E., Ingabire, N., . . . Nsabimana, E. (2022). Evaluating the impact of community-based sociotherapy on social dignity in post-genocide Rwanda: Study protocol for a cluster randomized controlled trial. *Trials, 23*(1). https://doi.org/10.1186/s13063-022-06994-3

Jaouad, S. (2021). *Between two kingdoms: A memoir of life interrupted*. Random House.

Kagimu, M., Guwatudde, D., Rwabukwali, C., Kaye, S., Walakira, Y., & Ainomugisha, D. (2013). Religiosity for promotion of behaviors likely to reduce new HIV infections in

Uganda: A study among Muslim youth in Wakiso district. *Journal of Religion and Health, 52*(4), 1211–1227. https://doi.org/10.1007/s10943-011-9563-8

Kahn, S., & Denov, M. (2019). "We are children like others": Pathways to mental health and healing for children born of genocidal rape in Rwanda. *Transcultural Psychiatry, 56*(3), 510–528. https://doi.org/10.1177/1363461519825683

Kamya, H. (2012). The cultural universality of narrative techniques in the creation of meaning. In R. A. McMackin, E. Newman, J. M. Fogler, & T. M. Keane (Eds.), *Trauma therapy in context: The science and craft of evidence-based practice* (pp. 231–246). American Psychological Association. https://doi.org/10.1037/13746-000

Kamya, H. (2013). Engaging spirituality in family conflict: Witnessing to hope and dialogue. *Journal of the American Academy of Matrimonial Lawyers, 26*(1), 15–30.

Kamya, H., & Trimble, D. (2002). Response to injury: Toward ethical construction of the other. *Journal of Systemic Therapies, 21*(3), 19–29. https://doi.org/10.1521/jsyt.21.3.19.23338

Kelly, B. L., Lanza, C., Travis, R., & Ellis, T. (2024). A vision for engaging the arts in social work practice. In S. Cohen Konrad & M. Sela-Amit (Eds.), *Social work and the arts: Expanding horizons* (pp. 189–210). Oxford University Press.

Koenig, H., McCullough, M. E., & Larson, D. (Eds.). (2001). *Handbook of religion and health.* Oxford University Press.

Konrad, S. C. (2007). Hard stories in the workplace. *WORK: The Journal of Prevention, Assessment & Rehabilitation, 28*(4), 371–378. PMID: 17522458

Langer, S. K. (1957). *Philosophy in a new key: A study in the symbolism of reason, rite, and art* (3rd ed.). Harvard University Press.

LaSala, M. C., & Goldblatt Hyatt, E. D. (2019). A bioethics approach to social work practice with transgender clients. *Journal of Gay and Lesbian Social Services, 31*(4), 501–520. https://doi.org/10.1080/10538720.2019.1653804

Laszloffy, T. A., & Platt, J. J. (2024). Divided we fall: Constructive dialoguing about our political differences within family therapy training. *Journal of Marital and Family Therapy, 50*(3), 523–544. https://doi.org/10.1111/jmft.12721

Lee, J. H. (2019). Integration of spirituality into the strengths-based social work practice: A transpersonal approach to the strengths perspective. *Journal of Sociology and Social Work, 7*(2), 25–35. https://doi.org/10.15640/jssw.v7n2a4

Leimumäki, A. (2012). What does falling ill mean? Illness narratives as elucidation of experience expertise. In E. Cohen, L. Toker, M. Consonni, & O. E. Dror (Eds.), *Knowledge and pain* (pp. 257–292). Brill.

Loftus, E. F., Miller, D. G., & Burns, H. J. (1978). Semantic integration of verbal information into a visual memory. *Journal of Experimental Psychology: Human Learning and Memory, 4*(1), 19–31. https://doi.org/10.1037/0278-7393.4.1.19

Lorde, A. (Ed.). (2015). Learning from the 60s. In *Sister outsider: Essays and speeches* (pp. 134–144). Crossing Press.

Lorde, A., & Smith, T. K. (2020). *The cancer journals.* Penguin Books.

Luterman, S. (2023, September 13). Marriage could mean losing life-saving benefits for people with disabilities. So, they're protesting. *The 19th.* https://19thnews.org/2023/09/disability-advocates-marriage-equality-commitment-ceremony

Madsen, W. C. (2007). *Collaborative therapy with multi-stressed families* (2nd ed.). Guilford Press.

Mangram, J. A. (2022). The elephant is the room: The art and peril of navigating Whiteness. In K. V. Hardy (Ed.), *The enduring, invisible, and ubiquitous centrality of Whiteness* (pp. 37–48). Norton.

Marsten, D., Epston, D., & Markham, L. (2016). *Narrative therapy in wonderland: Connecting with children's imaginative know-how.* Norton.

Maslow, A. H. (1968). *Toward a psychology of being* (2nd ed.). D. Van Nostrand.

Mbiti, J. S. (1990). *African religions & philosophy.* Jordan Hill: Heinemann.

McKenzie-Mohr, S., & Lafrance, M. N. (2017). Narrative resistance in social work research and practice: Counter-storying in the pursuit of social justice. *Qualitative Social Work, 16*(2), 189–205. https://doi.org/10.1177/1473325016657866

Merriam-Webster. (n.d.). Language. In Merriam-Webster.com dictionary. Retrieved September 8, 2025, from https://www.merriam-webster.com/dictionary/language.

Miller, D. L. (1999). *Principles of social justice.* Harvard University Press.

Miller, J. F. (2007). Hope: A construct central to nursing. *Nursing Forum, 42*(1), 12–19.

Monk, G. (1997). How narrative therapy works. In G. Monk, J. Winslade, K. Crocket, & D. Epston (Eds.), *Narrative therapy in practice: The archaeology of hope* (pp. 3–31). Jossey-Bass.

Moore, K., Talwar, V., & Moxley-Haegert, L. (2015). Definitional ceremonies: Narrative practices for psychologists to inform interdisciplinary teams' understanding of children's spirituality in pediatric settings. *Journal of Health Psychology, 20*(3), 259–272.

Morgan, A. (2000). *What is narrative therapy? An easy-to-read introduction.* Dulwich Centre.

Morson, G. S., & Emerson, C. (1990). *Mikhail Bakhtin: Creation of a prosaics.* Stanford University Press.

Mueller, C. (2010). Create sacred space with stories: Storytelling as a formational tool and spiritual practice. *Health Progress, 91*(6), 16–18, 20–21.

Mugisha, J., Hjelmeland, H., Kinyanda, E., & Knizek, B. L. (2013). Religious views on suicide among the Baganda, Uganda: A qualitative study. *Death Studies, 37*(4), 343–361.

Mukamana, D., & Brysiewicz, P. (2008). The lived experience of genocide rape survivors in Rwanda. *Journal of Nursing Scholarship, 40*(4), 379–384. https://doi.org/10.1111/j.1547-5069.2008.00253.x

Mukherjee, S. (2015). *The emperor of all maladies.* Scribner.

Mulvale, J. P. (2021). Six aspects of justice as a grounding for analysis and practice in social work. *Journal of Social Work Values and Ethics, 18*(1), 34–48. https://doi.org:10.55521/10-018-106.

National Association of Social Workers. (2021). National Association of Social Workers Code of Ethics [Online version]. https://www.socialworkers.org/About/Ethics/Code-of-Ethics/Code-of-Ethics-English.

National Constitution Center. (2015). *Obergefell v. Hodges.* https://constitutioncenter.org/the-constitution/supreme-court-case-library/obergefell-v-hodges

Ncube, N. (2010). The journey of healing: Using narrative therapy and map-making to respond to child abuse in South Africa. *International Journal of Narrative Therapy and Community Work, 1,* 3–12.

Nikuze, D. (2014). The genocide against the Tutsi in Rwanda: Origins, causes, implementation, consequences, and the post-genocide era. *International Journal of Development and Sustainability. 3*(5), 1086–1098.

Nunn, N. (2010). Religious conversion in colonial Africa. *American Economic Review: Papers and Proceedings, 100,* 147–152. http://www.aeaweb.org/articles.php?doi=10.1257/aer.100.2.147

Oxhandler, H. K., & Pargament, K. I. (2014). Social work practitioners' integration of clients' religion and spirituality in practice: A literature review. *Social Work, 59*(3), 271–279 https://doi.org/10.1093/sw/swu018

Pagel, M. (2017). What is human language, when did it evolve and why should we care? *BMC Biology, 15*(64). https://doi.org/10.1186/s12915-017-0405-3

Pamfile, D., Bourquin, C., Michaud, L., Brovelli, S., Pécoud, P., & Stiefel, F. (2024). What is in a chosen name? An exploratory study on the renaming experiences of transgender people. *International Journal of Transgender Health*, 1–19. https://doi-org.une.idm.oclc.org/10.1080/26895269.2023.2301318

Pargament, K. I., & Mahoney, A. (2021). Spirituality: The search for the sacred. In C. R. Snyder, S. J. Lopez, L. M. Edwards, & S. C. Marques (Eds.), *The Oxford handbook of positive psychology* (3rd ed., pp. 878–891). Oxford University Press.

Penn, P. (2001). Chronic illness: Trauma, language, and writing: Breaking the silence. *Family Process, 40*(1), 33–52.

Perry, A. D. V., & Rolland, J. S. (2009). The therapeutic benefits of justice-seeking spirituality: Empowerment, healing, and hope. In F. Walsh (Ed.), *Spiritual resources in family therapy* (2nd ed., pp. 379–396). Guilford Press.

Plante, T. G. (2007). Integrating spirituality and psychotherapy: Ethical issues and principles to consider. *Journal of Clinical Psychology, 63*(9), 891–902. https://doi.org/10.1002/jclp.20383

Pouchly, C. A. (2012). A narrative review: Arguments for a collaborative approach in mental health between traditional healers and clinicians regarding spiritual beliefs. *Mental Health, Religion and Culture, 15*(1), 65–85.

Powell, J. A. (2012). *Racing to justice: Transforming our conceptions of self and other to build an inclusive society.* Indiana University Press.

Prehn, J. (2025). An indigenous strengths-based theoretical framework. *Australian Social Work, 78*(2), 145–158. https://doi.org/10.1080/0312407X.2024.2340464

Price-Feeney, M., Green, A., & Dorison, S. (2020). Understanding the mental health of transgender and nonbinary youth. *Journal of Adolescent Health, 66*(6), 684–690. https://doi.org/10.1016/j.jadohealth.2019.11.314

Randall, W. L. (2011). Memory, metaphor and meaning: Reading for wisdom in the stories of our lives. In G. M. Kenyon, E. Bohlmeijer, & W. L. Randall (Eds.), *Storying later life: Issues, investigations, and interventions in narrative gerontology* (pp. 18–36). Oxford University Press.

Rappaport, J. (1987). Terms of empowerment/exemplars of prevention: Toward a theory for community psychology. *American Journal of Community Psychology, 15*(2), 121–145.

Reamer, F. G. (2014). Ethical issues and challenges: Managing moral dilemmas. In A. B. Dessel & R. M. Bolen (Eds.), *Conservative Christian beliefs and sexual orientation in social work: Privilege, oppression, and the pursuit of human rights* (pp. 233–254). CSWE Press.

Reichert, E. (2003). *Social work and human rights: A foundation for policy and practice.* Columbia University Press.

Reik, T. (1983). *Listening with the third ear: The inner experience of a psychoanalyst.* Farrar, Straus and Giroux.

Reimer, E. C. (2017). A relational approach to practice: An ethical alternative to working with parents in out-of-home care process. *Journal of Social Work Values and Ethics, 14*(2), 6–19.

Riessman, C. (2008). *Narrative methods for the human services.* Sage.

Rivett, M., & Street, E. (2001). Connections and themes of spirituality in family therapy. *Family Process, 40*, 459–467.

Roth, S., & Epston, D. (1996). Consulting the problem about the problematic relationship: An exercise for experiencing a relationship with an externalized problem. In M. F. Hoyt (Ed.), *Constructive therapies* (Vol. 2, pp. 142–162). Guilford Press.

Russell, S. T., Pollitt, A., Li, G., & Grossman, A. (2018). Chosen name use is linked to reduced depressive symptoms, suicidal ideation, and suicidal behavior among transgender youth.

*Journal of Adolescent Health, 63*(4), 503–505. https://doi.org/10.1016/j.jadohealth.2018.02.003

Saleebey, D. (1994). Culture, theory, and narrative: The intersection of meanings in practice. *Social Work, 39*(4), 351–359.

Saleebey, D. (1996). The strengths perspective in social work practice: Extensions and cautions. *Social Work, 41*(3), 296–305.

Sandage, S. J., Rupert, D., Stavros, G. S., & Devor, N. G. (2020). *Relational spirituality in psychotherapy: Healing suffering and promoting growth.* American Psychological Association.

Sandberg, S. (2016). The importance of stories untold: Life-story, event-story and trope. *Crime, Media, Culture, 12*(2), 153–171. https://doi.org/10.1177/1741659016639355

Scheinkman, M. (2017). Vulnerability cycle in couple therapy. In J. Lebow, A. Chambers, & D. Breunlin (Eds.), *Encyclopedia of couple and family therapy* (pp. 1–3). Springer International.

Scheinkman, M. (2019). Intimacies: An integrative multicultural framework for couple therapy. *Family Process, 10*(10), 1–19.

Scheinkman, M., & Fishbane, M. (2004). The vulnerability cycle: Working with impasses in couple therapy. *Family Process, 43*(3), 279–299.

Schutz, A., & Luckmann, T. (1974). *The structures of the life-world.* Heinemann.

Schwartz, R. C., & Sweezy, M. (2020). *Internal family systems therapy* (2nd ed.). Guilford Press.

Sedgwick, P. (2013). Nietzsche, illness and the body's quest for narrative. *Health Care Analysis, 21*(4), 306–322.

Sengupta, A., Follmer, K., & Louis, D. (2025). Leadership, spirituality and empowerment: Examining the experiences of women of color in Fortune 500 companies. *Equality, Diversity and Inclusion: An International Journal, 44*(5), 674–703. https://doi.org/10.1108/EDI-11-2023-0380

Shachar, R. (2010). Combining relaxation and guided imagery with narrative practices in therapy with an incest survivor. *International Journal of Narrative Therapy and Community Work, 1*, 35–55.

Sharp, D. N. (2021). Prickles and goo: Human rights and spirituality. *Journal of Human Rights, 20*(1), 36–51. https://doi.org/10.1080/14754835.2020.1856647

Shaw, M. (2013). The concept of genocide. In B. Ingelaere, S. Parmentier, S. J. Jacques Haers, & B. Segaert (Eds.), *Genocide, risk and resilience: An interdisciplinary approach* (pp. 23–35). Palgrave Macmillan. https://doi.org/10.1057/9781137332431_2

Shorter, A. (1975). *Prayer in the religious traditions of Africa.* Oxford University Press.

Siegel, D. (2010). *The mindful therapist: A clinician's guide to mindsight and neural integration.* Norton.

Siegel, D. (2012). *The developing mind: How relationships and the brain interact to shape who we are* (2nd ed.). Guilford Press.

Simblett, G. (2013). Dancing with the *DSM*: The reflexive positioning of narrative informed psychiatric practice. *Australian and New Zealand Journal of Family Therapy, 34*(2), 114–128.

Snyder, B. A. (2005). Aging and spirituality: Reclaiming connection through storytelling. *Adultspan Journal, 4*(1), 49–55.

Snyder, C. (2000). Genesis: The birth and growth of hope. In C. Snyder (Ed.), *Handbook of hope* (pp. 25–38). Academic Press.

Sobrino, J. (1988). *Spirituality of liberation: Toward political holiness.* Orbis Books.

Sontag, S. (2003). *Illness as metaphor.* Farrar, Straus, and Giroux.

Stainton, T. (2002). Taking rights structurally: Disability rights and social work response to direct payments. *British Journal of Social Work, 232*, 751–763.

Steger, M. F., & Park, C. L. (2012). The creation of meaning following trauma: Meaning making and trajectories of distress and recovery. In R. A. McMackin, E. Newman, J. M. Fogler, & T. M. Keane (Eds.), *Trauma therapy in context: The science and craft of evidence-based practice* (pp. 171–192). American Psychological Association. https://doi.org/10.1037/13746-000

Straus, S. (2004). How many perpetrators were there in the Rwandan genocide? An estimate. *Journal of Genocide Research, 6*(1), 85–98. https://doi.org/10.1080/1462352042000194728

Teilhard de Chardin, P. (1955) *The phenomenon of man*. Harper.

Thomas, J., & McDonagh, D. (2013). Shared language: Towards more effective communication. *Australian Medical Journal. 6*(1), 46–54. https://doi.org/10.4066/AMJ.2013.1596

Tordoff, D., Wanta, J., Collin, A., Stepney, C., Inwards-Breland, D., & Ahrens, K. (2022). Mental health outcomes in transgender and nonbinary youths receiving gender-affirming care. *JAMA Network Open, 5*(2), 1–13. https://doi.org/10.1001/jamanetworkopen.2022.0978

United Nations. (1948). *The United Nations' declaration of human rights.*

Van Hooft, S. (2014). *Hope.* Routledge.

Wade, A. (1997). Small acts of living: Everyday resistance to violence and other forms of oppression. *Contemporary Family Therapy, 19*(1), 23–39.

Wahlig, J. L. (2015). Losing the child they thought they had: Therapeutic suggestions for an ambiguous loss perspective with parents of a transgender child. *Journal of GLBT Family Studies, 11*(4), 305–326. https://doi-org.une.idm.oclc.org/10.1080/1550428X.2014.945676

Walsh, F. (2007). Traumatic loss and major disasters: Strengthening family and community resilience. *Family Process, 46*, 207–227.

Walsh, F. (2008). *Spiritual resources in family therapy.* Guilford Press.

Weedon, C. (1997). *Feminist practice and post-structuralist theory.* Blackwell.

Weingarten, K. (1991). The discourses of intimacy: Adding a social constructionist and feminist view. *Family Process, 30,* 285–305.

Weingarten, K. (2000). Witnessing, wonder, and hope. *Family Process, 39*(4), 389–492.

Weingarten, K. (2001). Making sense of illness narratives: Braiding theory, practice and the embodied life. In C. White (Ed.), *Working with the stories of women's lives* (pp. 111–125). Dulwich Centre.

Weingarten, K. (2010). Reasonable hope: Construct, clinical applications and supports. *Family Process, 49*(1), 5–25.

Weingarten, K. (2013). The "cruel radiance of what is." Helping couples live with chronic illness and disability. *Family Process, 52*, 83–101.

Weingarten, K., & Worthen, M. (2017). Unreliable bodies: A follow-up twenty years later by a mother and daughter about the impact of illness and disability on their lives. *Family Process, 56*, 262–277.

Weingarten K. (2022). Waiting and witnessing: Using reasonable hope to cope with uncertainty. *Journal of Medical Imaging and Radiation Sciences, 53*(2S), S9–S15. https://doi.org/10.1016/j.jmir.2022.02.010

Weis, R., & Speridakos, E. C. (2011). A meta-analysis of hope enhancement strategies in clinical and community settings. *Psychology of Well-Being: Theory, Research and Practice, 1*, 5.

White, M. (2004). Working with people who are suffering the consequences of multiple trauma: A narrative perspective. *International Journal of Narrative Therapy and Community Work, 1,* 45–76.

White, M. (2007). *Maps of narrative practice.* Norton.

White, M., & Epston, D. (1990). *Narrative means to therapeutic ends.* Dulwich Centre.

White, M., & Morgan, A. (Eds.). (2006). *Narrative therapy with children and their families* (pp. 1–56). Dulwich Centre.

Wiesel, E. (2006, January). *Questions unite people, answers divide them.* Interview with Oprah Winfrey on *The Oprah Winfrey Show* in Auschwitz.

Wolfe, B. G., & Hintz, E. A. (2024). Assessing the mediating role of disenfranchising talk on the well-being of female patients with chronic overlapping pain conditions. *Patient Education and Counseling, 127,* 108354.

Wong, W. Y., & Drake, B. (2021). Family responses to transgender and nonbinary young people: What helps and what hurts. *Journal of LGBTQ Youth, 18*(2), 169–192. https://doi.org/10.1080/19361653.2020.1803910

Yohani, S. C., & Larsen, D. J. (2009). Hope lives in the heart: Refugee and immigrant children's perceptions of hope and hope-engendering sources during early years of adjustment. *Canadian Journal of Counselling, 43*(4), 246–264.

# Index

Note: Italicized page locators refer to figures.

# About the Author

**Hugo Kamya, PhD,** is a professor in the School for Social Work at Smith College. He lives in Arlington, Massachusetts, where he also maintains a clinical practice. Dr. Kamya is a psychologist, clinical social worker, and couple and family therapist. He received AFTA's 2003 Distinguished Contribution to Social and Economic Justice Award in recognition of his work addressing trauma and supporting diverse populations. His scholarship and practice focus on care across communities, community capacity building, and the impact of social determinants of health on youth and families. He also works to strengthen social, cultural, and human capital among immigrant and refugee populations. As a Fulbright Scholar, Dr. Kamya has collaborated on partnership development and program design in Uganda, Rwanda, Kenya, South Africa, and Australia. Dr. Kamya is a founding member of the Boston Institute for Culturally Affirming Practices (BICAP). His current projects examine African-centered approaches to decolonization, historical trauma, and resilience. He is also the recipient of NASW's 2014 Greatest Contribution to Social Work Education Award.